Prostitution and the State
in Italy, 1860–1915

A Volume in the Crime, Law, and Deviance *Series*

Prostitution and the State in Italy, 1860–1915

Mary Gibson

RUTGERS UNIVERSITY PRESS
New Brunswick and London

Library of Congress Cataloging-in-Publication Data

Gibson, Mary, 1950–
Prostitution and the state in Italy, 1860–1915.

(Crime, law, and deviance series)
Bibliography: p.
Includes index.
1. Prostitution—Italy—History—19th century.
2. Italy—Moral conditions. I. Title. II. Series.
HQ203.G53 1986   306.7′4′0945   85–30440
ISBN 0–8135–1172–0

British Cataloging-in-Publication
Information Available.

To my father in memory of my mother

Contents

Contents

Tables

Tables

Acknowledgments

I would like to thank those individuals and organizations that contributed to the preparation of this book in both the United States and Italy. I owe a special dept to William Cohen, who ten years ago initially suggested the topic of prostitution and wholeheartedly supported my venture into the then rather new field of Italian social history. He offered careful and constructive criticism of an early version of the manuscript, as did David Pace, Leonard Lundin, Peter Bondanella, Anthony Molho, and Judith Walkowitz. I am especially grateful to Harry Kavros for his skillful editorial assistance. My initial research trip to Italy was greatly facilitated by Edward Bayne, Patricia Weaver, and Karen Rautenstrauch, all of the Center for Mediterranean Studies. They introduced me to the joys of Roman life as well as to important professional contacts. Sources for the history of prostitution were not easy to track down and were sometimes uncatalogued; for their assistance in unearthing government records, I would like to thank Mario Missori of the Archivio Centrale dello Stato and the cooperative staff of the Archivio di Stato di Bologna. I owe a special note of appreciation to Steve Hughes, who generously informed me of the availability of police files in the Bolognese archives. Grants from Indiana University and Grinnell College sustained the research for this project. Doris DeVito worked untiringly and efficiently to type the final draft of this manuscript. Finally, it has been a pleasure to work with Marlie Wasserman of Rutgers Press, a cheerful and skillful editor.

Prostitution and the State
in Italy, 1860–1915

Introduction

There is only one remedy for prostitution and that is to get rid of it; but because prohibitionist laws only multiply prostitution and push it into secrecy, with dangerous moral and physical effects, it is better to bring prostitution out of the shadows in order to discipline it and make it less harmful.

Pietro Castiglione, 1872

On July 28, 1886 Guadelina Bistocchi was arrested in Bologna for prostitution. The police said they brought her into custody "because she is an idle vagabond without means of subsistence, identification, or a home, and she is a clandestine prostitute."[1] The arrest certificate offered no proof of soliciting, much less of accepting money for sexual services. When the police checked their records, they found Bistocchi to be a legally registered prostitute; she was, nevertheless, given a sentence of five days for having stayed outside her brothel after the 10:00 PM curfew for prostitutes. After serving her time, she disappeared rather than return to her brothel, causing police to issue two warrants for her arrest. Picked up on August 9, she was returned to jail for fifteen days. Dropping from sight again after being released from prison, she did not turn up until November 22, when she was rearrested and given a vaginal examination. Found to have venereal disease, she was sent to the *sifilicomio* of San Orsola, a special hospital for prostitutes. Fifteen days in jail awaited her after treatment and recovery at the sifilicomio. Thus ended Bistocchi's police dossier for 1886.

The case of Bistocchi is not unusual and illustrates some of the major characteristics of the relationship between prostitutes and the Italian state in the late nineteenth and early twentieth centuries. First, prostitution was legal for women who registered with

1

police, underwent biweekly health examinations, and submitted voluntarily to treatment of venereal disease in the sifilicomi. This policy of "regulated" prostitution was embodied in laws that minutely prescribed the daily lives of legal prostitutes, for instance setting a curfew and limiting movement throughout the city. Prostitutes who defied these restrictions or failed to register with the government were subject to automatic arrest and sentencing by police. Police could arrest a woman for prostitution simply on the grounds that she was homeless and unemployed, for these traits alone marked a woman as immoral. The arresting officers made no attempt to claim or even imply that Bistocchi had been caught in the act of prostitution, although Bistocchi probably was a prostitute, having had a previous record of registration. But any lower-class woman, especially one found alone on city streets in the evening, might be arrested on similarly flimsy evidence. Arrest was often followed by forced registration as a prostitute. In addition, women in police custody usually underwent a routine vaginal examination with or without their consent. If found infected, they were escorted by police to the sifilicomio, for symptoms of venereal disease constituted further proof of prostitution.

In her resistance to this system of regulation, Bistocchi was typical. Born in a village near Forlì, in the province of Bologna, she had traveled a relatively short distance to find work. Since her file does not include her original papers of registration, it is not clear if she initially requested inclusion on police lists as a legal prostitute or was placed there by force. Once registered, however, Bistocchi took every opportunity to elude police surveillance. Despite the threat of punishment, she stubbornly resisted the efforts by the state to confine her to one of the "tolerated brothels." Her life, then, became one of subterfuge punctuated by periodic internment in prison or the sifilicomio. Registered or unregistered, a prostitute could not entirely escape the discipline of the law. Yet the lack of cooperation by Bistocchi and many of her colleagues disrupted the regulation system to such an extent that it can now be evaluated only as a failure.

Why the government of the new Italian state instituted regulation in 1860 and why the policy persisted despite its failings are the main questions this study seeks to address. That Prime Minister Camillo di Cavour promulgated the first legislation on prostitution in the midst of the wars of unification demonstrates its importance to his vision of the new kingdom. This legislation reflected—along with the laws on police, health, prisons, *opere pie* (charities), and education—Cavour's concern with rationalizing social programs. Standard analyses of the *Risorgimento*, the movement toward Italian unification, have generally ignored this social counterpart to political unification. A process dating back to the eighteenth century, the Risorgimento sought not only territorial unity, but the making of a new Italian citizenry imbued with a homogeneous moral and social vision. Thus after 1860 Cavour sought to remove all threats to the stability of the young nation, and these threats included not only political opponents but also the "dangerous classes," who were thought to live in idleness and crime. If the thief was becoming a major target of repression by the expanding propertied classes who ruled the new Italy, his female counterpart was the prostitute.[2] In 1871 Giovanni Bolis, police chief of Bologna and briefly national director of police in Rome, explicitly drew the connection between these two marginal groups: "The same causes which push men into crime throw women into the arms of vice and prostitution. . . . [Thieves and prostitutes] have a strict pact of alliance with immorality. Held in contempt and rejected by civil society, they form a class apart. Common interests and passions guide and determine their conduct. They are in permanent war with the laws of honesty, and both live at the expense of other citizens."[3] While the thief endangered property, the prostitute threatened other fundamental middle-class values: public order, morality, and health.

The ruling classes believed their cities were being swamped with prostitutes, but it is impossible to ascertain from available statistics if per capita prostitution indeed rose after unification. It is clear, however, that growing numbers of women were leaving the farms and villages, which could no longer support the burgeoning population. While many men—at least by the end of the century—emigrated to the Americas, women tended to move to the nearest big city. Since all respectable women had traditionally been under the tutelage of men, the nineteenth-century mind found it hard to conceive of any way to catagorize these young, single, working-class migrants other than as prostitutes. And, indeed, a certain proportion of migrating women, cut off from the financial and psychological support of their families, had little choice but to turn to prostitution. The increasing visibility of these "independent" women on city streets reinforced general anxieties about female emancipation. It is not suprising that an era that uneasily witnessed changes in the status of women should be preoccupied with female deviance. Thus in the nineteenth-century iconography of the dangerous classes, a female figure, the prostitute, claimed a prominent place.

Italy was not alone in formulating new legislation to control prostitution. The debate about prostitution raged at international conferences and in the pages of legal, criminological, medical, and feminist journals read throughout Europe and the United States. Commissions were dispatched from one capital to another to observe the workings of foreign laws. Experts and lawmakers divided into three international camps advocating either the prohibition, regulation, or decriminalization of prostitution. For Italy, Cavour's choice of regulation was decisive, for with modifications it remained intact until 1958. The other two policies, however, had adherents within Italy and dominated the legislative strategies of some neighboring states. To establish the international context, therefore, I briefly describe these three policies that framed the discourse on prostitution during the nineteenth century and continue to do so today. These three rather schematic ideal types provide a basis for exploring Italian regulation in more detail in the following chapters.[4]

Prohibition, the oldest of the three policies in Christian Europe, has traditionally forbidden the act of prostitution and advocated the prosecution of offenders as criminals. According to prohibitionist ideology, the crime of prostitution lies in the immorality of the act of sexual intercourse performed outside the institution of marriage. While in theory extramarital sex constitutes a sin for both women and men, most prohibitionist statutes have punished the female prostitute and not her client. As implied in the phrases *donna caduta* (fallen woman) and *donna perduta* (lost woman), prohibitionists locate the cause of prostitution in the moral failings of certain individual women who are wholly to blame for their own fate. In this ideology only moral reform and repentance can promise redemption. Punishment for prostitutes has varied widely and decreased in severity over the centuries, from floggings and brandings to small fines and short jail terms. Prohibitionist legislation, most typical in pre-Enlightenment societies where church and state collaborated in crusading against vice, has remained intact in only a few countries, most notably the United States.[5]

Rejecting the moral crusades of prohibitionists, regulationists have preached the acceptance of prostitution as an unpleasant but inevitable fact of social life. What has made prostitution universal, they have suggested, is the strong and uncontrollable nature of male sexuality. In their view, prostitution does not challenge the sanctity of marriage, as prohibitionists claim, but reinforces it by providing a safety valve for a male sex drive that might otherwise be directed against "honest" women. Thus, whereas prohibition theoretically rejects extramarital intercourse for both sexes, regulation explicitly acknowledges the double standard. Believing prostitution to be necessary for the preservation of social equilibrium, regulationist states have legalized and controlled its practice. Regulation was the object of some medieval and early modern communal legislation as well as that of a large part of continental Europe in the nineteenth and early twentieth centuries, although the latter type of "modern" regulation claims to be unique in its reliance on rationality and science.

Decriminalization is the most modern term for those instances in which the state has refused to intervene directly either to prohibit or to regulate the private act of prostitution. Reform movements preaching various degrees of decriminalization (called "abolition" in the nineteenth century) have sprung up repeatedly during the last 150 years in opposition to both prohibition and regulation. Like regulationists, abolitionists classify prostitution as a "vice" rather than a "crime"; unlike them, however, they have refused to accept it as inevitable and necessary to the proper functioning of society. Believing that environment rather than innate moral failings in women or the biological sex drive of men causes prostitution, they have preached the reform of society rather than the prosecution or regulation of individual women. According to supporters of decriminalization, the state should not interfere with the right of women to choose prostitution as a profession, since they are constrained by economic necessity; when social reform eliminates this necessity, prostitution will diminish.

During the late nineteenth and twentieth centuries, some type of limited decriminalization legislation has replaced regulation in most European countries.

Little is known about the practical functioning of any of these three strategies historically and geographically. This study focuses on the vicissitudes of only one—regulation—in Italy between unification and World War I. I intentionally concentrate on a limited time and place because too many studies have presented prostitution as a static social phenomenon without history. "The oldest profession," a phrase invariably coupled with prostitution, conveys this sense of fixity. As two contemporary sexologists, John Gagnon and William Simon, have correctly pointed out, "female prostitution is as much, if not more, vulnerable to the process of social and scientific simplification than are other kinds of sexual relationships."[6] Such simplification arises in part from the tendency to view human sexuality, and male and female sex roles, as immutably rooted in biological imperatives. Research on women has especially suffered from physiological determinism, which has reduced the variety of female experience and the multiplicity of female consciousness to a common denominator of instinctual response. Historians, criminologists, and sexologists have, until recently, explained female behavior, whether normal or deviant, with clichés supported by little rigorous research but nonetheless presumed to be universal.[7] Instead, I have attempted to embed prostitution, and the discourse surrounding it, in the complex political, economic, and social conditions that characterized Italy in the nineteenth and early twentieth centuries.

The bibliography on prostitution has been unimpressive, reflecting, for the most part, traditional assumptions about the trade.[8] Older histories have been anecdotal rather than analytical, offering sweeping panoramas of prostitution that reach back to the beginnings of Western civilization.[9] In these works, prostitution appears static, detached from the changing political, economic, and social context in which it existed. Sociologists and psychologists have offered more theoretical approaches, but they have often failed to recognize that their data and conclusions are anchored in present-day Western society and thus not indicative of universal truths.[10] Only very recently has a new wave of social historians turned to the careful investigation of prostitution in a specific time and place; most notable here is a cluster of new publications on France, Britain, and the United States during the fifty years before World War I.[11] This study fits into this latter category and seeks to illuminate the Italian experience, which has so far been virtually neglected by historians.[12]

I have organized my investigation into two major sections: one on the state and the other on the women who were, or were accused of being, prostitutes. The first section examines chronologically the policy of regulation as embodied in Italian law and implemented by bureaucrats in the Ministry of the Interior in Rome. Since the state had the power to define prostitution and to label women as prostitutes, I had to look closely at both the theory behind prostitution policy and the modifications this theory underwent in practice. The labeling function of the state did not go unchallenged, however, and this section also explains the campaign by various groups of the Left, including feminists, to replace regulation with abolitionist legislation. From its critics' point of view, the Italian system was illiberal in restricting the civil rights of prostitutes and sexist in disciplining women and ignoring their clients. While succeeding governments did modify and liberalize the original Cavourian statute, reformers failed to move the Italian kingdom out of the regulationist camp.

The second section shifts the focus to the lives of Italian prostitutes, especially as they came in contact with the state. I begin by reconstructing a social profile of prostitutes and comparing them to Italian women in general in age, civil status, education, and former profession. These data draw heavily on the rich records of Bologna, supplemented by national statistics. When possible, I compare Bologna to the other major cities on the peninsula: Naples, Milan, Rome, Turin, Palermo, Florence, Genoa, and Venice. I then follow the life cycles of these prostitutes as they "interacted" with the officials who enforced the regulation laws at the local level: police and public health doctors. By looking at such routine, daily contact on the streets, in police stations, and in sifilicomi, I can begin to measure the repressiveness of the system and evaluate whether it benefited prostitutes in areas such as health care for venereal disease. This section also details how both registered and clandestine prostitutes increasingly resisted the regulation system and foiled its efficient operation.

The study of prostitution, an extremely complex phenomenon, involves the intersection of research on crime, women, sex, disease, law, and bureaucracy and thus invites analysis from diverse perspectives. I have approached the subject as a practitioner of social history, women's studies, and criminology, drawing on all three disciplines. Social history teaches us not to ignore the powerless or unorganized but to value their experience as vital to understanding the past. As a feminist, I was drawn to the study of one such marginal group, prostitutes, whose lives lay practically untouched by the new social history when I began this project a decade ago. The progress of women's history from focusing on the victimization of women to recognizing their real, if limited, power also influenced my thinking: rather than emphasize exclusively the domination of the state as an institution of social control, I concurrently document the attempts of prostitutes actively to shape their lives within or against the regulation system. Far from being passive victims, nineteenth-century prostitutes exhibited a surprising vitality, flexibility, and ingenuity.

Finally, my reading in the history and sociology of crime has led me to look beyond the deviance of individual women for the etiology of prostitution. Michel Foucault's history of French prisons, *Discipline and Punish*, provides a model of disciplinary power applicable to the tolerated brothels of Italy.[13] While Foucault's work is top heavy in its concentration on the *pouvoir* (power) and *savoir* (knowledge) of the state, it brilliantly analyzes how prisons create delinquents or, applied to this case, how the regulation system creates prostitutes. I also profited from criminal sociology, especially the work of the labeling and interactionist theorists, who encouraged me to reconstruct the daily, face-to-face encounters between government officials—police and doctors—and prostitutes.[14] While the unevenness of historical sources limits this strategy, I try to show how the dialectical interaction between the state and prostitutes profoundly affected both parties. Neither state legislation nor the conduct of individual women can alone explain Italian prostitution of the period; only the interaction of the two, both embedded in specific political, economic, and social conditions, accounts for the etiology, form, and extent of prostitution in late nineteenth- and early twentieth-century Italy.

Introduction

Debate continues about prostitution, and historical studies can shed light on a political issue that remains emotional, uncomfortable, and perplexing. While prostitution legislation in Europe and the United States has failed on its own terms, lawmakers have been unable, or unwilling, to develop innovative alternatives. It is prostitutes themselves, rather than governmental officials, who are now beginning to speak up and put their plight on the political agenda. As the Conclusion explains, prostitutes in Italy have recently formed their own Committee for Civil Rights to lobby for modification of the Legge Merlin, the 1958 law decriminalizing prostitution. Similar movements spearheaded by prostitutes and seeking decriminalization are underway in other nations such as France, Britain, and the United States. In February 1985 an international conference on prostitution was held in Amsterdam; its international character recalls those of the last century, yet it differs in being organized by prostitutes rather than police, doctors, or middle-class feminists.[15] The world of Guadelina Bistocchi may seem quite distant, but the fundamental problems of poor women as well as the discourse on prostitution have changed little in the past century. Perhaps an understanding of her life can help us better comprehend and evaluate the protests and proposals of prostitutes today.

I

The State

1

Regulation:
The Cavour Law of 1860

On February 15, 1860, in the midst of the wars of unification, Prime Minister Cavour promulgated a law on prostitution for the new Italian nation. His homeland, the Kingdom of Piedmont, was in the process of liberating the rest of northern Italy from Austrian rule, and he hastened to substitute his king's authority for that of Austria. According to Cavour's vision of the Risorgimento, the conservative, but constitutional, monarchy of King Victor Emmanual of Piedmont provided the strongest rallying point for the Italian peninsula, which had been fragmented for several centuries. As prime minister, he moved quickly to centralize power. Thus the law on prostitution became known as the Regolamento Cavour (Cavour Regulation) because it emanated directly from a ministerial decree rather than legislative action. It took effect in Piedmont and those provinces already annexed: Lombardy, Tuscany, Modena, Parma, and the Romagna. It was later extended to the Papal States and the Kingdom of the Two Sicilies in 1861, Venice in 1866, and Rome in 1870 as unification was completed. The Cavour Regulation, and the relationship it prescribed between the state and prostitution, would remain in effect until 1888.

The new law pleased administrators, such as prefects, police, and government doctors, involved in implementing official policy on prostitution. Most perceived prostitution as a growing problem and despaired of dealing effectively with it by means of the disparate legislation on the books of the old Italian states. As Bolis wrote in 1871 upon the completion of unification by the acquisition of Rome: "Until these last few years, prostitution in Italy was nearly left to itself; no fixed norm, no regulation, no special services were established. All regular surveillance was neglected and prostitutes were left entirely to the caprice of agents of the municipal police, who in several cities, either directly or by means of their own wives, ran houses of prostitution."[1] Indeed, not only the diversity of legal codes but also ineffective and corrupt administration had characterized state policy toward prostitution on the Italian peninsula before 1860.

During the early years of the nineteenth century, the various royal and papal rulers of Italy had employed either prohibition or regulation to manage prostitution. Historians have not yet clarified the confusing map of prostitution during this period, but observers of the era offer a few uniformly pessimistic glimpses into the situation in a few states.[2] An example of prohibition could be found in Rome, where the pope denounced prostitution as a sin and, consequently, a crime. Although the medieval papacy had periodically tolerated prostitution, in the nineteenth century Pope Pius IX compared the official recognition of brothels to "the licensing of an illicit trade in human flesh, unworthy of civilized and Christian peoples."[3] Yet according to a French observer, Dr. Jacquot, papal authorities enforced prohibition in an inconsistent, ineffective, and sometimes brutal manner:

> The most despotic arbitrariness, influenced by the ignorance of wordly matters and by the hesitations or hypocrisy of the popes, vicarate, inquisitors, and governors, has led alternately to the relaxation or tightening of the law, now toward temporary and apparently tacit tolerance, now toward the most brutal measures. . . . Meanwhile, prostitution has never ceased to exist in Rome in spite of imprisonment, fines, torture [and] every type of harassment.[4]

On the contrary, Rome continued to be a notorious center of European prostitution, where women openly plied their trade "in the streets, in dark corners, in brothels, under deserted porticos [and] along remote thoroughfares."[5]

Several states had drawn up legislation based on the policy of regulation the French had introduced during the Napoleonic occupation; enforcement, however, was equally inefficient. For example, in Palermo an ordinance of 1823 ended centuries of sanctions against prostitutes and charged police and health officials with vigilance over newly tolerated brothels. Yet in practice, according to historian Antonino Cutrera, "the lower ranks of the police were completely corrupt; their dishonesty and venality prevented the laws and regulations from being enforced."[6] Since public health officials also lacked "zeal and honesty," he concluded that members of both administrations "closed their eyes" to the increasing numbers of unauthorized prostitutes.[7] Under a similar system, Bologna established a health office and a special hospital for infected prostitutes, but in the opinion of Bolis, these services constituted only a "shadow" of what was really "indispensable" for the effective containment of venereal disease.[8]

Cavour replaced this patchwork of law and custom with a homogeneous statute applicable to all communes, urban or rural, that harbored prostitutes. His statute made regulation, rather than prohibition or decriminalization, official policy. From its beginnings, then, the unified Italian state labeled prostitutes according to regulationist criteria. Underlying the legal philosophy of the Cavour Regulation was the premise that, as regulationist Giuseppe Sormani explained, "prostitution is not a crime, and therefore cannot be prosecuted according to the penal code; but it is a vice, morally and hygienically dangerous to Society. The exercise of prostitution can therefore be considered from the same point of view as that of unsanitary industries, which Society, with every right, subjects to special regulations and special surveillance."[9] Accordingly, Cavour sidestepped the penal code and issued a special regulation that legalized prostitution but with strict controls. Admitting that the private act of prostitution did not constitute a crime, he nevertheless feared the consequences for public order, morality, and health. To protect "Society," the law required that prostitutes register with police, undergo biweekly health checks, and report to special hospitals for the cure of venereal disease—the so-called sifilicomi—if found infected. Thus the

15

Italian state labeled prostitutes as deviants rather than criminals, but deviants dangerous enough to justify and indeed necessitate special government intervention.

What circumstances can explain Cavour's preoccupation with an issue like prostitution in the midst of war, with unification not yet even assured? Why did the articulation of the relationship between the state and prostitution assume such urgency? The standard histories of the Risorgimento rarely mention social questions in their accounts of the military and political maneuverings of Cavour, Giuseppe Garibaldi, and other nationalist leaders. Yet the Cavour Regulation formed part of a wave of legislation, as yet largely unstudied, that constituted the social counterpart to political unification. Before examining the regulation in more detail, I must explain the urgency of its promulgation. First, I review the enormous changes occurring in the social and economic structure of nineteenth-century Italy. In many ways, these developments were common to other Western nations and explain why the debate on prostitution took on international dimensions by midcentury. Second, I examine the military and political circumstances more specific to Italy that explain the choice of regulation by Cavour and the timing of its proclamation as law. The sum of these elements—social, economic, military, and political—propelled the prostitute to the forefront as a dominant symbol of the dangerous classes.

The Prostitute and the "Dangerous Classes"

The tremendous changes of the nineteenth century enabled the Italian ruling classes, and in particular the new bourgeoisie, to consolidate their political, social, and economic hegemony. Yet these changes also provoked anxiety and fears that crystallized around figures of the so-called *classi pericolose* (dangerous classes). According to Bolis's definition, "the dangerous classes of society are formed from all those individuals who, being destitute of the necessary means of subsistence, live in idleness and vagabondage at the expense of other citizens. Trampling on the supreme law of man, which is that of work, they constitute a permanent danger to social order; the danger is even greater in those cases where the idle abandon themselves to perverse instincts."[10] Bolis, like other writers of the period, singled out the prostitute as the most representative female figure of this lumpen proletariat. Three revolutions—in demography, economy, and the family— underlay the prominent position of the prostitute in the iconography of the dangerous classes.

Like other areas of Europe, Italy experienced marked demographic growth in the nineteenth century. Between 1811 and 1911 the population more than doubled, growing from 18 to 37 million. Expansion accelerated after unification, at which time residents of the peninsula numbered roughly 26 million.[11] This dramatic increase was due primarily to a drop in the death rate, especially child mortality, resulting from a variety of factors including increased food supply, improved sanitation, and the end of the cyclic epidemics typical of preindustrial Europe. While demographers disagree on the levels of fertility during the nineteenth century, several claim that a short-term increase in the birthrate accelerated population growth before the long-term decline in fertility typical of twentieth-century Europe took effect. All agree, however, that the predominant characteristic of this period, which preceded the widespread adoption of birth control, was an overall growth of the population.

With land and labor opportunities in the countryside inadequate for supporting the swelling population, many peasants migrated to urban centers. The nine major cities that form the focus of this study expanded rapidly (Table 1.1); all except Venice showed a demographic growth of over 50 percent between unification and World War I. Turin, Rome, and Milan more than doubled in size.[12] Moreover, migration to the cities involved women as well as men, most notably young, single women looking for work. As rural holdings grew smaller or peasants lost their land altogether, fewer families could provide daughters with dowries or even afford to keep them at home. Unlike many of the men, single women did not emigrate to the Americas, and only a small number traveled to France, Germany, or Switzerland to find employment. Most went no further than the nearest large town or city in their region, a pattern that gave rural families hope of retaining ties to their daughters.[13]

Because of the economy, however, migration to the city did not

17

Table 1.1. *Population of Nine Communes*

	1861	1911	Percentage increase
Naples	449,050	678,031	51
Rome	244,354[a]	542,123	122
Milan	242,457	599,200	147
Turin	205,378	427,106	108
Palermo	194,463	341,088	75
Genoa	151,348	272,221	80
Florence	143,213	232,860	63
Venice	130,997[a]	160,719	23
Bologna	109,395	172,628	58

SOURCES: Direzione Generale della Statistica, *Censimento della popolazione del Regno d'Italia al 10 febbraio 1901*, 5 vols. (Rome: G. Bertero, 1902–1904); Ufficio del Censimento, *Censimento della popolazione del Regno d'Italia al 10 giugno 1911*, 3 vols. (Rome: G. Bertero, 1914).
[a]Population in 1872.

always solve the problem of unemployment, particularly in Italy, where the industrial take-off did not occur until the late 1890s and even then failed to match developments in the other major western European countries. Furthermore, industry grew significantly only in the northern cities like Milan and Turin, while the urban populations of central and southern Italy continued to depend on commerce (Naples) or government and church bureaucracies (Rome) for employment. That urbanization and industrialization were not inextricably linked is clearest in the case of Rome, where the population increased over 122 percent between 1861 and 1911, a fifty-year period which saw little change in the economic base. The crisis created by industrial development's lagging behind demographic growth was most apparent in the waves of emigration from Italy. In fact the gap was so great that emigration did not cease with the industrial take-off of the 1890s but increased until cut off by World War I and the immigration restrictions legislated by the United States in the 1920s.[14]

Lacking the outlet of emigration, women competed fiercely for the available jobs in Italian cities. Since factory employment, especially in skilled or heavy industry, was generally restricted to

18

men, women congregated in domestic service and garment making
or other sweated trades based on piecework. In short, women's
work, although carried out in an urban rather than a rural environment, changed little, remaining the most unmodernized sector
of a slowly industrializing economy. The only major exception to
this pattern was the textile industry, which was largely located in
medium-sized cities of the North and employed, at least until the
turn of the century, large numbers of women.[15] Yet the large urban centers involved in this study, like Milan and Turin, remained relatively unaffected; and where new textile factories were
established, the wages of women workers were extremely low,
averaging one-half to two-thirds those of men in equivalent occupational categories.

As a result of demographic growth and high rates of migration,
family patterns also began to change during the nineteenth century. In the premodern period, the family was characterized by
what two historians, Joan Scott and Louise Tilly, have called the
"family economy."[16] In both peasant and artisan households, all
members worked together to produce what the family consumed.
Teenage daughters could often earn their keep by spinning and
weaving until they were old enough to receive an appropriate
dowry and marry or else join a convent. If the family could not
feed all its children, several were sent out to work on neighboring
farms either as apprentices, farmhands, or more often in the case
of girls, as servants. These children remained part of the family
economy since they worked close to home, sent back extra earnings, and returned when the household could financially reab-
sorb them.

As the century progressed, the "family wage economy" gradually replaced the traditional producer economy as an increasing
proportion of the members in each household began to work for
outside employers. This shift occurred in both rural areas, where
land shortages reduced peasants to day laborers, and cities,
which were marked by industrialization and growth of the tertiary sector. Scott and Tilly stress the continuity between these two
types of family economies because, in both, all individuals contributed to the group whether as producers or wage earners. As
young women migrated further and further away to find work,
however, a growing number—perhaps unintentionally and to

19

their dismay—lost contact with their families. Unless they had relatives in the city, they had difficulty finding not only a place to work but also a place to live. This precariousness of housing may partially explain the attraction of domestic service, which paid badly but included room and board. Positions in the houses of strangers in large cities, however, did not offer the protection and security that had typified the rural households of family friends. Lacking male protection, new female migrants were at the mercy of domestic employers who were often as exploitative as industrial overseers or the merchants who organized the sweated trades.

The almost hysterical fear of prostitution in the nineteenth century can be understood only against this background of economic and social change that brought visible numbers of single, unemployed, and homeless women to Italian cities. To middle- and upper-class observers, they were all prostitutes—or potential prostitutes—because they did not fit into any of the traditional female categories: daughter, mother, wife, or perhaps, nun. Unlike the new migrants, women in the old typology were in some degree defined by their relationship to men. The prostitute was a woman alone, and to many she embodied a cluster of traits— idleness, illegality, immorality, and female autonomy—that were antithetical to the bourgeois ethic of the nineteenth century. The symbol of the prostitute assumed its potency from this overlapping of several marginal groups—the idle poor, the criminal, the sexual deviant, and the woman—in one figure.

First, in the eyes of respectable society, prostitutes formed part of the ranks of the idle poor, those able-bodied young men and women who crowded into the cities without jobs or homes. Bolis graphically described the sense of submersion felt by the urban ruling classes in the face of widespread emigration from the countryside: "As a wave runs to the sea, so to the large cities flow all those perverse and roving people who shun work and disdain the slender salary of a laborer."[17] Like his contemporaries, he attributed this "roving" not to demographic growth and limited economic opportunities but to absence of "all moral sense" in the newcomers.[18] Rejecting the discipline of honest work, these "disgusting worms which infect society" flocked to the cities' "most dirty streets," which resembled "polluted and filthy sewers."[19] Of course prostitutes did indeed have a profession, but they were lumped with this idle crowd because their lives lacked discipline, routine, and stability. To control these wandering masses, the nineteenth-century state developed new policies for the poor, who had traditionally been dependent on the benevolence of the church. For the "deserving poor," those who could not work because of age or health, the government established, expanded, and and rationalized a cluster of institutions: foundling homes, orphanages, insane asylums, and hospitals. The idle poor, on the other hand, received only repression and repatriation to their hometowns as the state strictly enforced new laws against vagabondage.[20]

Second, prostitutes were thought to have close ties to criminals, the element of the dangerous classes that had degenerated from laziness to illegality: "The man who is dissipated today will be a thief and swindler tomorrow in order to feed his wicked passions. Idleness [is] the first link in a long chain which ends in dishonor and prison."[21] Although current estimates of crime rates in the nineteenth century differ, state officials of the period perceived an explosion of delinquency. As the middle class grew and accumulated possessions, theft became a special focus of new legislation and police repression. The fear of crime encompassed prostitution because experts believed that both phenomena sprang from the same depraved impulses. More specifically, as Giovanni Gozzoli, the author of a treatise on prostitution, observed, "Authors of crime often find refuge in houses of prostitution."[22] Against crime, as against the idle poor, the state took measures. To increase surveillance on the streets, it established urban police forces; to discipline the criminal, it initiated a building program for prisons and reformatories.[23]

Third, prostitutes fell into the marginal category of sexual deviants. While historians disagree as to the severity of sexual repression in everyday life, it is clear that prescriptive literature of the nineteenth century increasingly isolated, defined, and condemned extramarital sex.[24] Restrictions were especially severe for women, who were, ironically, considered to be dominated by their sexual organs and yet passionless. According to this line of reasoning, if biology determined the natural role of women to be motherhood, then puberty, menstruation, pregnancy, and menopause logically controlled their physical and emotional life cycles. Diagnoses of doctors and psychiatrists affirmed that sexuality was

21

the key to understanding the female body and mind. Yet in normal women this biological imperative found fulfillment in motherhood rather than in individual or egotistical sexual satisfaction. In his study of prostitution, Giuseppe Tammeo emphasized the naturalistic basis of marriage: "The monogamous union is the ultimate form of sexual selection, which, slowly, by way of interminable struggles, formed and raised marriage to a social institution whose perfectibility is always increasing as the struggle for life augments the moral and material inheritance of the peoples."[25] Such writers used science, first Comtean positivism and later Darwinian evolutionism, to reinforce rather than challenge the traditional religious prescription of the female role.

Promiscuous and usually single, the prostitute came to be viewed in the nineteenth century as not only morally but also biologically deviant. Ironically, many of the same writers who eulogized marriage also confirmed the need for prostitution in order to satisfy the male sexual drive, which was also "natural" and frustrated by the passionlessness of marriage.[26] But necessity did not make prostitution normal; the consequence of a heightened reverence for motherhood was a marginalization of alternate forms of female sexuality. Thus, as a form of sexual deviance, prostitution came under close scrutiny and control by the nineteenth-century state, as did other "perversions" such as birth control, abortion, homosexuality, and all forms of childhood sexuality.

Fourth, prostitutes bore a special onus because they were women. The category of women is not strictly comparable to those of the idle poor, criminals, and sexual deviants because most women were integrated into "normal" society as daughters, wives, and mothers. Yet even in these roles they were legally subordinate to their male relatives, thus prevented from full participation in the mainstream of public life. Even more liminal were "independent" women, those who lived, by choice or by necessity, without the protection of a man. Historians have documented the difficult struggle of independent women in the middle and upper classes to gain entrance into universities, professional occupations, and the political sphere. Yet they have often ignored the fact that many lower-class female migrants to the city were also, if often unwillingly, autonomous. Fear of this second uprooted group centered on the prostitute, who was obviously detached economically, emotionally, morally, and sexually from the nuclear family and male control. Not only the new legislation on prostitution but also the establishment of orphanages and reformatories for homeless girls illustrated the preoccupation of the nineteenth-century state with protecting society from the destabilizing influence of lower-class, autonomous women. It sought either to separate these women from respectable citizens by enclosure in institutions or to reform and reintegrate them into families.

Thus the prostitute constituted a powerful and in some ways unique symbol of deviancy in nineteenth-century Italy.[27] In the context of the economic and social transformations of the period, this symbol became a target for state efforts to assert hegemony and restore order. But while demographic, economic, and social developments explain the general preoccupation with prostitution in nineteenth-century Italy, military and political considerations determined the exact form and specific timing of state intervention. Since the factors described above were, to some extent, common to other western European nations and the United States, the debate about the proper relationship of the state to prostitution took on international proportions involving not only public officials but organizations of doctors, police, lawyers, and feminists. The simultaneous "discovery" of prostitution as a serious social problem by an entire block of countries can be understood only against the shared backdrop of the dislocations caused by urbanization and industrialization. Yet Western nations did not adopt identical strategies of social control, and the timing of state initiatives, rather than converging on one decade, ranged throughout the century. In Italy, the political requirements of unification accounted for Cavour's establishment of regulation in 1860, but the origins of this policy may be found in Piedmont during the 1850s and in the preparations for war.

As prime minister of Piedmont after 1852, Cavour considered a modern, well-trained, and well-equipped army essential to his goal of unifying Italy. After the failures of nationalist uprisings in 1848, it was clear that spontaneous revolution and a patchwork military force were incapable of toppling Austrian rule in the North and asserting Piedmont's hegemony over the lower peninsula. Many of Cavour's reforms in the 1850s—the extension of

23

railway lines, initiation of an arms industry, and establishment of banks—were geared, at least in part, to providing the transportation, weapons, and capital necessary for a war of unification.[28] Cavour also needed a healthy army, and his focus on the military aspects of the Risorgimento led him to a preoccupation with the high rates of venereal disease in the Turinese garrison.[29] To minimize the debilitating effects of infection on the performance of his soldiers, he authorized his minister of the interior, Urbano Rattazzi, to investigate the problem. Rattazzi recommended the adoption of regulationist legislation.

The recommendation was not surprising since regulation as a policy had originally been developed to meet military needs. In 1802, after years of war, Napoleon I had initiated the inspection of prostitutes following his armies in an attempt to control venereal disease.[30] This new strategy had been further elaborated in successive pieces of French legislation and then adopted by several other European nations, most notably Belgium and Prussia. Underlying the philosophy of both Napoleon and Cavour was the assumption that prostitution constituted the "most certain and diffuse means of the transmission of infectious diseases of the sexual organs and particularly of syphilis."[31] Characterized as "the principle source of the germs of infection," prostitutes became the only section of civil society to undergo forced registration, examination, and treatment.[32] Regulationists simply assumed that the elimination of disease from brothels would secure the good health of the army.

While regulationist legislation applied only to female prostitutes, it is interesting to note that one group of men—the lower ranks of the military forces—also underwent periodic examination and required treatment for venereal disease. In the Italian army and navy, health inspection took place once a week, on Sundays.[33] Since special military discipline restricted the rights of members of the armed forces, they occupied a very different legal status from members of civil society. The military's submission to examination was not required by civil statute and therefore did not form an exact parallel to the treatment of prostitutes, or justify it. But the singling out of these two groups for inspection by government doctors demonstrated the importance of the initial link between military necessity and the introduction of regulation.

Sormani explicitly pointed out this relationship when he blamed "the triad"—soldiers, sailors, and prostitutes—for keeping alive the germ of syphilis throughout the centuries.[34]

From the military point of view, then, the prostitute represented the overlapping of not four, but five, liminal and potentially threatening groups. To the idle poor, the criminal, the sexual deviant, and the woman, was added the category of the sick. Contagion, in fact, provided a rich metaphor that encapsulated all five categories since the prostitute was considered morally as well as physically infectious. Prophylactic measures against prostitutes, the assumed carriers of venereal disease, were first developed in Italy to shield the army but later extended to ever wider circles of civil society. The defense of regulation on the basis of benefits to health appears especially important in the light of Foucault's suggestion that the "healthy body" became the hallmark of the middle classes in the nineteenth century. Lacking the "pure blood" that defined the limits of the nobility, the bourgeoisie substituted the notion of a body uncorrupted by the indulgences of the decadent aristocracy and uncontaminated by the infections of the poor.[35] The advance of medical knowledge and the professionalization of doctors multiplied the value placed on health as the century progressed. The state, assuming the role of guarantor of good health, responded with the expansion of hospitals and the founding of university clinics, both of which played a central role in the fight against venereal disease. Thus, as long as prostitutes were blamed as the propagators of infection, regulation continued to be defended as the best screen to medically shield the rest of the population.

Legislative History of Regulation

In the ideological framework of the 1850s and 1860s, regulation seemed a modern and innovative policy that fit quite nicely into Cavour's general strategy for reforming Piedmont and uniting Italy. Admittedly, Rattazzi modeled Piedmont's new prostitution legislation on that of France and Belgium; his proposal would not have been accepted, however, had it been antithetical to Cavour's basic philosophy. British historian Denis Mack Smith has defined this philosophy as a combination of "theoretical liberalism" and "practical Machiavellianism," both of which contributed to Piedmont's eventual ascendancy to leadership of the Risorgimento.[36] The basis for Piedmont's claim to liberal leadership lay in its Statuto, the only constitution granted by an Italian ruling house during the revolutions of 1848 that was not later revoked. In the 1850s Cavour sought to enhance the enlightened reputation of his kingdom through a series of reforms such as the curtailment of ecclesiastical immunities, the granting of asylum for exiles from other Italian states, modernization of the penal code, and the encouragement of capitalist economic development. Within ten years Cavour "beat, molded, and transformed" a backward Piedmont into "a magnetic and central element of the new liberal Italian politics."[37] At the same time, Cavour's "practical Machiavellianism" reinforced the power and prestige of the monarchical state. Internally, he not only centralized and rationalized the bureaucracy but established in 1852 a new police force, the Guardie di Pubblica Sicurezza (Public Security Guards), to guarantee order.[38] To raise Piedmont's profile in foreign affairs, he modernized the army and inserted himself into European politics, first at the Paris Peace Conference of 1856 at the end of the Crimean War, later through the Plombières agreement with Napoleon III arranging an alliance against Austria and clearing the way for an Italian kingdom in the North. This realpolitik assured that the wars of unification in 1859–1860 would not repeat the mistakes of 1848–1849.

From a broader historical perspective, Cavour's "liberalism" and "Machiavellianism" might be equated with what Foucault has identified as the two major legacies of the Enlightenment: a passion for civil rights and a respect for discipline. In his *Discipline and Punish*, Foucault has pointed out that European philosophes revered classical Rome precisely because they believed that it embodied these two qualities: "in its republican aspect, it was the very embodiment of liberty; in its military aspect, it was the ideal schema of discipline."[39] He goes on to describe how the French state, in the nineteenth century, established or reorganized various institutions such as the prison, the school, and the military training camp according to this double model inherited from the eighteenth century. Not surprisingly, this double model aptly characterized the philosophy of first Piedmont and later the unified Italian state, both of which looked explicitly to France for a legislative and administrative blueprint.

The new Piedmontese policy of regulating prostitution reflected, at least in theory, this philosophy because it took into consideration liberty and discipline and struck a certain balance between them. In the spirit of Cesare Beccaria and enlightened penal reform, Piedmont legalized the act of prostitution, which in and of itself did no harm to other individual members of society. As a nineteenth-century representative of this "classical" school of enlightened criminology explained, "immorality in itself is not punishable, because the State is in a position only to judge conduct manifested in external acts, not the disposition of the soul appertaining to the internal life."[40] Regulationists, who were secular and usually anticlerical, denounced religious crusades against prostitution and excessive punishment such as torture, branding, and flogging. Prostitutes whose conduct remained within the limits prescribed by regulationist legislation should undergo no retribution. Those who broke the law deserved moderate, measured, and humane punishment: short periods of arrest or small fines. To its supporters, then, regulation offered a progressive and rational step in the process of penal reform begun in the eighteenth century.

Concurrently, regulationist legislation did not guarantee total liberty to prostitutes, since it disciplined the practice of their profession in the name of social good. Sormani expressed the regulationist point of view when he affirmed that "society has every right to impose special restrictions on the liberty of prostitutes in order to protect itself against the harms that these females continually present to the social body."[41] These "harms" fell into three categories: those against public order, public morality, and public health. To protect the "social body" from the negative side effects of prostitution, the Piedmontese state submitted prostitutes to registration, examination, and treatment in the sifilicomi. Critics of regulation claimed to see no difference between the traditional, "despotic" treatment of prostitutes and the new discipline, but regulationists defended their policy as rational rather than arbitrary, moderate rather than harsh, secular rather than religious, and necessary to the construction of the modern state— first Piedmont and later Italy.

Two pieces of legislation, both drawn up by Rattazzi, defined Piedmont's new system of regulation.[42] On July 20, 1855 Rattazzi promulgated the first, experimental measure, the Ministerial Instructions concerning Prostitution. Based on the recommendation of Casimiro Sperino, a well-known specialist in the treatment of venereal disease at the University of Turin, the Ministerial Instructions relied heavily on the three-pronged strategy enshrined in the codes of Paris and Brussels: registration, examination, and treatment.[43] A special *polizia dei costumi* (morals police), drawn from the ranks of the Guardie di Pubblica Sicurezza, were put in charge of the system; registration and cancellation from official records was at their discretion. They also controlled the movement of prostitutes, granting permissions for change of residence, scheduling examinations, and ordering the sick to hospitals for recovery. Doctors performed the health checks but under strict subordination to police.

On January 1, 1857 the new Regulation on Prostitution for the City of Turin, also called the Rattazzi Regulation, replaced the Ministerial Instructions within the jurisdiction of the capital. The concentration of the new law on Turin reflected a preoccupation with the health of the garrison stationed there. In addition, new provisions were intended to meet the criticism by liberals that the instructions of 1855 "still preserved too much of the old regime," that is, despotism.[44] Critics thought the government should lower the profile of the police while emphasizing the public health functions of the system and assuring the prostitute that the purpose of police registration was humanitarian: to protect her from venereal disease. In response, the Turin regulation established a new institution, the Ufficio Sanitario (Health Office), to administer the law. To improve medical care, the regulation also created the special post of ispettore sanitario (health inspector) to direct the team of doctors who regularly examined the registered prostitutes. Finally, in line with the ongoing rationalization of the Piedmontese bureaucracy, brothels were classified for tax purposes, and standard prices for licenses and medical checks were fixed throughout the city. It is questionable whether the institution of the Health Office represented true reform. While the spatial separation of prostitution services from police headquarters was innovative, an officer from the Public Security Division continued to supervise the medical staff.

This second statute, the Turin regulation, provided the model for the Cavour Regulation promulgated on February 15, 1860.[45] Like the Statuto and law codes, the Cavour Regulation represented the transplanting of Piedmontese legislation to the new nation with few modifications. This transfer took place under the aegis of Piedmontese administrators and occurred almost automatically without parliamentary discussion or careful study of local conditions. Because of this process of "Piedmontization," the fundamental laws of the new Italian state never succeeded in gaining respect and consensus among large strata of the population.[46] Even the small minority with the right to suffrage was given no opportunity to shape social programs to suit the diversity of the peninsula. Critics would later charge the Cavour Regulation with authoritarianism on the grounds that it resulted not from legislative action but from administrative decree.

Pragmatism, rather than ideological rigidity, motived Cavour to impose centralized legislation, like the Cavour Regulation, on the new Kingdom. Before unification he had been an admirer of English local government and vocally supported decentralization as a model for united Italy. With the rapid acquisition of so many diverse territories and with the immediate outbreak of brigandage in the South, however, the Piedmontese decided that only centralized control could preserve unity.[47] As historian William Salomone has pointed out, this strategy of Cavour and his successors of the Liberal Right proceeded "almost as if Italian society were another antagonist to be subdued" and encouraged "an erosive 'social war.'"[48] In the crackdown against opponents, the demarcation between political and common criminals was often blurred, as illustrated by the campaign against the "brigands" of the South.

The Cavour Regulation reflected this preoccupation with the homogenization of the Italian population and the suppression of subversion. Rather than copying the municipal nature of other European regulationist codes, it instead established a national system directed from the Ministry of the Interior. Thus the Cavour law was unique in its aim to identify and control every prostitute, urban or rural, throughout the country. Under the Italian system, no gaps would be left in surveillance, no place of hiding left for prostitutes. Theoretically, the Cavour Regulation insured that one group of deviants—prostitutes—would not trouble the social order and public morality of the new state.

With the transition from the Turinese to the Italian statute, administrators broadened their perspective not just from urban to national but also from military to civilian. Certainly, the good health of the army continued to be important as long as the South harbored secessionist sentiment and Venice and Rome remained outside the union. But rather than simply extending regulation to all garrison towns or potential war zones, Cavour enveloped the entire population. The government took on the obligation to protect all respectable society from disease, especially those middle classes that would provide the bulwark of the new Italy. As Sormani pointed out, syphilis did not just punish the immoral sections of society but could infect innocent women and children: "Who among us would concern himself with protecting the health of the libertine or the prostitute, if syphilis stopped at the libertine, if those innocent of impure contacts did not also risk great dangers in a contaminated society, if infection could not be transmitted to offspring with great damage to the human race?"[49] While military necessity prompted the introduction of regulation in Piedmont, broader concerns about the destabilizing effects of disorder, immorality, and disease on the civilian population of the new nation assured its perpetuation.

Like the Turinese statute, the Cavour Regulation embodied the seemingly contradictory values of liberty and discipline that underpinned the political philosophy of the ruling party, the Liberal Right. As the following detailed scrutiny of the law illustrates, components of state control greatly outweighed protection of civil rights for prostitutes,[50] and in this sense the prostitution legislation typified the general tendency of the new kingdom to put constraints on the liberty of its citizens. Yet the modernity of the Cavour Regulation should not be overlooked. Its leading proponents were not drawn from the ranks of the traditional ruling classes, that is, the conservative landed aristocracy and the church. Little interested in social reform, these feudal elements continued to condemn prostitution as immoral and tended to favor the policy of prohibition sanctioned by the pope. Instead, regulationists represented a group of bureaucrats, police officials, and doctors who sought to build a new state based on the principles of science, reason, and efficiency. In social origins, they were middle class or, like Cavour, liberal aristocrats who had been influenced by Enlightenment thought and favored moderate change. Thus regulationists occupied, at midcentury, the center of the political spectrum, between the feudal classes on the right, who favored prohibition, and the Mazzinian democrats on the left, who championed abolition. The political position of the Liberal Right becomes clearer through analysis of the elements of liberty and control in the Cavour Regulation.

The Cavour Regulation based its claim to enlightenment on the legalization of prostitution. Dropping the blinders of moralism, regulationists prided themselves on recognizing prostitution as a "necessary and ancient social evil."[51] Lamenting prostitution as a "deplorable necessity," numerous tracts warned readers that proper analysis could proceed only from a realistic and reasonable acceptance of its existence as a fact of history.[52] They pointed out that prostitution had been known to all human societies despite moral crusades and harsh laws against it. Furthermore, sex roles, which regulationists thought to be determined by the immutable principles of biology, required the continuation of prostitution. Possessed by a strong sex drive, men, especially single soldiers and sailors, needed an outlet for their passions. Prostitution provided a sexual safety valve for young men who might otherwise be driven to seduce or molest "honest" girls and married women, causing individual ruin and social chaos. As one writer concluded, prostitution constituted, "in the end, the antidote to, and preservation from, evils which would return men and the family back to barbarism and the conditions of brute animals."[53] On the basis of these assumptions about male sexuality, most regulationists denied the possibility of ever entirely eradicating this evil from society. Sormani spoke for an exceptional few when he wrote that he had "greater faith in the future of Humanity and in the future of women" than to accept the eternal nature of prostitution.[54] Yet even he supported the Cavour

Regulation because the government had to deal with society as it was in reality, "with its failings, with its prostitutes, with its syphilis."[55]

By legalizing prostitution the Cavour law promised to free prostitutes from the grip of the criminal underworld. Regulationists believed that, in the past, brothels had fostered gambling, drunkenness, and brawls as well as provided havens for thieves.[56] To disassociate prostitution from vice, the statute forbade "games of any sort and the serving of food or drink of any type" in tolerated houses.[57] Police, who set the hours for opening and closing, were authorized to make unannounced inspections "wherever they are believed necessary for the maintenance of public order."[58] In this way, delinquents could be easily rooted out of their hiding places. To minimize the deviant character of brothels, regulationists recommended that madams take as their model the small business and its principles of efficiency, cleanliness, rationality, and order. The state assumed that prostitutes would be grateful for the opportunity to systematize their lives according to bourgeois values.

The Cavour law also promised to protect individual employees from exploitation by madams.[59] When a woman entered a brothel, the owner was required to pay for the furnishings of her room, her clothes and linen, her biweekly health exams, and treatment for nonvenereal diseases (cure in the sifilicomi was free). The owner had to make a list of the possessions brought by an entering prostitute and return them at her departure along with "all those things which she had bought with her own money and which had been added to the inventory."[60] Explicitly forbidding the maltreatment of prostitutes, the state not only fixed the price each brothel could charge but also the percentage of profit the owner could take from her employees. Prices were set according to class of brothel: customers paid five lire or more in first-class brothels; two to five lire in second-class brothels; and less than two lire in those of the third class. Of this, the prostitute kept one-fourth. Any disputes between madams and employees —for example, over money—were to be referred to the Health Office "for the necessary measures of conciliation."[61] Finally, the law required that managers inform the police of any woman who wished to leave prostitution; the employer could not keep a women against her will, even if the employee owed her money.

Through these stipulations, regulationists claimed that their system benefited and in fact protected prostitutes.

The majority of the articles in the Cavour Regulation, however, prescribed controls on the prostitute rather than guaranteed her liberty. While proponents differed as to the exact balance that should be struck between the rights of prostitutes and the protection of society, regulation, as its name implies, put more weight on the latter. To protect society, the Cavour Regulation employed the same strategies Foucault has described as characteristic of the administration of nineteenth-century prisons—enclosure, discipline, surveillance, and the collection of information—and the law can thus be analyzed in terms of these four strategies.

First, the regulated brothels, significantly called in popular jargon the *case chiuse* (closed houses), provided for enclosure. Although the Cavour law made some allowances for the practice of "isolated prostitutes" who lived and worked alone, it recommended that police chiefs give permission for such private practice "with much reserve and only with the agreement of the landlord."[62] The state preferred that prostitutes congregate in the tolerated houses since concentration facilitated control by police and doctors. Integrated into the "family" of the brothel supervised by a madam, prostitutes would lose their threatening status as independent women. To seal off these brothels, the law stipulated that their windows remain shut, covered with smoked glass in winter and persian blinds in the summer, "fixed and closed to the height of two meters measured from the floor of the room."[63] To prevent communication between outside and inside, prostitutes were forbidden to stand in the windows or doorways of their houses.

Enclosure prevented both the moral and physical pollution of society by contact with prostitutes. Whereas streetwalkers offended the moral sensibilities of the middle and upper classes, brothels made vice invisible. As an extra precaution, police were not to permit the opening of brothels "near schools, public buildings, and churches."[64] The opaque walls of the brothel were meant not only to hide sin, however, but also to contain disease. Since regulationists considered prostitutes the primary carriers of venereal disease, they hoped to decrease diffusion by limiting the area within which prostitutes could practice.

Second, as the regulationist Pietro Castiglione commented, "It is not enough to register or take note of and examine prostitutes; it is necessary to discipline them."[65] In brothels, as in the prisons Foucault described, discipline was intended to produce "docile bodies," to transform "the confused, non-utilitarian or dangerous multitudes into ordered multiplicity."[66] For example, procedures for entering a brothel involved a kind of self-mortification—the vaginal examination—that may have served to break the independence of the newly registered.[67] While the purpose was manifestly medical, vaginal examination constituted an invasion of privacy and even, according to public opinion of the period, a degradation. Once certified as healthy, a woman entering a brothel generally gave up her clothing and possessions to be kept by the madam, an act that further eroded her sense of identity. For the duration of her stay, she used the linen, clothes, and furnishings provided by the madam.

Discipline in brothels extended to the routine of the everyday, or as Foucault called it, "the discipline of the minute."[68] To prevent disorder and public immorality, detailed regulations restricted the movement of prostitutes. The law "absolutely" prohibited prostitutes from loitering in public streets and squares; wandering through neighborhoods near their brothels, especially "in the hours of vespers"; and going outside "without just cause" after eight at night in the winter and ten in the summer.[69] When they did leave the brothel, prostitutes were warned to be sober, dress modestly, and refrain from "following passersby through the streets" and "soliciting them with words and gestures."[70] The theater was off-limits. To guarantee public health, the law prescribed that government doctors examine prostitutes twice a week, either at the brothel or in the Health Office. Prostitutes who failed to comply with these regulations were subject to arrest.

Third, surveillance constituted the method of enforcing both enclosure and discipline. As Foucault pointed out, the early modern practice of cruel and unusual corporal punishment was replaced after the eighteenth century by "the uninterrupted play of calculated gazes."[71] Under the Cavour law, the Health Offices provided the base from which police could fan out over the city to insure that registered prostitutes obeyed disciplinary regulations and to root out clandestine prostitutes, that is, those not registered on police lists. Castiglione described his vision of a perfect system of surveillance as follows: "Surveillance [of prostitutes] for political and moral purposes is hardly possible unless the State has thousands of agents, all disciplined, all taking orders from the center, spread throughout the entire territory of the Kingdom, corresponding among themselves and ready to act at a moment's notice."[72] To facilitate this type of total surveillance, the law required that prostitutes seek permission from the morals police in order to change residence, absent themselves from their brothel for more than three days, enter a hospital, or leave the profession. Even if a woman succeeded in the difficult task of removing herself from police lists, surveillance over her behavior continued for three months to make sure she was no longer dangerous.

The vaginal examination constituted the sanitary equivalent of police surveillance. In prisons, Foucault found that "the examination is highly ritualized" and "it manifests the subjection of those who are perceived as objects and the objectivization of those who are subjected."[73] The vaginal examination separated the sick from the healthy, the dangerous from the innocuous. According to the law, it was to take place twice a week and be carried out "with the greatest care and employing all the means which the present state of science recognizes as useful for rendering more certain the diagnosis of venereal disease."[74] Despite these instructions, the primitive state of medical knowledge concerning the etiology and cure of venereal disease often prevented the correct classification of sick and well. That government doctors ignored their critics who pointed out this deficiency only underscored the double purpose of examination: the exercise of power as well as the protection of public health. The central ritual of regulation, examination, reenacted biweekly the subjection of the prostitute to the state. To prevent any "shadows" or gaps in health surveillance, brothels were subject to additional, unannounced inspections at the will of the police.

Fourth, surveillance served the purpose not only of enforcing enclosure and discipline but also of collecting information. Foucault emphasized this aspect of the examination when he wrote, "In it are combined the ceremony of power and the form of the experiment, the deployment of force and the establishment of truth."[75] Prompted by the desire to understand the phenomenon of prostitution, administrators issued eight forms to be filled out by police and doctors, a number that jumped to thirteen, excluding budgetary records, in 1880.[76] This abundance of forms included registers of prostitutes, results of examinations, admittances to the sifilicomi, and permissions to transfer residence. Four times yearly the *questore* (provincial commissioner of Public Security) compiled these forms and sent the resulting tabulations to the prefect, who relayed the most important data to the minister of the interior. Thus, from its inception, regulation involved prostitutes "in a whole mass of documents that capture[d] and fix[ed] them."[77] Surveillance, then, can be seen as not only a repressive force but also a creative one that produced information and conveyed it to the upper levels of the state. The purpose of this accumulation of knowledge was to improve the network of discipline, thus creating a circular relationship between "*pouvoir*" and "*savoir*," power and knowledge.

An analysis of the tolerated brothel in terms of the four Foucaultian strategies is useful but not complete. The peculiar nature of the brothel—a dangerous but also a necessary social space—created gaps in control and blindspots in knowledge. Unlike other total institutions, the brothel promoted the mixing of deviants with normal society, that is, male clients. Alternately, prostitutes regularly made excursions out of the closed house into respectable society, although their behavior was circumscribed by many rules. The role of the madam, as an intermediary between police and prostitute, also mitigated control; she had to be relied on to enforce the minute provisions of the law. Police and doctors were stationed outside the brothel, and the opaque walls that protected the public also hindered their "gaze." Prostitutes could and did exploit these gaps in power and knowledge to expand their autonomy. While the Cavour Regulation created, on paper and in intent, a system of almost total control, practice failed to measure up to the promise.

In theory, nonetheless, regulation suited the wider program of the Liberal Right to maintain and strengthen the fragile unity of Italy. An ambivalent figure, the prostitute offered a special challenge because official discourse recognized her role as necessary as well as subversive: necessary to meet male sexual demands yet subversive to public order and morality. In response, regulation, using the rhetoric of secular reason and science, promised to dicipline and make invisible a group that threatened to spread disorder, immorality, and disease. The system ingeniously combined repression toward individual prostitutes with a preservation of the institution of prostitution. The popularity of the prostitution policy of the Liberal Right came from its ability to preserve a practice desired by a great number of Italian men yet at the same time extend the power of the central state over its female practitioners.

The strategy of regulation steadily gained adherents, not only in Italy but throughout Europe, during the 1860s and 1870s. As more states adopted this policy, its supporters—most vocally doctors—urged the adoption of international accords. As Castiglione pointed out at the Congress of the Italian Medical Association in 1870, "All the local provisions [for regulation] are not yet sufficient without a large system of international prophylaxis,"[78] one that would leave no hiding place for the clandestine prostitute in all of Europe. Already in 1867 the members of the International Medical Congress, meeting in Paris, had approved a resolution that instituted the study of such a project. When the congress met two years later in Florence, the chairmen of the study commission, Dr. Crocq of Brussels and Dr. Rollet of Lyons, recommended the institution of an international system of regulation.[79] Discussion of this topic continued in the successive congresses in Rome (1871) and Vienna (1873); during the latter, one speaker optimistically predicted that "from the moment when prostitution shall become a regular and recognized institution, admitted and regulated by the State, its perfect organization will become possible."[80] By the mid-1870s this regulationist offensive seemed on the verge of victory.

2

Abolition:
The Crispi Law of 1888

The establishment of regulation in an increasing number of European nations during the middle decades of the nineteenth century did not go unchallenged. Opponents quickly founded a new movement, also international in scope, to fight the implementation of a pan-European regulation system. Members of this movement called themselves "abolitionists" because they wished to abolish regulation and, instead, decriminalize the private act of prostitution. They also drew a parallel between the American abolitionists' successful campaign against slavery and their own crusade to end the so-called white slave trade, the international traffic in women for the purpose of prostitution. In Italy, for example, the feminist Fanny Zampini Salazaro compared prostitutes to black slaves, lamenting, "Oh, that we now had in Italy a woman with the genius of Harriet Beecher Stowe, to describe vividly the horrors of the slavery of women!"[1] For abolitionists, "slavery" was the result of the system of regulation as well as of the white slave trade because the tolerated houses, they thought, provided the merchandise for international procurers.

The Italian movement for abolition posed a stiff challenge to the Cavour Regulation, a challenge that showed the ruling classes divided in their estimate of the proper relationship of the state to prostitution. If regulation represented official state policy, it did not receive unanimous support from all groups in a position to influence the formulation of prostitution legislation. Yet the political structure of the new kingdom made reform of existing laws extremely difficult. Pressure had to come from Parliament, which was weak compared to the centralized and hierarchical administrative bureaucracy of the Ministry of the Interior. The legislature, based on severely restricted suffrage, represented an elite that still exhibited the ideological and geographical fragmentation characteristic of the peninsula before 1860. Even if united, however, senators and deputies could only indirectly affect prostitution laws because the latter's formulation remained the prerogative of the prime minister. Parliament, therefore, rarely provided a forum for abolitionist challenges to the government. Rule by ministerial decree, rather than legislative approval, in fact characterized the closed nineteenth-century Italian state. Despite these obstacles, abolitionists did force the repeal of the Cavour law, but the struggle took twenty-eight years and they ended up with only partial reform.

Like that for regulation, the push for abolition was a progressive movement with roots in the Enlightenment. In calling for reform, however, abolitionists were more concerned with the protection of civil rights than the extension and rationalization of state power. Thus the bitter confrontations between regulationists and abolitionists symbolized the tensions inherent in the Enlightenment tradition that emphasized both freedom and discipline. While abolitionists found prostitution as repugnant as regulationists, they defended the right of women to choose this profession. Regulation, they charged, unjustly relegated prostitutes to second-class citizenship in states that claimed to be founded on the principle of equality before the law. Just as the regulationist philosophy made some concessions to civil liberty—for example, eliminating harsh, physical punishment for prostitutes—abolitionists did not completely ignore the need for discipline in the name of social good. They believed, however, that strict application of the penal code to prostitutes would adequately guarantee public order and morality. In addition, the submission of prostitutes to the laws applicable to all citizens would assure equity of treatment.

Not surprisingly, the international leader of abolition, Josephine Butler, came from Great Britain, a nation with a strong tradition of individual freedom and limitations on central authority. Even the British Parliament, however, passed a series of regulation statutes in 1864, 1866, and 1869. Called The Contagious Diseases Acts, these laws imposed police control on prostitutes in certain garrison and port towns where large numbers of soldiers and sailors were stationed. As in Italy, concern for the health of the military constituted the initial pretext for the introduction of regulation.[2] In 1869 Butler organized the English Ladies' Association against the Acts to oppose the extension of regulation to civilian areas and to fight for repeal of the existing laws. She could soon count among her supporters influential liberals such as John Stuart Mill, John Bright, Harriet Martineau, and Florence Nightingale.[3]

Although Butler first limited her organizing and petitioning to England, she soon realized that the schemes for international regulation, currently being discussed at the congresses of medicine, could be successfully challenged only by a more broadly based association. To spread her doctrine she personally toured several continental countries, including Italy, during the years 1874–1875. Finding a positive response in regulationist nations, Butler founded, upon her return to Britain, the British, Continental, and General Federation for the Abolition of Government Regulation of Prostitution. The federation, which later shortened its name to the International Abolitionist Federation, began publication of its own journal, *Le Bulletin Continental*, in January 1876. Geneva in 1877 hosted the first international congress of the federation, to which delegates were sent by branches recently established in Europe and America.

In reporting on her trip to the Continent, Butler claimed that "her own work abroad had had very little of a creative character, but had rather served to bring out and give expression to sentiments and convictions already existing in various countries she had visited."[4] This was certainly true of Italy, where several groups had protested the Cavour law since its promulgation fifteen years earlier. This indigenous opposition to regulation was firmly rooted in the political logic of the more general critique of Cavour's realization of the Risorgimento. Butler built on the foundation of this already existing movement against the Cavour Regulation, meeting with its proponents and holding public lectures to advance the cause. Italian abolitionists benefited greatly from the prestige and publicity generated by Butler's visit. These Italian reformers were drawn from three groups: the political Left, the nascent feminist movement, and the working class.

Early denunciation of regulation came from the political Left, a loose coalition of opponents to Cavour and his successors of the ruling Liberal Right. The Left was charged with acting out of "party-spirited motives," but its attack on regulation conformed with the general spirit of its political traditions.[5] Although of middle-class origins like much of the party in power, proponents of the Left had preferred a republican to a monarchical conclusion to the Risorgimento, and after unification they called for a liberalization of the Statuto. To democratize the kingdom, they demanded extension of the suffrage (2 percent of the population could vote in 1861); an elected senate to replace the one appointed by the Crown; compulsory, state-supported education; and the replacement of indirect taxes—such as the grist tax, which fell heaviest on the poor—with a direct, progressive income tax.[6] Less consensus existed on the issue of decentralization; before unification, part of the Left insisted that only a strong, national government could overcome the power of conservative, provincial elites, while others believed that regionalism would better insure liberty. Although these differences of opinion persisted during the early years of unity, members of the opposition increasingly deplored the "Piedmontization" of Italy and supported some degree of decentralization to break the monopoly of power held by former officials of the Kingdom of Savoy.[7]

Not only did opposition to regulation fit comfortably into the program of the Left; it had the support of prominent leaders such as Giuseppe Mazzini and Garibaldi. They believed the principles of the Cavour Regulation were antithetical to their concept of the Risorgimento as a spiritual rebirth of Italy rather than simply a mechanical unification. Regulation not only denied equal rights to women but institutionalized the corrupt status quo instead of encouraging the "moral education of society."[8] In 1870, only a year after its founding, Mazzini sent a letter of support to the Ladies

Association in England: "Can you doubt me! Can you doubt how eagerly I watch from afar, and how heartily I bless the efforts of the brave, earnest British women who are striving for the extension of the suffrage to their sex and for the repeal of the vice-protecting Acts [Contagious Diseases Acts] which last question is but an incident in the great general question of justice to women?"[9] He concluded by stressing how both regulation and exclusively male suffrage had the negative effect of weakening women's loyalty to the state and, consequently, national unity: "If you punish the accomplice, leaving the sinner untouched, you destroy, by arousing the sense of injustice, every beneficial result of punishment. If you assume the right to legislate for any class, without allowing the class voice or share in the work, you destroy the sacredness of law, and awaken hatred or contempt in the heart of the excluded class."[10]

While Mazzini and Garibaldi lent the prestige of their names to the abolitionist cause, other men of the Left more directly battled regulation in Parliament, in the press, and as political organizers. Already in the 1860s the anarchist Salvatore Morelli, perhaps the most dedicated promoter of women's rights in the early years of the Chamber, challenged the state's policy of tolerating prostitution. He also opposed the construction of a new sifilicomio because he considered these institutions repressive and medically ineffective.[11] Another early reformer, the democrat Giuseppe Nathan, organized the Roman branch of the International Abolitionist Federation.[12] Agostino Bertani was one of the first medical doctors to criticize regulation; as a republican deputy, he attacked the government in a famous open letter addressed directly to Prime Minister Agostino Depretis in 1881.[13] His other abolitionist activities included attendance at the first international abolitionist congress in Geneva in 1877 and also the organization, along with Aurelio Saffi, of a meeting on the same theme for the Democratic Association of Bologna in 1881.[14] Other politicians of the Left who joined the campaign against regulation were Benedetto Cairoli, Giovanni Bovio, and Ernesto Nathan.[15]

During her trip to Italy, Butler met with several of these members of the political opposition, encouraging their efforts and seeking new converts. A few, such as Giuseppe Nathan and

Aurelio Saffi, had already met or corresponded with her about the situation in Italy.[16] In one letter, Nathan had described to Butler his motivation for rescue work among prostitutes:

> I wish you were here to teach me how to act in this case. I would ten times sooner face the mouths of twenty guns than a poor girl who feels that she has lost all right to respect; though not in *my* eyes! No! God is my witness that I judge *no* woman unworthy of respect; her womanhood outraged is in itself more than sufficient claim for the respect of every man. Had not one of *my* sex robbed her of her peace, withered in its bloom all happiness, all that made life a blessing to her, she might now have been happy and making others happy.[17]

Butler also inspired high flights of rhetoric in a book by Mazzinian Tito Mammoli, who called her "the new apostle of liberty" whose "cry of moral revolt" signaled "the beginning of a new faith."[18] Her public meetings received favorable reviews in a number of newspapers: *Il Dovere* and *L'Emancipazione* (Rome), *La Gazzetta di Milano* and *L'Ambrosiano* (Milan), *La Rivista Subalpina* (Cuneo), and *Il Pungolo* (Naples).[19]

The second group to oppose regulation during the early decades of unity were women involved in the broader campaign for female emancipation. During the 1860s and 1870s these women, like the men of the first group, generally came from the ranks of the Mazzinian Left. Those who adhered early to abolition—for example, Anna Maria Mozzoni, Sara Nathan, Jessie White Mario, Kate Crawford, and Giorgina Crawford Saffi—were veterans of the largely unsuccessful campaign to guarantee equal civil rights to women during the initial creation of the new state.[20] They had been disappointed by the Civil Code of 1865, which sanctioned women's legal inferiority to men, but refused to abandon the cause. Feminist issues such as abolition were publicized in *La Donna*, a republican women's journal founded in 1869 by Alaide Gualberta Beccari.[21]

While the Mazzinian feminists gave enthusiastic support to Butler during her visit in 1874, they were a relatively small proportion of Italian women. Not only were they middle class but they included a disproportionately large number of Protestants and Jews. Several, like Jesse White Mario and Giorgina Crawford Saffi, were foreigners, Englishwomen who had married Italian men and lived in Italy. Others were familiar with England because British liberals had given fervent support to the Risorgimento and housed revolutionaries, such as Mazzini, during periods of exile from the Italian peninsula before 1860. These characteristics facilitated contacts between Italian feminists and Butler, whose husband was a Protestant minister,[22] but they also marked these women as in some ways outsiders in Catholic Italy. One could say, then, that in the 1860s and 1870s Italian feminists existed but organized feminism did not. Only in 1881 did an autonomous organization for women's rights appear, the League to Promote the Interests of Women, founded by Mozzoni in Milan. The blossoming of the women's movement took place a decade later, in the 1890s.[23]

Early Italian feminists were, however, crucial to the establishment of abolition, which was itself a small movement. Butler's meetings with Mazzinian women, as with the male politicians, consolidated contacts made before her visit. Already in 1869 she had begun correspondance with Mozzoni, an active and prominent feminist, asking for a report on regulation in Italy. Mozzoni's reply, published in both Britain and Italy, lamented the small attention given to social questions by Italian women. She accused housewives of having a narrow vision of prostitution and of accepting their husbands' visits to brothels as necessary to the maintenance of family harmony.[24] Convinced of the injustice of regulation, she agreed to head the Milanese branch of the International Abolitionist Federation when she met Butler in 1874.[25] Beccari also appealed for women to support Butler's cause through an article in *La Donna* entitled "An Indispensable Duty" published in 1875.[26] In 1877 Mozzoni and White Mario attended the first abolitionist congress in Geneva, along with Giuseppe Nathan and Bertani. In her memorial to the congress, Mozzoni continued to bemoan the hesitancy of Italian women to support the abolitionist campaign: "We are lacking one ally which we need. Without this ally, the outcome of this struggle is in doubt, and the undertaking itself could seem crazy. The ally which we lack is the mass of women."[27] Few Italian women yet had the courage to support, much less speak publicly about, a cause that involved not only a social but also a sexual issue such as prostitution.

45

A third group of at least potential support for abolition was the working class, especially lower-class men. In Great Britain, Butler consciously and successfully drew male, urban workers into her movement by emphasizing the class nature of regulation.[28] In a letter to the Roman newspaper *L'Emancipazione*, an Italian worker reproduced her argument:

> These gentlemen who make such a noise about the necessity of prostitution too often forget, I think that in order to satisfy that necessity, *the dishonour of the daughters of the people* is indispensable, for as yet no society of worshipers of the medical theories has been found ready to declare themselves willing to be sacrificed in order to satisfy this necessity; instead of this, we do find that gentlemen have employed every method of seduction that the mind of man or devil could invent, in order to drag poor girls of our class into the mud.[29]

Giuseppe Nathan was most responsible for spreading this message in Italy, giving speeches "closely reasoned and full of conviction and fire" to meetings of workers throughout the peninsula.[30] Mammoli also appealed, as the son of a worker, for support from the men of the lower classes: "Now come out and fight . . . and if you wish to assure the glory of your country, first assure the glory of your family."[31] The "glory" of a family resided in the virtue of its female members, a virtue abolitionists claimed was under attack from both middle-class men and the middle-class state. The routine vaginal examination alone subjected lower-class women arrested for prostitution to a procedure shunned as demeaning by their middle-class sisters.

According to abolitionist accounts, the campaign for lower-class support was highly successful. Giuseppe Nathan sent Butler periodic reports on the adhesion of working-class organizations to the abolitionist cause; in 1876, he triumphantly wrote that in "Savona alone, a small town of Liguria, we have over 1,300 working men who are ardent adherents of our cause."[32] While Butler directed her efforts in England toward constructing an alliance between middle-class women and lower-class men, Italian feminists sought to publicize abolition also among working-class women. In response to proreform articles in *La Donna*, Beccari claimed in 1876 to have collected the signatures of three thousand women, not all of them bourgeois, for an abolitionist petition. She never published the list of names, however, in order to guarantee anonymity to those women who had dared to support a cause their male relatives and friends often opposed.[33] The female sections of workers' societies, generally Mazzinian in political orientation, also provided a platform for abolitionist appeals and held votes of confidence in the movement. When Mozzoni attended the international abolitionist congress in Geneva in 1877, she went not only as a leading feminist but also as the representative of two hundred workers societies located in cities throughout Italy.[34]

While abolitionists gained some adherents from the lower classes, their publicity most likely overemphasized a rather modest support. In her book on British prostitution, Judith Walkowitz has emphasized the innovative and successful campaign of middle-class abolitionist women for the support of working-class men. Unlike Britain, whose industrial revolution had begun a century earlier, however, Italy could claim only a small number of organized workers in the 1860s and 1870s. The majority of the urban lower classes, newly arrived from the countryside, lacked any experience with, or expectation of, political activism. High rates of illiteracy hindered the dissemination of ideas through print. Thus the working-class pool from which Italian abolitionists could draw support was smaller than that of their British counterparts.[35]

These three groups that formed the constituency for abolition were related yet unequal in political power. Only the first, the men of the Left, had the right to vote, much less a direct voice in Parliament. The other two could petition and protest but had ultimately to rely on the initiative of male politicians to effect legal reform. Feminist women often had close ties to men of the Left through marriage or, more generally, in middle-class political and social circles, and they therefore possessed a channel of communication to those with political power. It is no coincidence that many of the leading male proponents of abolition, like Saffi and the Nathans, were related by blood or marriage to feminists who educated them to the cause. Other male reformers, like Bertani and Gramola, acknowledged publicly the role of women like Mozzoni in inspiring and informing their own adherence to abolition.[36] Workers had contact with the first two groups in the

47

Mazzinian societies, which were interclass in nature. There is no evidence, however, that workers took a leading role in the abolitionist crusade; they generally remained subordinate to their middle-class allies.[37] These bourgeois abolitionists—male and female—were responsible for elaborating a critique of regulation and for laying the theoretical foundations for a new relationship between the state and prostitution.

Theory of Abolition

While the discourse propounded by Italian abolitionists echoed the general themes put forth by Butler, it also constituted a specific rebuttal to the Cavour Regulation. It challenged the philosophy and practical effectiveness of this law in regard to both liberty and discipline. According to abolitionists, the former, liberty, should be the fundamental principle informing all legislation of the new Italian state. Not only did they criticize the relatively low priority framers of the Cavour statute had placed on liberty, but they also denied that the few sections intended to guarantee the rights of prostitutes were conscientiously enforced. Similarly, they denounced regulation for its preoccupation with discipline; furthermore, opponents argued, the oppressive control of prostitutes did not achieve the regulationists' aim of protecting public order, morality, and health. Based on this critique, abolitionists developed their own "label" for prostitutes and their own proposals for creating a new state policy on prostitution.

Underpinning the abolitionist appeal for liberty was a challenge to regulationist assumptions about male sexuality. In his tract on prostitution the reformer Antonio Gramola asked "if the male instinct, to which the existence of prostitution is attributed, can or cannot be overcome?"[38] He, and other abolitionists, answered a resounding yes, claiming that upbringing, not biology, caused men to think that they needed more sexual fulfillment than women.[39] Through proper education and conscious self-improvement, men could tame their sexual instinct and thus remove the "necessity" of the social safety valve of prostitution.[40] As for female sexuality, abolitionists tended to repeat the regulationists' eulogies of purity. In the words of Mammoli, "The modesty of a woman constitutes the shield of personal dignity, the honor of the family, and the moral poetry of the nation."[41] The passionlessness of women proved their current moral superiority, which men should emulate in the struggle of the spirit over the body, a struggle necessary for the progress to a higher level of civilization. Abolitionists preached the end of the double standard and looked toward a future that would de-emphasize sex and limit it, for both men and women, to monogamous marriage.

Opponents of the Cavour law also pointed out the social injustice inherent in the regulationist assertion that history had shown prostitution to be a permanent aspect of culture. According to Mammoli, "The acceptance of organized prostitution as a necessary part of the social system is a national crime."[42] It was hypocritical for the Italian state to proclaim the inviolability of civil rights and at the same time sanction the slavery of a special class of women in order to meet the "natural" sexual needs of men.[43] Mozzoni took up the theme of hypocrisy when she pointed out that the horror of her countrymen at American slavery, the oppression of Christians by Turks, and the African slave trade did not often extend to the regulation of prostitution. She admonished them: "Be logical and fair. Examine and think about regulation by the morals police. Ponder the cynicism, the brutality, the juridical absurdity of it, and then tell me if primitive forms of barbarity could have been more disgraceful than this."[44] Repeating another favorite abolitionist argument, Gramola noted that every prostitute was someone else's wife, sister, daughter; he then demanded to know which regulationist was willing to sacrifice his female relatives to the "necessity" of prostitution?[45]

Having denied the naturalness of the male sex drive and the necessity of prostitution to society, abolitionists saw no barriers to the expansion of liberty for prostitutes. While agreeing with regulationists that prostitution did not constitute a crime, they called for decriminalization rather than regulation. Decriminalization would prevent the two major abuses inherent in the Cavour law: the restriction of the civil rights of prostitutes and the unequal application of the law according to sex.

As evidence of the first major abuse, Bertani pointed to the denial to prostitutes of certain freedoms guaranteed to other citizens: for example, the freedom to change residence, to move

49

freely throughout the city, and to choose when and where to seek medical attention. He concluded that, rather than protecting prostitutes, "the ideal aim of sanitary regulation is nothing less than that of subordinating all prostitution to it, of having all prostitutes within reach."[46] Abolitionists decried as a contradiction of the professed liberal principles of the Italian state this reduction of prostitutes to a subclass with restricted rights.[47] Furthermore, they likened tolerated brothels to prisons in which madams, in connivance with police and in violation of the law, exploited their employees. According to abolitionists, proprietors tried to keep resident prostitutes in debt by selling them clothes and furnishings at high prices. Once indebted, prostitutes could not leave the profession, or even change brothels, unless "sold" to another madam who would assume the debt. Although the Cavour Regulation forbid this practice, reformers charged that the morals police looked the other way.[48]

In a more general way, abolitionists believed that the regulation system encouraged prostitution, which as a profession was inherently exploitative and demeaning. By officially registering, taxing, and setting rules for brothels, the state was sanctioning a social evil and perpetuating the degradation of women.[49] Abolitionists warned that more men tended to seek out brothels in a society where they were plentiful and apparently approved by the government.[50] More important, regulation compounded the dehumanization inherent in prostitution by reducing women to "machines which are checked, cleaned, and polished by the State" or to "a *thing* stamped and guaranteed by the state for the market of public vice."[51] Despite administrators' lip service to reform in the Cavour law, abolitionists blamed them for being more interested in the efficient discipline of prostitutes as objects than in their redemption and growth as free individuals.

The second abuse opponents complained of was that the repressive aspects of the Cavour Regulation applied only to women. As Bertani emphasized, "Legislators, princes, popes, procurers, and libertines are all men and all claim the right to the free use of their own body, to respectability, and to the protection of their own health; only the woman, whose body is infected and violated by men, is defenseless and condemned to degradation; only the women are victims and must pay for everything and everyone."[52] It was illogical to place prostitutes under police surveillance in the name of public health while men with venereal disease retained exercise of their full civil rights. But, as Bertani concluded, "such is the logic of sanctioning regulation: the diseased woman is criminal; the man is unfortunate."[53] According to Mammoli, it was equally irrational to subject only the prostitute to health examinations in order, as regulationists argued, to protect innocent wives and children from venereal disease: "What prostitute has ever entered into an honest family and personally infected the mother, or, through the mother, the children? No, the husbands and fathers are the only destroyers of the domestic sanctuary."[54] Yet, as Gramola remarked, "No one had been able to suggest a way to make the more *noble* sex accept surveillance."[55] The sexism of the Cavour law explains to a great extent the increasing attraction the abolitionist movement had for feminists.

In condemning the Cavour Regulation not only for its lack of liberty but also for the failure of its disciplinary measures, abolitionists refuted, point by point, the state's claim that its system of registration protected public order, public morality, and public health. Reformers charged that regulation failed to eliminate noisy brothels and annoying solicitation by streetwalkers. They complained that many policemen not only refused to submit brothels to their authority but also spent many evenings in such houses in collusion with madams. Furthermore, large numbers of clandestine prostitutes escaped detection even in areas that were efficiently patrolled. Instead of breaking their ties with the underworld, these prostitutes were only reaffirming their criminal identity by hiding from the police.

According to abolitionists, police were also guilty of overlooking displays of public immorality. Registered or nonregistered, prostitutes continued to appear publicly on city streets. Reformers attributed this to an inherent contradiction within the regulation system: it sanctioned prostitution but forbade public solicitation. To legalize a business but proscribe advertising was not only absurd but unworkable. To make a profit, prostitutes had to break the law to draw attention to themselves and their brothels. Caught in such a contradiction, police ignored these indiscretions to insure a flourishing trade in their government-sponsored domain.

51

Thus, rather than becoming invisible to the public eye, prostitutes continued to embarrass honest women and entice young men.

Abolitionists even contested the most fundamental and central claim of the state: that regulation protected public health. They countered that registered prostitutes, under pressure from madams, had more sexual contacts per day than clandestine prostitutes and therefore infected a greater number of clients. State guarantees that prostitutes had been inspected only encouraged visitation by men who would otherwise be restrained by the fear of infection.[56] In response to the regulationists' scientific attempts to prove the efficacy of their system through statistics, abolitionists produced their own figures documenting opposite trends. They also pointed to the increasing number of clandestine prostitutes who avoided examination altogether.[57] Even if regulationists would not admit the weakness of their theory, abolitionists challenged them to defend the effectiveness of health examinations when administered to only a fraction of practicing prostitutes.

Proceeding from this critique of the Cavour Regulation, abolitionists advanced alternative proposals for government action. Despite their emphasis on liberty, they did not counsel a completely laissez-faire attitude in respect to the social ramifications of prostitution. As one proponent wrote, "Abolition means only the abolition of regulation, not the abolition of prostitution; abolition does not require that prostitution be ignored, overlooked, tabooed, or treated in a spirit of prudery as non-existent; it is entirely consistent with thorough inquiry into the whole phenomenon, and constructive social action aiming to deal with it."[58] Reformers agreed with regulationists that moral crusades of prohibition could not uproot prostitution and hastened to distance themselves from such efforts. The abolitionist Lorenzo Mei made this clear when he wrote that "it is not my intention to launch a war to exterminate this terrible force [prostitution] which devastates the social body." Yet he added, "If it is not possible to totally get rid of this devouring cancer, it is at the same time not impossible to slow the corrosive process and limit its dominion."[59] Abolitionists condemned the hypocrisy of regulationist theory riddled with a contradiction between "morality which condemns a vice and the law which tolerates it."[60] Instead, they promised slowly to reduce prostitution, not through repression, but through social and moral reform.

The abolitionist analysis stressed prevention of prostitution by eliminating its causes. After talking to hundreds of prostitutes, Bertani concluded that a major cause was economic: "Women's work is everywhere poorly paid; even when her work is equal in time, skill, and value, it is always paid less than that of a man."[61] Mozzoni emphasized the same problem when she wrote, in her report to the Geneva congress, "Everyone has the right to live from his work, but women seem to have more of a right to die since it is so difficult for them to find honest and sufficient work."[62] While abolitionists lacked any concrete program of economic reform, they urged investigation into the causes of and remedies for poverty in the swelling cities. They called for more and better orphanages and schools to train poor girls in economic skills so that they would not need to turn to prostitution. As middle-class reformers, however, they hesitated to put forth a more radical and sweeping critique of the economic system.[63]

Abolitionists proved more innovative in their promotion of sex education. Although implying moral uplift rather than physiological explication, the idea of sex education nevertheless shocked much of middle- and upper-class society. In a narrow sense, sex education was counseling young people, especially adolescent males, about the spiritual and physical evils of prostitution. More fundamentally, however, sex education sought to transform basic social relationships between men and women. Realizing that male demand as well as female poverty accounted for the persistence of prostitution, abolitionists argued that young men should be taught to regard women as free, intelligent, and equal beings. Ceasing to regard women merely as objects for their sexual pleasure, men would then eschew contacts with prostitutes.[64] Again, this program of reform was perhaps too general to be effective, but abolitionists wisely realized that there would be a supply of female prostitutes as long as male demand continued.

To foster this shift in attitudes and moral values, abolitionists expected the state to legislate equal rights for women. Mozzoni convincingly and repeatedly argued that regulation was buttressed by a series of other laws that were sexist and encouraged prostitution. She cited as examples the legal nullity of oral and written promises of marriage made by seducers of young girls; the prohibition of the legal investigation of paternity by unwed mothers; the lack of any sanction against husbands who abandoned their wives and children; and the implicit right of husbands to take concubines. Furthermore, while a girl could not marry before thirty years of age without parental consent, she could register herself as a prostitute at sixteen.[65] Few Italian feminists of the 1860s and 1870s went as far as their English counterparts and demanded women's suffrage; the idea was entirely too radical in a nation where the majority of men lacked the vote. Nevertheless, most abolitionists linked their campaign with the broader movement to bring sexual equality before the law.

In theory, then, abolitionists put forth a comprehensive program that promised to transform markedly the relationship of the state to prostitution. They did agree with the regulationists' refusal to label prostitutes as criminals; they also shared their opponents moral revulsion at the promiscuity of prostitutes. There the two analyses diverged because abolitionists insisted that, though morally deviant, prostitutes deserved full protection of their civil rights, which included the liberty to pursue any profession, including the morally repugnant one of prostitution, as long as they observed the sections of the penal code regarding public order and public morality.[66] Abolitionists urged that the phenomenon of prostitution be fought not with repressive measures but through a general shift in laws, economy, sexual morality, and attitudes toward women. As Mozzoni put it, the International Abolitionist Federation professed not only the "circumscribed" aim of defeating regulation but also a more long-range plan for "social transformation."[67] Abolitionist successes in Italy were only partial, however, and even the first, more modest goal was never fully reached.

The Crispi Regulation

Opposition to the Cavour Regulation based on the abolitionists' theoretical foundation developed immediately after the law's promulgation. In response to sharp criticism from Parliament,

Rattazzi, upon assuming the post of prime minister in 1862, nominated a commission of inquiry. Presided over by Conte Augusto Ponza di Martino and composed largely of prominent physicians, such as Sperino, Pietro Gamberini of Bologna, and Pietro Pellizzari of Florence, this commission was directed to study charges that the Cavour law was "insufficient and immoral."[68] But owing to the fall of the Rattazzi government in December, the results of the commission "were never known."[69] On September 12, 1866 Prime Minister Bettino Ricasoli appointed a second commission, but its work was ignored by a government preoccupied with war for the acquisition of Venice.[70] After returning to power in 1867, Rattazzi charged the third commission of the decade to investigate the possibility of decentralizing the administration of the sifilicomi. He appointed Maurizio Bufalini president of the committee, which included Pellizzari and Pietro Castiglione.[71] As with the previous two efforts, however, executive disinterest in liberalizing prostitution policy and governmental instability relegated the investigation to irrelevancy by 1868.

With the parliamentary "revolution" of 1876, in which the Left replaced the Liberal Right as head of government, abolitionists hoped for immediate victory. As Salomone has pointed out, "the Left's *trasformismo*, after the fall of the Right in 1876, seemed momentarily pregnant with great possibilities of renovation of Italian life."[72] Inspired by the recent visit of Butler, abolitionists expected that the party that stood for political equality and the end of social injustice would immediately abrogate the repressive Cavour law. In response to this pressure from abolitionists, who constituted the left wing of his party, the new prime minister, Depretis, authorized another investigation. The commission, appointed on May 13, 1876, began its work by gathering information at the local level about the functioning of the Cavour Regulation.[73] It became known as the "Nicotera commission" since it was coordinated by Minister of the Interior Giovanni Nicotera.

The Nicotera commission was the first to draw up a detailed report on the functioning of the regulation policy and to elaborate a new law to replace that of Cavour. After approving the work of his commission, the minister of the interior presented its findings to Parliament on November 22, 1877. Nicotera claimed that the proposed legislation balanced the "right of society" to preserve public health, order, and morality against the right of prostitutes to "unrestrained liberty".[74] In other words, he had tried to work out a compromise between regulation and abolition. On the one hand, he admitted the need for continued registration and examination of prostitutes. As Giovanni Catella, one member of the commission, pointed out,

> Prostitution, a real social cautery, must be tolerated in order to avoid greater evils; prostitution is protean in its manifestations, very mobile, hard to discipline, and infests the human race with a terrible virus, of which it is the most active propagator. It is necessary to have a concealed, diligent, and untiring operation by various branches of the public Administration in order to contain prostitution within the limits of an undesired but necessary toleration; in this way it will not endanger security, morality, or public health."[75]

Yet on the other hand, abuses in the present system convinced Nicotera that current policy had to be "radically modified."[76] He denounced the "excessive meddling" of the police, which exposed any woman suspected of prostitution to "unlimited and uncontrolled arbitrariness."[77] Frequent mistakes made by police in registering "honest" women brought shame to the individual and her family. Finally, the government was demeaning itself by regulating the price of prostitution and by collecting excessive taxes so that the perpetuation of this vice was assuming the character of a fiscal measure.

To minimize these abuses, Nicotera suggested decentralization of the regulation system. He held that municipal police, who knew local brothel districts, could best assure that all prostitutes were registered. Municipal authorities, who were most interested in preventing outbreaks of venereal disease in the local population, would more zealously enforce the health stipulations. To prevent police harassment of women, the local Health Offices could register an unwilling woman only after the deliberation of a five-member commission presided over by the mayor. The decision could then be appealed to the prefect. As with other diseases, the communes and provinces were to take over the funding and administration of special dispensaries, to be annexed to the sifilicomi. Nicotera also proposed reform of the taxation of brothels, although he admitted that financially the government could not afford to eliminate this source of revenue completely. Taxation rates would be modified, however, so that income from brothels would not exceed expenditures for the administration of the Health Offices and other services related to prostitution.

Despite the fact that the law proposed by Nicotera in 1877 sought, through decentralization, to perpetuate rather than abolish regulation, it never reached the floor of the Chamber. With the fall of the first Depretis ministry in December 1877, Nicotera was replaced as minister of the interior. Although Depretis formed the succeeding government, he acquiesced in maneuvers by supporters of the Cavour law to block the discussion of the proposed legislation.[78] He further proved his disinterest in the abolitionist cause by issuing, as his own minister of the interior in 1880, his set of Istruzioni provvisorie per regolare il servizio degli Uffici Sanitari, la ricossione ed il versamento degli introiti (Provisional Instructions for Regulating the Services of the Health Offices and the Collection and Paying in of Revenues) that reinforced the principles of the Cavour law. The only significant alteration of the previous statute was a requirement to keep thirteen additional informational registers, most dealing, as the title indicated, with the processing of taxes and fees levied on brothel owners and prostitutes. Rather than pulling the government out of the business of prostitution, as abolitionists wanted, Depretis sought to increase the knowledge, power, and profits of the regulationist state.

In response to the promulgation of the Istruzioni provvisorie, Bertani published an open letter of protest dedicated to "Agostino Depretis, Lawyer, Legislator, Father of a Family."[79] As a longtime friend and political colleague, Bertani reminded Depretis that neither of them was a sentimentalist or especially puritanical. As a liberal, however, he chided the prime minister for not repealing regulation as he had promised when taking office. Bertani could not countenance the hypocrisy of a government of the Left that championed liberty while perpetuating a "market of human flesh":[80] "I am fighting only the state, which, as educator and custodian of the public virtue, makes itself minister of prostitution and authorizes and guarantees enterprise in it. I combat exclusively the brothel-owning government, the supreme procurer, the great manager of the managers of the houses of depravity."[81] He concluded that Depretis had sacrificed his liberal principles for the financial gain of the state: "because money comes from prostitution, public modesty must adapt itself."[82]

Refusing to admit defeat, forty abolitionist deputies, led by Nicola Fabrizio, demanded that Depretis again nominate a commission during his fourth ministry in 1883. "Pushed with his shoulders to the wall by such a vast movement," as Tommasoli put it, he selected a committee composed mainly of legal and medical experts, presided over by Ubaldino Peruzzi.[83] After two years of study, the commission published a two-volume report widely judged as objective, conscientiously compiled, and accurate.[84] Although less than half the members were abolitionists at the time of their appointment in 1883, the majority report concluded in 1885 that "the Regulation of 1860 is contrary to morality and law; it goes against the offices of the state; it exercises a pernicious influence on the public administration; and it does not deliver the health benefits which had been promised."[85] Consequently, the committee formulated a set of proposals intended to replace it. Embodied in a document whose title translates as "Provisions for Public Morality, Order, and Health," the proposals of 1885, like those of 1877, offered a compromise between regulation and abolition. While the Nicotera commission had leaned toward regulation, however, the Peruzzi report recommended a more radical break with the past. Pointing out that the state had never developed an adequate definition of a prostitute, the committee denied it the right to register, or label, individual women under this rubric. Police could arrest women only for offenses already enumerated in the penal code, such as corrupting a minor or public nudity. In terms of health, the commission deemed it unlawful to force any woman to undergo a medical examination or enter a hospital against her will.[86]

The idea of police surveillance was not completely dropped, however, since, as the report noted, "It is puerile for the State to pretend that prostitution does not exist, when it can create a public danger."[87] Instead of individuals, though, police could only designate places—an apartment, group of apartments, building, or section of the city—as objects of special regulation and control. Commission members believed that brothels, like restaurants and hotels, fell in a legal category between private homes, which were inviolable to state intervention, and public sites, which police were free to patrol. As with other "places of public use," the government had a right to impose "special vigilance" and restrictions in order to protect society.[88] Since brothels were considered a favorite meeting place of the "dangerous classes," the commission thought it reasonable to allow a certain degree of police control. Consequently, the proposed law provided that patrolmen had the right to inspect all *rooms* of brothels at any hour, to designate which hours brothels could be open, to forbid games or the sale of food and drink, and to order the closure of any house that became disorderly or employed minors.

The proposed law was perhaps most revolutionary in its health section. After inspecting a number of Health Offices and sifilicomi, the commission recommended the abolition of both. Instead of being treated in separate institutions, prostitutes with contagious syphilis were to enter the clinics that specialized in the cure of skin and venereal diseases and were annexed to general hospitals. Where these clinics did not already exist, the government would finance the building of new ones. For both female and male victims of noncontagious syphilis or other types of venereal disease, the state was to establish outpatient dispensaries to provide free medical care. These provisions signaled a radical shift in public health philosophy: instead of focusing on prostitutes as the font of disease, the treatment of venereal infections was to be extended to the general population, all of whom were now considered possible carriers. To encourage the cooperation of prostitutes in fighting venereal disease, the state would make treatment free, accessible, and anonymous. The commission believed that only education in the symptoms and dangers of syphilis, not force, would increase the numbers of prostitutes and other citizens seeking medical advice and cure.[89]

Despite the wealth of statistics and arguments gathered by the commission to support its conclusions, Depretis again refused to demand repeal of the Cavour law. Abolitionists charged that he conspired with "the interests"—the police, doctors of the sifilicomi, and influential protectors of madams—to block reform. After the report was printed, Senator Corrado Tommasi-Crudeli claimed that opponents "seized this edition and sequestered it."[90] Although the report was finally delivered to the Chamber, its contents were never discussed or voted on. As previously, the administration managed to prevent open parliamentary debate on prostitution by ignoring commission reports; procrastinating until the government fell, which happened often; or even "stealing" proposals for new legislation.

With the death of Depretis, however, abolitionists gained a new hearing from Francesco Crispi, who succeeded as prime minister. As a former Garibaldian, Crispi initially seemed bent on carrying out the program of the left wing of his party. He accelerated social reform by promulgating legislation on police, health, penal law, local administration, and communal suffrage.[91] In this spirit of renewal, he promised the Chamber that, after one final investigation, a version of the law proposed by the report of 1885 "would be approved as soon as possible and put into effect."[92]

In a seeming replay of the Depretis era, one commission inquiry turned into two. Again, the first report about the health services, written by Enrico Albanese, disappeared before its contents were made public.[93] Yet those who had read it agreed that it called for repeal of the Cavour Regulation and found the sifilicomi to be "an overflowing sink of corruption."[94] The second committee generally supported the report of 1885 and drafted a similar law. Contrary to all past experience, Crispi finally approved this proposal, which went into effect, again by ministerial decree, on July 26, 1888.[95]

Like the proposed law of 1885, the new Crispi Regulation did not completely fulfill the demands of abolitionists. While police could not inscribe individual women, they retained the power to register "places" of prostitution and keep them under surveillance. The new legislation also required brothel managers to supply police with the names and other identifying information about their employees, thus effectively compromising the legal principle that the state could register only places and not persons. In accordance with abolitionism, however, police could arrest isolated prostitutes only for violations of the penal code. Free and equal treatment for venereal disease would become available to both sexes through new outpatient dispensaries and special hospital wards. Finally, one section of the law strengthened the duty of police to protect prostitutes working in brothels and to facilitate the rehabilitation of those who wished to leave.

The promulgation of the Crispi Regulation followed the repeal of the British Contagious Diseases Acts by five years. These two events signaled the defeat of the movement for international regulation, which had been gaining momentum in the 1860s and 1870s. European opinion seemed to have turned from favoring regulation to abolition. Unlike the total repeal in England, however, the new Italian law was only partially informed with abolitionist principles since the core of regulation, the registration and surveillance of brothels, remained intact. Why did Italian abolitionists have to struggle longer and end up with only a compromise measure while their British counterparts could claim complete victory? Some answers may be found in four aspects of the Italian experience that differed substantially from the English: the nature of the political Left, state administration, the women's movement, and religion.

First, unlike Britain with its increasingly articulated system of political parties, Italy's division between Left and Right became more muddled after unification. The Left, rooted in the diverse and sometimes contradictory philosophic impulses of the Risorgimento, had never constituted a cohesive political party in the modern sense. With the parliamentary revolution of 1876, it even lost that unity which came from being in opposition. Once in power, the prime ministers of the Left, beginning with Depretis, instituted a policy of *trasformismo* (transformism) or collaboration with certain politicians of the Right. As Crispi lamented, before becoming a master of trasformismo himself, "Since 1878 we have had no political parties in Italy . . . only political men and groups, and each group, instead of comprehending an order of ideas, has been just an association of individuals whose opinions have constantly changed. This state of affairs has been actively encouraged by the government."[96] Comprised of moderates, radicals, republicans, socialists, and anarchists, the Left splintered into small groups such as the pentarchy, the *estrema sinistra* (extreme left), and the *Fascio della democrazia* (Democratic League).[97] Polarization along class lines, reflecting the extreme poverty of the Italian masses, as well as among geographical regions, most notably the North and South, further weakened the ruling party. In this political context it was difficult for abolitionists to marshal a united front in Parliament. Depretis's failure to repeal regulation was symptomatic of the more general antagonism between the moderate Left, which he represented, and the more radical wing of the party from which men like Bertani were drawn. Thus abolitionists received support only from the left wing of a party that, itself, was not well-organized and disciplined.

Second, the controversy between regulationists and abolitionists assumed in Italy the character of an administrative-legislative battle in which the latter group held a decidedly weaker position. Divided among themselves, liberal senators and deputies had to assail a bastion of centralized power in the Ministry of the Interior. Police and government doctors strongly defended the Cavour law because it gave them wide discretionary authority in the name of protecting public order and health. While the prime ministers came out of Parliament, they quickly came to identify with their position in the executive and to fear loss of political and social control by the state. This was true not only of Depretis but also Crispi, who, after his early period of legislative reform in the 1880s, became in the 1890s a firm believer in a strong, centralized state.[98] Furthermore, abolitionist legislators legally had very little opportunity to bring the subject of prostitution up for debate. Cavour had promulgated his law by the common method of ministerial decree, so that the Parliament never discussed the merits or drawbacks of regulation. Revision or repeal, according to Article 86 of the Legge di pubblica sicurezza (Law on Public Security), was also reserved to the prime minister.[99] Under pressure, the government did periodically authorize parliamentary investigations, but the reports were often suppressed or simply ignored by the administration.

Third, the weakness of feminism in Italy, compared with Britain, undercut the abolitionist movement. While Italy could claim articulate, intelligent, and dedicated feminists, their numbers and degree of organization lagged behind the English. Giorgina Crawford Saffi noted this in a speech dedicated to the successes of Butler: "Do we women of Italy wish to be among the last to respond to the call?"[100] But even she was inhibited by the traditional Italian attitudes toward women, having excused herself at the beginning of the speech for her "absolute incapacity for speaking in public."[101] The prejudice against women assuming public roles was also reflected in the occupation by men of many of the top posts in the Italian branch of the International Abolitionist Federation; the presidency, for example, was held first by Giuseppe Nathan and then, after his death in 1882, by his brother Ernesto.[102] This contrasts with England, where women established a separate abolitionist organization under their own leadership.[103] While the contributions of Italian feminists should not be underestimated, their political strength did not yet rival that of their British colleagues.

Fourth, one potentially influential ally, the Catholic church, failed to join ranks with Italian abolitionists. Officially Pope Pius IX condemned regulation, but after his defeat by the new, secular state, he withdrew as a "prisoner" into the Vatican and refused to take part openly in Italian politics. Even if involved in politics, however, the Catholic hierarchy was not a natural ally for the liberal, feminist, and often non-Catholic leaders of the abolitionist campaign. Instead, the church espoused the legal prohibition of prostitution. British abolitionists, on the other hand, enjoyed the firm support of Nonconformist, Methodist, and part of the Anglican clergy.[104] The British movement, then, had access to an institution that could spread the message of abolition to a large part of the population.

In Italy, moreover, Catholic views of male sexuality often coincided with those of regulationists rather than abolitionists. Since the Middle Ages, many canon lawyers had accepted the necessity of prostitution as an outlet for the inevitable male sex drive.[105] During certain periods, the Papal States had even exercised a type of tolerance and control of prostitution in some ways similar to that of the Cavour law.[106] Thus, Catholic insistence on prohibition was relatively modern, and many churchmen continued to accept the existence of prostitution and perhaps regulation. Official papal condemnation of state policy may have been undercut by the regulationist sentiments of the lower clergy, which were transmitted to lay congregations through counseling and confession.[107] This continuity between traditional religious and modern regulationist concepts of male sexuality certainly helps to account for the widespread acceptance of the latter in Italy, an overwhelmingly Catholic nation. In Britain, the relation between religious and reforming ideas on sexuality was very different, for the increasing insistence on male continence that was typical of most Protestant sects in the late nineteenth century coincided perfectly with the abolitionist analysis.

Despite these obstacles to success, Italian abolitionists did provoke the repeal of the Cavour Regulation in 1888. While the new Crispi Regulation retained compromises with the old law, abolitionists hailed its promulgation as a victory for their cause. The ministerial decree did not require legislative discussion or approval in order to take effect; the deputies of the lower house, however, met to give their formal consent to the reform they had longed called for. The abolitionist delegate Tommasi-Crudeli proposed a motion in which the Chamber expressed its confidence that the minister of the interior would "continue energetically to apply the new regulations for the limitation of syphilitic disease," that is, the Crispi statutes.[108] Following a brief discussion, the legislature approved the motion and, thus, the principle of abolition. The abolitionist triumph, however, would prove to be short-lived.

3

Return to Regulation:
The Nicotera Law of 1891

If abolitionists hailed the Crispi law as the first step toward the complete dismantling of the regulation system, they underestimated the power of the bureaucracy they wished to reform. Regulationists refused to cede victory to their opponents, taunting that their fuzzy-headed liberalism would only result in "free syphilis in a free state," a pun on Cavour's prescription for the relationship of church and state.[1] According to Sormani, members of the International Abolitionist Federation, while noble and well-intentioned in their desire to end prostitution, wrongly blamed regulation for its existence: "The Federation wishes to rid us of the Regulations but leave us the prostitutes. I counsel them to do something far more useful: *rid us of the prostitutes, and the regulations will fall by themselves.*"[2] Thus the promulgation of the Crispi Regulation did not signal a smooth passage from regulation to abolition but opened an era of renewed competition between these two strategies championed by different sectors of the dominant classes.

By 1915 and the entrance of Italy into World War I, this competition had not resulted in a clear victory for either side. It did, however, produce three important developments in legislation. First, in 1891 the regulationists in the Ministry of the Interior overturned the Crispi law and replaced it with one that carried the name of the new minister, Nicotera. While not constituting a complete return to Cavour, the Nicotera Regulation placed Italy squarely back into the regulationist camp. Second, increasing concern among abolitionists about the white slave trade encouraged the government to sign international accords in 1904 and 1910 pledging cooperation with other states in arresting traffickers in women. Third, the Health Statute of 1905 sanctioned the separation of the functions of the police and health bureaucracies in matters of prostitution; police surveillance over brothels remained intact, while the administration of venereal disease services was liberalized along abolitionist lines. These three legislative initiatives resulted in a complex picture: Italy continued to be a regulationist nation, but one in which the law was tempered by important concessions to abolition.

Broader aspects of Italian politics and society help to explain the seemingly contradictory trends toward both regulation and abolition after 1888. The promulgation of the Nicotera statute indicated the continuing dominance of the bureaucracy over the legislature in prostitution policy. The two succeeding initiatives, which smacked of abolitionism, did not essentially undercut administrative power but redefined its methods. The campaign against the white slave trade, although widely supported by feminists, ultimately provided a rationale for further state intervention in the area of sexual morality. By the turn of the century, adolescent sexuality had become a particular focus of anxiety among a collection of diverse groups: criminologists, Catholic moral reformers, and feminists. To "protect" young girls from white slavers, all these groups advocated the extension of "preventive" policing or surveillance over all female juveniles. Finally, the separation of medical services from those of the police did lighten the burden of government restrictions on prostitutes. Yet changes in medical philosophy, rather than the pressure of abolitionists, stimulated the rejection of regulation by the Division of Public Health. And physicians expected to gain, rather than lose, jurisdiction over prostitution policy at the expense of the morals squads. Thus the creeping abolitionism of the early twentieth century did not reflect a declining concern with prostitutes as a dangerous class but represented experiments in new types of control.

The Nicotera Regulation

Immediately after their defeat in 1888, regulationists, based in the Ministery of the Interior, reasserted their strength against the liberals in the legislature. They fought the Crispi law in two ways, by subverting its implementation and then by engineering its replacement by the Nicotera statute. Admittedly, the failure to enforce the law of 1888 properly was partially due to the honest misunderstanding of its provisions by many employees of the public security and public health departments. While the government boasted that its new law combined the best of regulation and abolition, this compromise confused bureaucrats at the local level. The confusion is evident in the responses to a questionnaire sent out by Tommasoli to state employees involved in the control of venereal disease. He received one hundred different answers to the question "Is prostitution free or regulated?" Furthermore, many of the responses were diametrically opposed, indicating that enforcement of the new law at the local level varied greatly among communes.[3]

Yet there is strong evidence that, at all levels, state personnel resisted the kind of implementation of the Crispi legislation that would have truly tested its merits. At the top of the administrative hierarchy, Prime Minister Crispi, according to critics, circulated copies of the new law "with timidity and almost clandestinely so that it appeared that the Government lacked courage."[4] Only in July 1889, almost a year after promulgation, did the statute take effect in all provinces.[5] Crispi was aware of ineffective enforcement of his legislation according to an unpublished circular in which he castigated his subordinates for their laxity. Yet he caved in to bureaucratic pressure not to send it out. Across the top of this document, which pinpointed problems and threatened reprimands for uncooperative employees, a high official at the Division of Public Health had scrawled that it was not "the moment to publish this circular."[6]

Furthermore, the government crippled the establishment of the new program of free care for venereal disease by failing to appropriate adequate funds. While the Division of Public Health closed 275 Health offices as stipulated by the new law, it opened only 160 dispensaries to replace them.[7] Since the Health Offices had dealt only with female prostitutes, while the dispensaries were to serve the entire population, the number of the latter was certainly inadequate. The creation of special wards for syphilitic patients proceeded even less successfully because many communes were unwilling or lacked the expertise to treat this disease. Even in major cities such as Milan, Florence, and Palermo, the outmoded sifilicomio buildings continued to be used until civil hospitals could be enlarged. Because the sifilicomi had formerly treated only prostitutes, the general public hesitated to use such disreputable facilities. The situation was worse in other communes where no hospital existed, after the closing of the sifilicomi, to treat venereal disease.

In addition to Crispi's passive resistance to rigorously enforcing the new law, subordinates directly contravened it. According to abolitionists, Vice-Minister of the Interior Fortis recommended that the police reinstate preventive health examinations for any woman suspected of prostitution.[8] At the bottom of the administrative hierarchy, many doctors and police abetted the defiance of their superiors. On the one hand, owing to pressure by these superiors, some continued to act according to the repressive tenets of the Cavour law. For example, based on the responses to his questionnaire, Tommasoli concluded that many doctors employed by the Division of Public Health feared retribution if they began to treat prostitutes on the basis of liberty rather than force: "Many of these Colleagues, whom we always suppose to be very respectable in every way, either do not have a full and precise understanding of their duties as doctors or, while understanding the sum of their proper duties, hold it honestly permissible to fail to carry them out for fear of bringing harm to themselves."[9] On the other hand, some members of the morals squads refused to carry out even those duties of registration and surveillance of brothels that the law continued to require, claiming that "they could do nothing, given that the new Regulation gave all to the women to do evil but nothing to the police, and that with such a Regulation, immorality could congratulate itself on enjoying the most absolute liberty."[10] Rather than embodying the moderation of the Crispi code, local enforcement seemed to waver between traditional authoritarianism and complete laxity.

In Parliament Crispi repeatedly professed ignorance of malpractice by administrators and attested to the sincerity of his abolitionist sentiments. He admitted in June 1889 that the law might be improved but pledged that the principle forbidding the forced examination of prostitutes would never be reversed under his administration. Six months later he assured the Chamber that "he would not give up any of the ideas affirmed in his regulation"; a year later he again stood before the deputies to promise "that he would never renounce that which represented a progressive act."[11] While his actions belied his words, even Crispi's weak defense of abolition disappeared with the fall of his ministry in January 1891.

Opponents of abolition in the Division of Public Health gained a willing ear in the new minister of the interior, Nicotera, who had already displayed his support for regulation, albeit in a decentralized form, in his proposed law of 1877. He listened to the insistence of his subordinates that the Crispi law had already failed, most notably in decreasing the rates of venereal disease in the military. Abolitionists countered with their own statistics, denying any dangerous rise in infection.[12] Furthermore, they argued that any existing health problems should not be blamed on a law that had never really been enforced. A legislative committee headed by Tommasi-Crudeli reconfirmed the Chamber's faith in the Crispi statute. The administrators in the Division of Public Health, however, designed alternative regulationist legislation to replace it. Despite outcry from abolitionist deputies, the minister chose the bill of the bureaucracy over the recommendations of the legislative committee and promulgated it as the Nicotera Regulation on October 27, 1891.

As the Crispi Regulation had been a compromise between abolition and regulation, the Nicotera Regulation fell between those of Cavour and Crispi. According to the authors of the law in the Division of Public Health, the 1891 statute retained more of the spirit of the Crispi reform than that of the Cavour legislation, which "has always been deplored."[13] In legal terms, the spirit of Crispi did persist in the definition of proper objects for surveillance. Only "places" of prostitution—defined as "the houses, quarters, or other closed areas" in which "prostitution is exercised habitually"—not persons, were suitable objects of police registration. More than was true of the Crispi law, however, this

69

principle was hedged with exceptions. As in the previous legislation, a madam who registered her brothel had to provide police
with a list of the women working for her. But while the former
statute stipulated that police could designate only a place housing
two or more women as a brothel, the Nicotera law allowed the
surveillance of single women. In Article 15, which was to become
a point of misinterpretation, debate, and criticism in the following
years, the government approved the registration of those "isolated" women who had either been arrested previously for breaking the prostitution law or infected a customer. While supporters
of the law claimed that this new procedure was counterbalanced
by other guarantees against police abuse, abolitionists interpreted
this clause as a loophole by which police would regain their
former power to harass innocent women. Because of the laxity of
the morals squads under the Crispi regime, the administration felt
that this extra power was a necessary tool for police to decrease
clandestine prostitution.[14]

In the area of health, Nicotera retained the general lines of the
Crispi legislation while providing police with additional means to
increase their vigilance over the spread of venereal disease. Administrators reaffirmed the need for special wards and clinics to
treat both sexes. They tightened restrictions on brothels, however, requiring owners to provide the name of the physician who
would examine the prostitutes regularly and information concerning the measures to be taken by owners to meet the government
health regulations. The law demanded that each physician inform
the health authority in the commune of any cases of infection.
While the previous measure had allowed spot checks by government doctors to make sure that owners were fulfilling health requirements, the Nicotera law also stipulated that any woman
found diseased, either by the brothel doctor or health authority,
was required to report to a hospital. Prostitutes still had the right
to refuse examination, "but in this case they will be presumed to
be infected" and sent, by force, to a hospital. To mitigate this re-
treat from the abolitionist position, which denied a liberal government the right to force any person to undergo hospitalization, the
law provided an alternative. If a brothel owner could guarantee
to police that the infected employee would be kept isolated and
that a private doctor would be called to cure her, then she could

forgo admittance to a hospital. But those treated in the government wards for venereal disease had to remain hospitalized until fully cured, or they would be returned by police escort.

Thus, within three years after the passage of the Crispi law, administrators of the Ministry of the Interior had engineered a return to regulation. Members of Parliament tried to defend abolition, but their weapon, the commission report, was only advisory and therefore not a powerful one. Loathe to loosen his control over prostitutes, each new minister turned a deaf ear to his former colleagues in the Chamber of Deputies and heeded the cries of alarm from the bureaucracy. After 1888 these cries of alarm again centered on the military, whose health was thought to be imperiled by abolition. In an age of virulent nationalism and rampant imperialism, the state could not risk the weakening of the army and navy by disease. The humiliating Italian defeat by Ethiopians at Adowa in 1896, for example, seemed to substantiate warnings about physical degeneration among military personnel. Only at the turn of the century did abolition reappear as a force in Italian politics, and this time in the guise of the anti–white slave trade campaign.

Campaign against the White Slave Trade

In 1911 a southern newspaper, *La Giovane Calabria*, published an article that accused a married couple of white slavery. In the words of the reporter, they made a practice of "shipping to the North American market poor girls who are deceived by mirages of easily accumulating large sums of money or, more likely, of probable marriage. And the poor unfortunate girls fall into the skillfully strung net, and depart unaware of the slavery which they go to meet, and of the inhuman exploitation to which they will be subjected."[15] This was only one of the hundreds of articles that exposed the trickery of white slave traders to the Italian public during the first fifteen years of the twentieth century.[16] Like abolition, of which it was an offshoot, the campaign against the international traffic in women was initially inspired by the British example and quickly became international in scope.[17] Because of the luridness and sensationalism of the tales of white slavery,

71

however, the crusade against it gained much wider popularity than simple abolitionism had in the late nineteenth century.[18] In fact, even traditional Catholic charitable organizations staffed by monastic or lay women gave their support to the new cause, a support that favored its success but blurred and complicated the ideological thrust of the movement. To understand how the campaign against the trafficking of women both strengthened and weakened abolition, one must examine in detail the reforming efforts of, first, Catholic women and, second, secular feminists.

Traditionally prohibitionist, Catholics had shunned the abolitionist movement, dominated, as it was, by democratic leftists and feminists. To the church, the abolitionist insistence on sexual equality and protection of the civil rights of prostitutes was anathema; prostitutes did not deserve liberty but required redemption. The white slave campaign appealed to this moral concern, since crusaders sought to save innocent, young girls from the influence of evil procurers of both sexes. Narratives, like the newspaper story quoted above, presented a simplistic picture of prostitution with the opposing forces drawn in black and white: girls "fell" because of the immoral designs of a few readily identifiable persons rather than a complex interplay of social and economic motives. Thus a number of prohibitionists joined the white slave campaign to advance their own final aim, ridding the world of prostitution, by punishing the malicious procurer and redeeming the sinning woman.

Since the salvation of prostitutes had been a traditional concern of the church, especially during the Catholic reformation, several institutions already existed, which quickly took up the new cause.[19] For example, the Pio Monte della Misericordia of Naples, founded in 1601, continued to include among its charitable functions "the rehabilitation of young girls who have unluckily fallen into error and vice."[20] Other organizations dating from the same period revitalized themselves in the nineteenth century when prostitution reappeared as a central social question. One of these, the congregation of the Buon Pastore (Good Shepard), which reached back to the seventeenth century, opened a new chapter in Milan in 1868. This branch, later licensed as an opera pia by the Italian kingdom, had the purpose of offering recovery, education, and work to "young girls who are corrupted by poverty or another unfortunate adventure" and promised to "educate them to an honest life."[21] With the commencement of the white slave trade campaign, newer organizations, like the Associazione Cattolica Internazionale per la Protezione della Giovane (Catholic Association for the Protection of Young Women), sprang up. The association had its headquarters in Freiburg, Germany and branches in fifty Italian communes by 1912.[22] Although partial, this list illustrates that the Catholic redemption charities ranged from local to international. Women organized and staffed them all, although the municipal organizations tended to be ultimately responsible to the resident bishop or abbot.

As revealed by their charters, the religious charities that campaigned against the white slave trade held a conservative view of the appropriate role of women to which they hoped to restore prostitutes. Not surprisingly, they required religious and moral education for the redemption of those who had already fallen, or as a preventive measure for young girls "in danger of being demoralized."[23] In addition, inmates were to be trained in "the tasks which are indispensable to good housewives and mistresses of the family."[24] As the Istituto Don Giacomelli explicitly put it, "The scope of this new Institution is that of molding good and capable little housewives."[25] Preoccupied with preparing women for the traditional duties of wife and mother, the religious charities failed to offer training geared toward the workplace. This implicit disapproval of woman's work outside the home was impractical and self-defeating for prostitutes seeking an alternative means of financial support.

While the campaign against white slavery was a new issue for Catholic women, it represented a second phase of abolitionism for secular feminists. The first report of the progressive Comitato Italiano Contro la Tratta delle Bianche (Italian Committee against the White Slave Trade), for example, echoed in 1903 the assumptions and logic of earlier emancipationists like Mozzoni:

> The victim of the vile cunning of the traffickers in human flesh is usually the already unfortunate woman of the working classes. Profiting from the sad conditions which everywhere characterize the life of proletarian women, they [traffickers] seduce ignorant girls and women who are strug-

gling in vain to give bread to their children and entice them into prostitution with false promises. . . . We must not forget, however, that the vile trafficker exists and prospers because men do not know how to curb their sexual instincts but are always looking for depraved enjoyments and new sources of dissipated pleasures, which disseminate corruption and hasten the degeneration of the species.[26]

Between the campaign against the Cavour Regulation during the 1870s and 1880s and the first decade of the twentieth century, the abolitionist analysis seemed to have changed little: the causes for prostitution were still thought to lie in the poverty that afflicted lower-class women, the trickery of procurers, and male lust that had not yet been bridled by civilization. More specifically, abolitionists linked their cause to that of white slavery because they believed that the tolerated houses formed an indispensable link in supplying the merchandise for the international market in women. The case chiuse provided an impenetrable space for the initiation of innocent girls into prostitution: a prison from which the victims could not escape until they had lost their honor and, therefore, the possibility of returning to respectable society. Once "fallen," the girls were shipped from city to city and nation to nation by means of the chain of interconnected brothels. For abolitionists, their crusade against the closed houses had developed naturally into the campaign against white slavery.

Beneath the consistency of rhetoric, however, lay the reality of an Italian feminism that had undergone significant modifications during the fifty years since unification. By the twentieth century, the women's movement no longer consisted simply of a few eminent and active individuals, but of a variety of organizations that, through meetings and journals, publicized women's issues and attracted an increasing number of members.[27] The earliest of these organizations was the Lega Promotrice degli Interessi Femminili (League to Promote Female Interests), founded in Milan in 1881 by a feminist of the older generation, Mozzoni. In the 1890s a group of local Leghe di Tutela degli Interessi femminili (Leagues to Protect Female Interests), modeled on Mozzoni's effort, sprang up in several cities of Piedmont and Lombardy as well as in Venice, Florence, and Rome. A short-lived journal, *Vita femmin-*

ile (1895–1897), served as a bulletin for the leagues.[28] Milan was the birthplace in 1899 of another important organization, the Unione Femminile (Female Union), whose journal, of the same name, was distributed throughout Italy (1901–1905).[29] During the first years of the twentieth century, two truly national feminist groups were established: the Consiglio Nazionale delle Donne (National Council of Women) (1903) and the Comitato Nazionale Pro-suffragio (National Suffrage Committee) (1904). Both gained stature from their status as branches of larger international organizations, the International Council of Women and the International Suffrage Alliance, respectively.[30] Thus by the eve of World War I the women's movement had been institutionalized at the local, national, and international levels.

This increased power of organization and numbers, however, was accompanied not by ideological growth but rather by a retrenchment into positions more conservative than those of the earlier generation of feminists. In this previous phase, Mazzinian democracy had melded with pre-Marxist socialism and anarchism to produce a radical and progressive critique of sex and class privileges. This kind of analysis typified both the early, individual feminists, like Jesse White Mario and Mozzoni, and the leagues of the 1880s and early 1890s. In ideology and membership, these early feminist societies were interclass. In the 1890s, however, the women's movement broke into two tendencies, bourgeois and socialist, each of which retreated, in different ways, from a platform of equality for women. Franca Pieroni Bortolotti, a noted historian of women, has labeled this shift as one from nineteenth-century "emancipation" to twentieth-century "feminism."[31] First, bourgeois women's organizations, such as the Council of Women, became less political, less concerned with workers, more preoccupied with using respectable methods, and ultimately, after 1910, nationalistic. They focused their attention on welfare, education, and protection of the family. Even suffragists argued for the vote on the basis of the complementarity and equivalency of the female and male spheres rather than the fundamental equality of men and women.

Second, in the socialist camp, the newly formed Marxist party, the Partito Socialista Italiano (PSI), gradually absorbed the Mozzonian leagues and, according to Pieroni Bortolotti, "The

75

Italian socialists, among other things, liquidated the campaign for the emancipation of women."[32] There were various reasons for the Marxist ambivalence toward the woman question, prominent among which were the socialist emphasis on class, rather than sexual, analysis. In addition, positivism, which constituted a prominent strain in Italian socialism, taught that motherhood was women's natural role in evolution.[33] Socialist feminists did begin to organize and publish a series of journals, but usually within and subordinate to the overall structure and discipline of the party.[34] Only a few feminist organizations fell outside of this bourgeois/socialist pattern; the Female Union was one, and its leader, Ersilia Majno Bronzini, criticized the timidity of both camps. But even Majno Bronzini stressed the different roles assigned to the two sexes by "the laws of Nature" and proclaimed "the defense of motherhood" to be the overriding concern of the union.[35]

Against this background of increasing moderation among feminists, it is not surprising that the campaign against the white slave trade became a popular women's issue. While the crusade had links with nineteenth-century abolition, it also reflected more current concerns of the first decades of the twentieth century. Bourgeois feminists, disinclined to an economic critique of society, preferred, like Catholic women, the moralistic narrative that blamed evil procurers for the problem of prostitution. Socialist feminists did not shirk class analysis, but they shared with their middle-class counterparts an idealization of motherhood and a horror of childhood sexuality, two themes that permeated wide strata of public opinion after 1900. The image of the victim of white slavery being that of a young and innocent girl, women of all ideological positions could agree that she deserved defense, both from the trafficker and from her own unnatural desires. The sometimes conservative tone of the white slavery campaign derived from this ambivalence: the desire to protect, and yet at the same time keep under surveillance, all possible victims of procurement.

Feminists contributed to the campaign against white slavery either through their preestablished, general organizations or by founding new groups dedicated exclusively to the new cause. For example, the Council of Women created a special section, Morality and the White Slave Trade, to study and make proposals on the new issue. It also cooperated with the Unione Internazionale delle Amiche della Giovanetta (International Union of Friends of Young Women), a Protestant organization dedicated solely to the protection of female emigrants. Begun in Switzerland in 1877, the Friends had branches in sixty-two Italian communes by 1902.[36] The major chapters were in the large cities like Milan. Such a chapter would have "an employment office which sent out its own delegates to the train stations in order to be guides to young girls who are either arriving or departing."[37] For those migrants who were "isolated or in need of help," the Friends gave "temporary shelter and assistance at a low price."[38] According to the Venice branch, the organization supplied work for the unemployed as "servants, maids, governesses, etc."[39] While this orientation toward domestic service was rather traditional, the Union of Friends was distinguished from the Catholic organizations by its secular orientation and its practice of not discouraging, but encouraging, emigration for the purpose of finding employment.

Most distinctive of the Italian reform societies was the Italian Committee against the White Slave Trade. Founded in 1901, it had branches in Milan, Rome, Genoa, and Naples and coordinated its programs with the International Bureau in London. While most of the local chapters became relatively inactive after the first few years of feverish organizing, the Milanese committee distinguished itself by widening its agenda and establishing the Asilo Mariuccia, a reformatory that has remained open until the present day.[40] Not surprisingly, the indefatigable Majno Bronzini served as vice-president of the Milan section, which was run under the auspices of the Female Union. Like its parent organization, the committee held a complex feminist philosophy that was not reducible to the narrow moralism and sentimentality of many other redemption organizations. Adopting a wider perspective, it defined the campaign against the white slave trade not as simply a hunting down of procurers but as an attack on "the multiplicity of moral, social, and economic causes" of prostitution.[41] As one of its biennial reports, published in 1910, explained:

It is necessary to concern ourselves not only with the foreign and more apparent manifestations [of trafficking], that organization of international commerce; but also with the trade

77

which operates *within the borders of one State*, and, above all, with those forms of the trade which, by being less heard of, since they cannot be explained by the intervention of a regular international merchant, nevertheless, differ from the others neither in substance nor in consequences.[42]

From this broad point of view, the committee concerned itself not only with the "classical" figure of the international trafficker but also with all other persons who fostered prostitution: parents who abandoned their children, lovers who seduced and deserted their fiancées, husbands who sent their wives out to prostitute themselves, as well as pimps and madams.

Like other religious and lay organizations, the Milan committee established centers to give "moral and material aid" to those prostitutes who wished to return to an "honest" life.[43] To contact prostitutes, two female members visited daily the clinic for venereal disease to see if any women needed assistance. They successfully encouraged the hospital to employ a teacher for those prostitutes, and their children, who wished to learn to read and write; to open a small library; and to make knitting and sewing materials available so that the patients would have the "means to dedicate themselves to useful tasks and give up their habits of laziness."[44] In addition, they arranged for the police to recommend the services of the committee to any prostitute who expressed a desire to leave the profession. Members of the committee admitted that some people laughed at this idea of "individual saving" as a way to fight prostitution, and they realized that rescue alone would not eliminate the problem. Instead, the significance of the committee lay not only in the individual cases of rehabilitation but in its "reaffirmation of the dignity of women and the integrity of their human rights."[45]

The committee realized, however, that it could only pursue its fight against "the present domination of the unfair double standard [in sexual morality]" by attacking the causes of prostitution.[46] To get at the root of prostitution and white slavery, it directed its activity primarily toward prevention rather than rehabilitation. The Asilo Mariuccia, for example, took in not only former prostitutes but also the "endangered"—those who through poverty, loss of parents, or attempted seduction were in danger of becoming prostitutes. During the first ten years of its existence, the Asilo annually provided a home for fifty to sixty women. The committee also opened an office that offered free legal advice and that denounced to the police suspected procurers and pimps. It opened a dormitory and a job-placement office to assist migrants to the city who might otherwise end up in a rooming house or employment agency that was simply a front for procurers. Finally, the committee paid transportation costs for any girl wishing to return to her family.

To guarantee that "the physical and moral integrity of childhood be respected and defended," members called for changes in legislation and education.[47] Believing that experiences in early life initiated the chain of events that led to prostitution, they gave high priority to the protection of children. Legal reforms suggested by the committee included increasing penalities for corruption of minors; limiting the rights of fathers and husbands who encouraged their daughters or wives to prostitute themselves; prohibiting employment of young children as actresses and ballerinas; and punishing parents who abandoned or maltreated their children. In addition to better schools for children, especially for orphans, the committee requested that the minister of public instruction institute a course in "sexual and social hygiene" in all secondary schools and teacher colleges. This course would instruct students in the dangers, symptoms, and prevention of infectious diseases, with emphasis on venereal disease. Although the minister did not carry out this request, the committee claimed to have at least opened the question to public discussion. It also published an Italian translation of a book called *Hygiene and Morality*, written by an English doctor, in the hope that teachers would recommend it to their students.

The committee's progressive philosophy not only stressed prevention rather than rehabilitation but also insisted that the government, not private charity, was ultimately responsible for preventive measures. For members, their work was more important than "the comfort of doing a good deed."[48] The campaign against the white slave trade was not a sentimental crusade but the "*fulfillment of a social duty.*"[49] The committee, therefore, demanded that its services and institutions become part of the public assistance administration. This appeal for state intervention raises several important questions. How successful was the white slavery campaign in modifying state policy? Did such modifications represent a triumph of abolitionism over regulation?

As its most notable victory, the reform movement pressured the Italian government into signing two international accords condemning white slavery, which were drawn up in 1904 and 1910 following debate at two Parisian congresses. According to these accords, the signatory states promised to cooperate in combating the international traffic in women.[50] This cooperation included the exchange of information, immediate extradition of suspected procurers, and free transportation for victims to their country of origin. In Italy the chief of the Division of Public Security (PS) expressed his firm intention to enforce these accords, promising "the reorganization of the entire administrative section dedicated to the repression of the despicable trafficking, a section to which I intend to apply the greatest stimulus toward expansion."[51] Through a series of circulars to prefects, he directed police officials to conform to the spirit of the accords at the local level, putting special emphasis on the protection of minors.[52]

Reformers also gained satisfaction from the positive recognition the state began to grant their redemptive institutions. While the laws on prostitution had always instructed police to help any woman wanting to leave the profession, this provision had rarely received high priority in practice. In 1911, however, the director of the PS asked all prefects for a list of those institutions in each province that "dedicate themselves primarily to the aim of giving moral and social assistance to girls and adult women, in order to rescue them from vice and immorality and to redeem those who are already corrupted." He added that, in the fight against white slavery, "the cooperation of private initiatives and energies can be of great and precious aid to public authorities."[53] The responses to the circular indicated a great variation among provinces in terms of the number of such organizations: Milan listed ten, Rome five, while the prefect of Palermo wrote that "no committees, societies, or charitable institutions exist in this province" for the purpose of eliminating white slavery.[54] Access to prostitutes for reeducation, then, was not uniform across Italy, being greatest in the northern and central cities.

The police bureaucracy in Rome gave a favorable hearing to the complaints and suggestions of the anti–white slave societies, which constituted a pressure group dedicated to safeguarding the international accords. In 1910 the chief of the PS urged railway officials to allow delegates from the Union of Friends and the Italian Committee to post signs in stations offering assistance to women traveling alone. He explained that these societies, while private, "merited nevertheless unconditional support and consideration of the Government, since they both aim to deliver girls from vice and corruption."[55] In 1913 he checked with the prison administration, at the request of the Friends, to make sure that minors were separated from "fallen women" in the judiciary prisons and that they were guarded by nuns or female lay custodians rather than men.[56] At the demand of the Friends and the Catholic Association for the Protection of Young Women, he allowed "visitors" from these organizations access to local police stations to make contact with arrested women and to inspect the conditions of their confinement.[57] The state refused, however, to build new public reformatories for girls or take over the funding and running of the private institutions, as the Milanese committee had demanded. On the eve of World War I, the government still envisioned the reeducation of female prostitutes as an act of private charity rather than the "fulfillment of a social duty." Thus the section of the Nicotera law that promised state aid to those prostitutes wishing to leave the profession remained, in practice, a dead letter.

At the local level, PS agents stepped up their investigation of white slavery in line with requests from the Ministry in Rome. Beginning in 1913 police interviewed all foreign prostitutes who came in contact with the regulation system: those requesting registration, undergoing treatment in the venereal disease clinics, or under arrest. During the interviews, prostitutes were asked if they had been victims of white slavery or had heard of other cases of trafficking. The answers were noted on special forms, the *foglietti di indicazione* (information sheets), large numbers of which remain as testimony to the zeal of the police.[58] The morals squads also exercised special surveillance over ports, hotels, employment agencies, theatrical and dance companies, and any other public or private concern that might attract homeless and unemployed girls. They investigated tips from private citizens, newspapers, or foreign governments.[59]

As the accords envisioned, Italian police relied on correspondence with their counterparts in other nations to locate and identify traffickers. International cooperation, for example, helped police to track down Rosario Ferrara, a man who had convinced two girls from Messina, Rosa Giusto and Concetta Cafiero, that he would find them "honest work" selling pianos in Bombay. Halfway through the voyage to India, however, Giusto realized "that the story of the little pianos was a pretext and that instead he wanted to abuse me and Concetta Cafiero in order to force us into prostitution for his profit."[60] After revealing this to the captain of the ship, the girls escaped with his help, and Ferrara was immediately extradited from India. Efficient police action did not always suffice to punish suspected trafficking, however; Ferrara was absolved on appeal for lack of sufficient evidence.

Did the successes of the anti–white slavery campaign represent the triumph of the abolitionist forces of the dominant classes over those of regulation? The answer is quite complicated and must be approached from several directions. On the one hand, both the approval of the international accords and the unprecedented co-operation of the PS administration with reformers signaled a strengthening of the abolitionist movement, which considered the crusade against white slavery its natural offspring. In addition, the subject of prostitution received so much publicity in the press that abolitionists seemed to have defeated what one historian has labeled the "conspiracy of silence" surrounding sexual issues.[61] Most notably, large numbers of women were now willing to organize and speak out on a topic that several decades earlier was considered too delicate for their ears. Prostitution had become a women's issue, and as feminist groups multiplied, they forced the public to face the problem from the point of view of the female victim rather than the male client or the government administrator.

On the other hand, the propaganda of the anti–white slavery crusade diluted and perverted the philosophy of abolition. The adherence of Catholic women created a united front that strengthened, and helps to explain the successes of, the cause. Yet this alliance with Catholic women reinforced the moralism that had always formed part of the abolitionist analysis at the expense of a more complex social and economic critique. Even the progressive Italian Committee marshaled most of its resources and energies toward attacking immorality rather than poverty as the main cause of prostitution. Furthermore, this narrowing of focus —from prostitution in general to the white slave trade—gave abolitionists a winning issue but one that was overblown. While the charges of white slavery were sensational and won public support, proof of widespread trafficking in women against their will is lacking. Italian evidence, such as the testimony preserved on the questionnaires required of foreign prostitutes, supports the contention that the reality of white slavery never approached its notoriety.[62] Historians of prostitution who have studied other nations during the same period have come to the same conclusion.[63] Thus, Italian feminists and abolitionists channeled their energies into a problem much less widespread than the myriad other injustices to which prostitutes were subject.

It is also noteworthy that regulationists were more tolerant of the anti–white slavery campaign than they had been of abolition. Perhaps they realized that the former diverted attention from the latter and therefore lessened the attacks on the closed houses. For example, Sormani lauded the women of the International Abolitionist Federation, whom he otherwise considered enemies, when they focused on the redemption of prostitutes. He patronizingly wrote that it was fitting that these "most noble and highly educated ladies of our citizenry" should create female reformatories, rather than mix themselves up in politics.[64] Others hoped that private charity would fill the need for secular institutions of reeducation without incurring government expense. Anticlerical regulationists like Gozzoli complained that many prostitutes who wanted to leave the profession resented the rigor of monastic homes that had traditionally provided the only place of refuge. He criticized the nuns who ran these reformatories for "fanatical bigotry and a mania for submitting women, who only yesterday left a life of pleasure, to spiritual exercises, to long singing of psalms, to fasts, and to making crosses on the ground with their

83

tongues. In this way they [the nuns] want too much too quickly and end up by irritating rather than converting."[65] For Gozzoli and other regulationists, the establishment of private lay reformatories to meet this problem was a natural, womanly task for female abolitionists.

Furthermore, the repressive aspect of the anti—white slavery crusade attracted regulationists, whose ideology was based on the discipline of the dangerous classes for the good of society. I have already explained that ambivalence pervaded the attitudes of reformers toward the victims of white slavery: they desired to protect, but at the same time keep a close surveillance over, the sexuality of young women, especially those of the lower classes. The director of the PS showed an appreciation of redemptive organizations' preoccupation with social control when he wrote to his subordinates that

> I do not need to waste words in order to demonstrate how much interest the [public] authorities have in establishing contact with the private associations for the repression of the white slave trade. Distinguished by their discretion, seriousness, and practicality, they can provide us with precious information, confidential reports, and circumspect surveillance which are invaluable for the police and justice systems.[66]

He realized that the reform societies, through their redemption homes, agents at the railway stations, "visitors" in clinics for venereal disease, and inspectors in prisons, were privy to the same kind of "knowledge" about marginal women that interested police. Thus regulationists could find in the anti—white slavery campaign a new, common ground for cooperation with their traditional opponents. Pragmatism, more than idealism, motivated the concern of the state with the problem of white slavery; administrators could use the reformers' demands to legitimize and extend the scope of government surveillance. Ironically, while its origins lay in abolition, the anti—white slavery campaign ended up by winning the support of both Catholic prohibitionists and secular regulationists. This coalition of forces helps to explain the successes of the campaign in influencing government policy and public opinion relative to the more modest gains of abolition.

84

The Health Regulation of 1905

Although the Nicotera Regulation was never repealed during the period preceding World War I, several modifications in the Italian law on prostitution undercut its regulationist character. In the 1890s the director of public health began a process of "decentralizing" the system of dispensaries that offered free treatment for victims of venereal disease. The decision to hand over the functioning of the dispensaries to local authorities was the first step in the elaboration of a new, general policy based on the principle of separation of police and health functions. This detachment of the prophylactic service of the public health bureaucracy from the surveillance duties of the police did not overturn the regulationist character of the Italian system, but it did infuse it with certain abolitionist tenets. The change was sanctioned in a new health law dealing with venereal disease issued in 1905. In both the case of decentralization and that of the health regulation, it was internal developments in the Ministry of the Interior rather than the pressure of abolitionists that accounted for the softening of regulation.

The first modification of state policy, decentralization of the dispensaries, followed some years of disillusionment with the functioning of the Nicotera law of 1891. A general inspection of the regulation system ordered by the Superior Council of Health in 1896 revealed laxity among police and the inadequacy of medical facilities for the cure of venereal disease. In response, Minister of the Interior Antonio Rudinì issued a series of circulars in which he admonished police chiefs, provincial doctors, and mayors to oversee more rigorously the proper enforcement of the law.[67] Budget difficulties hampered the implementation of several provisions, especially those concerning the establishment of dispensaries and hospital wards to replace the sifilicomi. Owing to the financial crisis of 1893/1894 and the economic losses of the Ethiopian campaign of 1895/1896, the central government had not been able to fund all the health facilities required by law. For the same reason, Rudinì had to suspend two projected ministerial decrees that would have rationalized the system of dispensaries and increased their personnel.[68] Within the next several years, budget problems convinced the administration that the central state was incapable of maintaining even the present dispensaries. For the first time, it seriously studied a measure long championed by the Left: decentralization.

In elaborating the new policy of decentralization, the Ministry of the Interior abandoned neither complete control over nor full financial responsibility for the dispensaries. To Genoa and Palermo, two of the first cities approached with the plan, administrators promised to turn over the buildings and equipment of the existing national dispensaries and provide subsidies to their new communal counterparts.[69] Furthermore, the contract sent out to each city detailed the various regulations with which each local facility had to comply. While local in nature, the new institutions were required to forward to the Ministry statistics on the number of patients, types of disease, and rates of cure. Finally, the director of public health reserved the right to send provincial doctors on inspection tours of the dispensaries to insure compliance with government stipulations.[70] In effect, decentralization simply meant a shift from direct to indirect control by national authorities. As with many other "local" social programs, the Ministry of the Interior set certain standards to be maintained by each communal administration. In this way, the national health bureaucracy could hope to continue and even extend the prophylactic policy against the diffusion of venereal disease on a smaller budget. On March 1, 1901 the national dispensaries were officially closed, although negotiations for the transfer continued with various cities.

The decentralization of the dispensaries was one step in the general trend toward separation of the police and health aspects of the regulation system. Already in 1896, in a letter to Giuseppe Reisso, the director of the municipal health laboratory of Genoa, a national administrator distinguished between the coercive nature of the surveillance of brothels in the name of public order and morality, and the voluntary quality of the health services.[71] He was trying to convince Genoa to take over the administration of the dispensaries and set an example of successful decentralization for the other major cities. He emphasized that this action would accent the differentiation between the negative (police) and positive (health) parts of the regulation system and prevent the confusion of roles and duties among agents of public security and public health. If venereal disease was handled at the local level like any other "common" disease, patients would seek cure without fear of contact with police.

The innovative and forceful director of public health, Rocco Santoliquido, made the separation of police and health functions the major tenet of a new reform philosophy in the late 1890s. Speaking to international health conferences, he stressed again and again the necessity "to separate without delay police measures from measures of prophylaxis."[72] As an avowed abolitionist, he strove to free the public health services from police domination. Declaring that "the prophylaxis [of venereal disease] has a right to complete independence, to absolute autonomy," he redefined the state's stance toward prostitution by establishing a dichotomy in values and functions between the administrations of public security and public health.[73] Unlike previous abolitionists who strove to replace regulationist legislation, Santoliquido liberalized the health services within the confines of the existing legislation. By working within the ambiguities of the Nicotera law, he managed to move Italy closer to abolition than any preceding liberal protest by Parliament.

As a defense of his new policy, Santoliquido stressed utility rather than the justice of abolition. As he told one congress of doctors concerned with venereal disease, "My prophylactic theory is frankly abolitionist, and not in words, but in practice."[74] He moved Italy toward liberalization in an evolutionary fashion, waiting for the proper moment to pursue reform. By 1900 Santoliquido felt abolition to be especially timely as he noted a shift in the practice of prostitution away from full-time service in brothels to part-time, autonomous activity. This seemed to indicate that brothels were no longer money-making ventures for owners. Because of this restructuring of the profession, the control of brothels by police was affecting a diminishing percentage of female prostitutes.[75] Santoliquido opposed regulation, therefore, not so much because it restricted civil rights but because it was useless in the face of the proliferation of part-time prostitution. Yet he did not attempt to take away police functions but pragmatically accepted surveillance over brothels as proper for the purpose of guaranteeing order.

In terms of health, however, Santoliquido condemned regulation as inefficacious. When only a small percentage of prostitutes worked in public brothels, a program aimed simply at cleansing these foci of infection could never control venereal disease. With prostitutes spread throughout the city and difficult to detect, the government could never afford to support a large enough police force to assure registration and biweekly examinations. On these grounds, abolition offered the only alternative in the fight against infection. Public health measures would have to be made attractive to both prostitutes and other victims of venereal disease.

Santoliquido branded as unjust the view that abolitionists, like himself, "oppose all guarantees of the public health."[76] In fact, he intended to reverse the traditional regulationist argument to show that only abolition could prevent the diffusion of venereal disease. As a doctor he declared that *"salus publica suprema lex"* and accused the police system of being a barrier between doctors and the public.[77] Instead of espousing, as many abolitionists formerly had, the view that public health should be subordinated to the maintenance of personal liberty, he called for the subordination of repression to the pursuit of good health. Since "the adversary for us is disease," it was not the duty of the doctor to condemn the profession of the patient, that is, prostitution.[78] To educate the public to consider venereal disease as similar to any other, the police must renounce any contact with the dispensaries or hospital wards.

To curb venereal disease, government doctors and medical institutions had to gain the trust of the public. Besides making treatment noncoercive, Santoliquido made attendance at clinics as anonymous as possible for embarrassed patients. Dispensaries would be discretely marked or, whenever possible, annexed to general hospitals where one could register without one's ailment being suspected. In hospitals where patients were mixed, doctors would carefully conceal the diagnosis of a syphilitic patient. While the government required statistics on the numbers of patients and types of diseases cured in dispensaries, Santoliquido allowed that names of patients be withheld from official records. This discretion was seen as a temporary measure to attract those who felt that their disease was a sign of immorality. Santoliquido expected that proper education would insure that the next generation would regard all diseases as health, not moral, problems.

The regulation of July 27, 1905, which replaced and abrogated the sixth section of the Nicotera law, followed the general outline of Santoliquido's ideas as he had expressed them throughout Europe in the preceding few years.[79] At the communal level, municipal doctors were to provide free treatment and drugs for the poor suffering from venereal disease, just as for poor with other diseases. Cure in the dispensaries and special hospital wards for venereal disease would be available to all citizens without charge. The dispensaries, now decentralized, were to be funded and administered by the communes with subsidies from the central state; the wards continued to be nationally financed. Contrary to the principles of pure abolition, the provincial health authorities would continue surveillance on registered brothels, whose owners were required to provide regular examinations for their employees. Suspected prostitutes, however, could not be arrested by police for health reasons nor submitted to forced examination.

In liberalizing the Nicotera law, Santoliquido succeeded, where abolitionists had failed, for three major reasons. First, he worked from within the bureaucracy of the Ministry of the Interior rather than against it. Always jealous of its interests, the public administration was more willing and more constricted to modify its policies at the insistence of an insider. It had continually resisted and resented pressure from Parliament and reform organizations. Furthermore, Santoliquido refrained from tampering in the domain of public security. Since the police were still committed to regulation, he simply detached health policies from the scope of the Nicotera law, leaving PS authorities free to pursue traditional objectives.

To members of his own staff in the Division of Public Health, Santoliquido could promise that abolition would increase rather than limit their power. Certainly, doctors lost the right to have prostitutes arrested for medical reasons or to force patients with venereal disease to undergo treatment. In return for loss of this direct control over prostitutes, however, doctors could now consider the entire population their domain. As the indispensable experts the doctors would exercise indirect but ever expanding influence through strategies of prevention and treatment applicable to all members of society. A health service for all promised multiplication of medical institutions and many more jobs in the public sector than in the past.

Second, a basic change in public health philosophy also accounted for the Division of Public Health's abandonment of regulation. Having once been the staunch defenders of registration and control of brothels, many doctors had by 1900 shifted their attention to preventive medicine for the general public. With the growth of the cities and the increasing internal migration, many physicians realized that surveillance over brothels was not an adequate deterrent to the spread of venereal disease; only a new policy of prevention and cure for all could insure a decline in the rates of such disease. Santoliquido personified this new abolitionist outlook of health authorities that grew not from concern with principles of liberalism but from recognition that the old prophylactic policies had failed. As he emphasized to a medical conference in 1901, "The Italian administration has not arrived at the present system . . . on the basis of preconceived notions or a theoretical idealism; it has developed from the unacceptable results of the extreme regulation system that dominated previously; it has been arrived at according to an experimental system which is the most secure method."[80] Doctors had not deserted the scientific method for a leap into political idealism, nor did medical reform threaten to unleash a larger wave of liberal reforms that might threaten state power.

Third, Santoliquido managed to capture the sympathies of the prime minister, whose cooperation was indispensable for the modification of the Nicotera Regulation, as it was a ministerial decree. This prime minister was Giovanni Giolitti, who also held the portfolio of the Interior Ministry from 1903 to 1905.[81] With this government, which initiated a period dominated by Giolitti that lasted until World War I, Italy received, in the words of Salomone, "a strong wind of fresh liberalism."[82] But, as Salomone added, for Giolitti, "liberty never became a passion" but represented "a useful lubricant for the mechanical balance of conflicting forces."[83] In short, as a pragmatic liberal, Giolitti was a perfect recipient for Santoliquido's conception of practical and limited abolition. Already in 1904 Giolitti sent out a circular that echoed the logic of his director of public health; in regard to the functions of the police and public health personnel, he wrote

that "any confusion between the two becomes dangerous and constitutes an abuse. Therefore, it is an unlawful act to arrest a
woman, no matter what her profession, for the sole purpose of
verifying the state of her health, just as it is illegal to deprive a
woman in a venereal disease ward of her personal liberty."[84]
Earlier prime ministers had feared that any concession to abolition would result in a loss of power for the state. Giolitti, however, in order to mollify critics and increase public support, pragmatically propounded a progressive health policy based on free
and voluntary cure for all social groups, including prostitutes.
Behind the facade of this liberalization, however, he left untouched the disciplinary role of the police.

Did the Nicotera Regulation of 1891, the white slavery accords
of 1904 and 1910, and the Health Regulation of 1905 alter the
balance of forces between regulation and abolition? Had significant change occurred in the attitude toward prostitution held by
the dominant classes that formulated government policy? A comprehensive response would have to be negative, for Italy remained
a regulationist state whose fundamental system had been liberalized but not overturned. Santoliquido was partially correct when
he boasted that, by the twentieth century, his nation had con-
structed a unique system that was neither regulationist or abolitionist. Yet despite an innovative health policy, the cornerstone of
the regulation system, the closed houses, remained intact. Even
the liberalism of the medical bureaucracy, based as it was on
pragmatism rather than idealism, differed from true abolition; for
this reason, Alain Corbin has labeled a parallel shift in French
medical opinion "neo-regulationist" rather than abolitionist.[85]
According to Corbin, French doctors were not committed to the
principle of freedom but simply wished to substitute medical for
police control over prostitution. Italy experienced a similar ri-
valry of bureaucracies in which public health authorities successfully contested the hegemony of PS officials over prostitution policy. Formerly subordinate to the police agents who directed the
Health Offices, physicians came to have sole jurisdiction over the
dispensaries and wards. Thus the state had not ceased to regard
prostitution as a problem but simply medicalized it.

Italy, however, did not experience, during the first decade of
the century, the same moral hysteria against prostitution that

characterized the social purity organizations of the United States and Great Britain. In the former, abolitionist sentiment had never been strong, and prohibition, or what Mark Connelly has called "anti-prostitution," sentiment dominated the groups that opposed regulation.[86] After 1900 these banded together to crusade successfully for the closing of the vice districts in American cities. While Britain had been the birthplace of abolition, reformers switched their allegiance to the cause of social purity after the repeal of the Contagious Diseases Acts. When the repressive nature of the social purity movement, which included the campaign against white slavery, became evident, Butler and other feminists abandoned it. But social purity reformers found new allies in the medical establishment, and out of this coalition grew the social hygiene movement that dominated British discourse on prostitution in the late nineteenth and early twentieth centuries.[87] Compared with the fanaticism and moralism of the Anglo-American purity reformers, the Italian campaign against the white slave trade remained relatively faithful to its abolitionist roots. Feminists remained in the movement and had a moderating influence on its course. Not until the 1920s, and the advent of fascism, did Italy construct a new policy toward moral issues based on social hygiene and pass new prostitution legislation that reversed the tentative steps toward abolition taken during the Giolittian period.

II

Prostitution

4

Social Profile of Prostitutes

In general, prostitutes have little education, and therefore most of them are ignorant and illiterate. Possessing a bizarre, versatile, and restless character, they love uproar and quarrels; they take offense as quickly as they make peace. Prone to bad temper and lying, they know how to conceal the truth with a persistence which does not even yield in the face of the facts. . . . They do not take heed of the future and thoughtlessly squander their belongings.[1]

According to Bolis, these habits and inclinations, so alien to those of normal women, were "second nature" to prostitutes.[2] Almost forty years later, in 1907, the criminologist Salvatore Ottolenghi drew a similar portrait of the prostitute in his manual for police education. Under the rubric "psychological traits of prostitutes," he listed "stupidity, imbecility, fickleness, improvidence; laziness; vanity, passion for alcohol and debauch; obscenity; immorality."[3] As these two quotations illustrate, members of the ruling classes held continuously, from unification until World War I, an image of the prostitute diametrically opposed to that of "honest" women who made up the majority of the female population. Much has been written about the sexual ideology of the nineteenth cen-

95

tury, which divided women into two groups: virgins (or mothers) and whores. Yet historians are only beginning to question whether this ideology truthfully represented social reality. The problem of the relationship between prescription and the actual behavior of "normal" and "deviant" women can be approached from several angles. Does a social profile of prostitutes differ significantly from that of women in general? Did those women who became prostitutes retain ties with respectable society? How divergent was the life of a prostitute from that of an "honest" woman?

The second half of this study attempts to provide answers to these questions. Unfortunately the answers are partial and sometimes hypothetical because prostitutes of the pre–World War I era have left little direct testimony about their lives and attitudes. Whereas regulationists and abolitionists have left a wealth of written evidence of their beliefs, the point of view of the prostitute must be indirectly reconstructed from documents written by others. While conjectural, reconstruction is necessary for an understanding of prostitution as a phenomenon rooted not only in the labeling process of the state but in the particular economic and social conditions of women's lives. Why did certain women become prostitutes, and how did Italy's system of regulation impinge on this choice? This chapter draws a social profile of prostitutes as a group, comparing them to Italian women in general during the same time period. This group portrait provides the basis for an analysis, in chapters five and six, of the interaction between prostitutes and those representatives of the national government who enforced the regulation system, police, and public physicians. The form and extent of state intervention in the lives of prostitutes contributed to determining the distance, both geographical and social, between them and other women.

The life cycle of the prostitute provides a second thread of organization linking the three chapters of part two. I use the term *life cycle* rather than *career*, which is preferred by modern sociologists, because the latter implies a rigidity, organization, and formality lacking in nineteenth-century prostitution.[4] Yet the life cycle of prostitutes did have a rhythm that was, to a great extent, determined by their interaction with agents of the regulation system. The three chapters trace this rhythm. The first describes the condition of women before registration; the second and third trace their lives after becoming part of the regulation system through contacts with police and doctors. After the moment of registration, surveillance and examination continued to shape the contours of the daily activity of prostitutes. This regimentation ended only with marriage, removal from police lists, escape, or death.

Documentation

As a regulationist nation, Italy left a specific type of documentation that has both strengths and weaknesses for the historian trying to reconstruct the social outlines of prostitution. Compared with data from societies characterized by prohibition or abolition, however, the strengths outweigh the weaknesses. The *pouvoir* (power) of the state, exercised through constant surveillance and examination, generated an extensive array of *savoir* (knowledge) not available in countries that banned or decriminalized prostitution. In constant contact with prostitutes, police and doctors in the Italian system collected detailed information that was systematically recorded in various registers as required by law. Madams were also responsible for keeping ledgers containing the names of their employees as well as their ages, civil status, birthplace, and former profession. Unfortunately, most of the original forms kept in brothels, police stations, and hospitals for venereal disease are no longer extant. The archive of the Ministry of the Interior, however, has preserved many of the aggregate statistics forwarded from the various provinces. The reports of the parliamentary commissions provide a wealth of data based on the original municipal records. Local functionaries, like Cartenio Pini who worked as a physician in the Health Office in Florence, also published accounts of the activity of their own institutions.[5]

Reviewing these sources, I selected the data on prostitution in the largest cities of Italy, more precisely, those with a population of over one hundred thousand at the time of unification. Nine communes fell into this category: Naples, Milan, Rome, Turin, Palermo, Genoa, Florence, Bologna, and Venice (Table 1.1). They represented a wide range of urban types, from industrial

97

(Milan) to commercial (Naples) to bureaucratic (Rome). Notably, industrialization did not always accompany urbanization in pre–World War I Italy.[6] Each of these cities had the entire apparatus of the regulation system: Health Offices, sifilicomi, dispensaries, and clinics for venereal disease. Obviously, the conclusions of this study are not necessarily appropriate for defining the relation of the state to prostitution in rural areas. Middle-sized communes resembled large cities, but small villages usually lacked not only a Health Office and dispensary but even a local PS office and registered brothels. The mayor was then responsible for enforcing the regulationist laws, but the application was most likely very different and would require a separate investigation.

To get closer to the daily interaction between prostitutes and agents of the state, I did intensive research in the local archive of one of the nine cities, Bologna. Unlike most of the other major communes, Bologna has preserved many papers of both the prefect and the questore. One of the questori of Bologna, Giovanni Bolis, gave prostitution a central place in his tome on the dangerous classes, from which I quoted in part one. In addition, the health inspector for Bologna, Pietro Gamberini, left an invaluable series of reports on prostitution and the treatment of venereal disease for the period 1863–1888. These provide an unbroken series of statistics drawn from the original registers compiled in the brothels, Health Office, and sifilicomio of Bologna.

Since Bologna provides the case study for these three chapters, let me briefly outline its specific urban characteristics. Bologna both resembled and differed from the other cities under consideration. Yet the diversity among them was so wide that no one city can be said to typify the others. All experienced the demographic growth of the nineteenth century including Bologna, whose population jumped from 109,395 in 1862 to 172,628 in 1911. Although this 58 percent increase fell short of six of the other nine cities, it outstripped the national average of 43 percent. The early and widespread use of birth control in Bologna, noted by the economic historian Giorgio Gattei, may account for its relatively moderate demographic growth compared with the larger urban centers.[7] While the general Italian birthrate fell below 30 per 1,000 only after World War I, Bologna reached this low, "modern" rate by 1870. High rates of migration sustained the population, which continued to grow despite declining fertility.

Gattei has linked the demographic patterns of Bologna to its local code of sexual morality: "It seems that it can be argued . . . that the conduct of the inhabitants of Bologna in matters of love cannot easily be reduced to the canons of severe morality, be it Catholic or bourgeois."[8] As evidence of this unconventional sexual behavior, Gattei mentions, in addition to low fertility, the high rates of illegitimacy, bridal pregnancy, and prostitution. He concludes by hypothesizing that the excess of women over men in the Bolognese population, and the resulting inability of large numbers of women to find husbands, might explain the widespread illegitimacy and prostitution. A comparison with the other eight cities, however, reveals that Bologna was not aberrant in this respect. According to the censuses of 1881 and 1911, six of the communes showed a preponderance of women over men. Only Rome maintained a consistently male-dominated population during the entire period, perhaps because of the almost exclusive employment of men in the bureaucracies of church and state.

The picture does shift when narrowed to the age group fifteen to thirty, or that in which women were most likely to marry. In this case, the majority of cities, including Bologna, showed an abundance of males.[9] Bologna, therefore, was not actually atypical in its sex ratio that favored women in the overall population but men in the category of young adults (Table 4.1). This preponderance of young men over young women may not, however, invalidate Gattei's argument. Moving from city to city to look for work, the mobile young men did not provide the permanent and stable households desired by poor women. In fact, high rates of male migration and emigration may have increased prostitution because many women were left behind by their fiancés, often with a child to support. Prostitution offered an alternative to these women, not only in Bologna but in all the major urban centers.

The economy of Bologna modernized during the nineteenth century but did not undergo a true "revolution." According to the economic historian Luigi Dal Pane, the artisan sector, which was concentrated in silk and hemp production, declined in the eighteenth and nineteenth centuries.[10] The same period saw the

Table 4.1. *Sex Ratios for Nine Communes*

Communes	All ages			Ages 15–29	
	1881	1901	1911	1881	1911
Bologna	972	929	925	1,080	1,011
Florence	949	905	893	942	911
Genoa	985	1,024	1,011	982	1,059
Milan	1,031	982	980	1,131	1,056
Naples	974	949	959	987	1,008
Palermo	997	1,005	1,039	1,051	1,272
Rome	1,258	1,080	1,039	1,405	1,107
Turin	1,004	937	976	1,099	1,044
Venice	940	942	970	994	1,137

SOURCES: Direzione Generale della Statistica, *Censimento della popolazione del Regno d'Italia al 31 Dicembre 1881*, 2 vols. (Rome: Bodoniana and Botta, 1883); idem, *Censimento della popolazione del Regno d'Italia al 10 febbraio 1901*, 5 vols. (Rome: G. Bertero, 1902–1904); and Ufficio del Censimento, *Censimento della popolazione del Regno d'Italia al 10 giugno 1911*, 3 vols. (Rome: G. Bertero, 1914).

NOTE: Numbers are males per thousand females.

growth of new industries in metal, machines, and food products, but the enterprises remained small and employed few steam-powered machines. Bolognese trade shrank from national to regional in scope.[11] In this sense, Bologna resembled several of the other large cities that experienced urban growth without significant industrialization. Yet, while textiles declined, they still provided employment for a large part of the population, especially women. Thus textiles constituted the only industrial sector open to widespread female labor but, as in other cities, it could not absorb the waves of unemployed women arriving from the countryside.

Because Bologna, like any other Italian city, was in many ways unique, I compare the Bolognese data on prostitution with those of other cities whenever possible. A certain uniformity of information resulted from the national scope of the regulationist legislation. In other regulationist nations, like France and Germany, municipal codes prescribed the behavior of police and medical personnel, so that variability derived from law as well as the specific character of each city. Instead, all Italian communes were subjected to the same law, and police and doctors took orders from the Ministry of the Interior in Rome. Therefore, legal and administrative consistency partially counterbalanced the economic and social diversity of Italian cities that produced the historical data on prostitution.

A significant bias pervades the statistics compiled by the state from brothel, police, and medical registers. These lists provide the number and characteristics of officially registered prostitutes rather than all women actually practicing prostitution at a given time. All historians of crime face a similar problem of discerning the "dark figure" of real crime behind the government data on arrests, prosecution, and sentencing. But the divergence between the dark figure and the number of registered prostitutes is especially great because, being a "victimless" crime, prostitution left few complainants. Identification and arrest of nonregistered prostitutes was almost entirely up to the police. The state, aware of the problem, labeled those practicing the trade but not inscribed on official lists "clandestine prostitutes." Various officials, like Gamberini, made estimates of the numbers of clandestine prostitutes based on figures of those women arrested for violating the prostitution statutes or those seeking treatment for venereal disease. Although it is only approximate, I have juxtaposed this information on clandestine prostitutes to that on legal ones to make the social profile more complete.

This weakness in the government statistics does not, however, invalidate them as a source of information. While aggregate data provided by the state underestimate total prostitution, change in these numbers over time is a significant indicator of modifications in the organization of prostitution or the behavior of agents enforcing the law. More interesting than simple levels of the incidence of prostitution, however, is the information on birthplace, age, civil status, and former occupation. Those statistics provide a portrait of prostitution not available to the historian of nonregulationist countries. In the latter, descriptions of the social characteristics of prostitutes have tended to be qualitative because based on small samples of women such as those in jail or a venereal disease clinic at a given time. Certainly these small samples are less representative than the Italian. Most important, the Italian statistics offer an excellent description of the type of women the state considered dangerous and consequently appro-

101

priate targets of social discipline. The following group portrait, though not complete, thus explains much about the background of that mass of women whose lives were touched, in many cases permanently altered, by the regulation system.

Geographical Map of Prostitution

A social profile of prostitutes should begin with their numbers and distribution throughout Italy. For the kingdom as a whole, the number of registered prostitutes increased from 8,302 in 1870 to a peak of 10,422 in 1881. It then declined sharply, fluctuating roughly in the range of 5,500 to 6,500 for the decade after 1900.[12] The same pattern holds when prostitution is computed as a percentage of total population; this figure increased from .03 percent in 1870 to a high of .04 percent in 1882, only to fall to .02 percent by 1890. According to Gamberini's statistics, Bologna exhibited a similar curve, but one that peaked earlier, in 1873 rather than in 1881.[13] In short, a rising number of registered prostitutes characterized most of the period of the Cavour law, but a decline set in before its replacement by the Crispi, and later Nicotera, legislation.[14] Legal changes partially explain the falling registration rates after 1881. For example, the Crispi and Nicotera statutes made the registration of "isolated" women more difficult and raised the age of minority for prostitutes from sixteen to twenty-one. Consequently, two groups that had formerly been special targets of the morals squads—prostitutes working alone and teenagers—were now partially or totally excluded from official statistics. Yet the downturn in registration rates preceded the passage of the Crispi law, suggesting that structural changes in the profession, such as the rebellion of younger prostitutes against the system and the increasing proportion of part-time prostitution, were more significant determinants in weakening regulation.

Density of prostitutes in urban areas greatly exceeded that for Italy as a whole. While the proportion of the population registered as prostitutes was .03 percent for the kingdom in 1875, the percentage in nine cities ranged from a low of .11 in Bologna to .31 in Naples. In fact, almost one-half of all registered prostitutes lived in the nine largest communes.[15] The predominantly rural province of Umbria and the Basilicata counted fewer than 100 prostitutes out of a total of 10,422 for the nation in 1881.[16] Probably more numerous than these numbers indicate, rural prostitutes may have been integrated into small communities and, therefore, less threatening to authorities. Furthermore, since small communes lacked Health Offices and morals squads, no special officials carried out registration and surveillance. From the state's perspective, prostitution was primarily a problem of the cities and was closely connected to other urban vices such as indolence, crime, and immorality.

Whether in large cities or small communes, registered prostitutes fell into two legal categories. According to the Cavour law, they could live either in groups in the *postriboli tollerati* (tolerated brothels) or alone as *meretrici isolate* (isolated prostitutes). Isolated prostitutes practiced their trade either at their own lodgings or in special rooms they rented only in the evenings. Police preferred the brothels where prostitutes lived in groups, because these institutions were easy to identify and control. That authorities favored the organization of prostitution in brothels is evident, for example, in a letter addressed to the local military commander from the questore of Bologna in 1886. In response to the complaint of the former about rising rates of venereal disease among the troops garrisoned in the city, the police commissioner promised to encourage isolated prostitutes to move into tolerated houses.[17] Pressure from the PS agents could bring results. The provincial doctor of Rome boasted in 1897 that, within six months, the number of brothels had jumped from 23 to 40 owing to the "increased activity" of the morals squad. As a result of this successful campaign against isolated prostitution, 89 percent of all registered prostitutes in Rome lived in brothels of more than one person.[18]

Despite the official preference for the systematization of prostitution in the tolerated houses, however, few other cities reached the high concentration of Rome in 1897. Even in the face of police persuasion to the contrary, many women preferred to live in private apartments and work independently. In 1881, the year for which there is the best data, only 64 percent of all registered prostitutes lived in the closed houses (Table 4.2), with provincial totals ranging from 43 to 82 percent.[19] In that year, Italy counted

Table 4.2. *Prostitutes Living in the "Closed Houses," 1881*

	Total number of prostitutes	Prostitutes in brothels	Percentage in brothels
Piedmont	1,019	642	63
Liguria	357	251	70
Lombardy	1,037	590	57
Veneto	585	445	76
Emilia	490	323	66
Umbria	97	64	66
Marches	138	95	69
Tuscany	487	397	82
Rome	646	340	53
Abruzzi/Molise	268	200	75
Campania	2,014	1,376	68
Puglia	809	519	64
Basilicata	89	65	73
Calabria	565	241	43
Sicily	1,659	1,033	62
Sardinia	162	72	44
Kingdom	10,442	6,643	64

SOURCE: Direzione Generale della Statistica, *Annuario statistico italiano* (Rome: Eredi Botta, 1884), p. 707.

1,119 tolerated brothels, a number that quickly dropped to 916 by 1885 but again exceeded 1,000 during the next decade.[20] As government administrators unhappily admitted at the time, however, an increase in the number of brothels did not necessarily indicate the concentration of individual prostitutes in tolerated houses. Since the total quantity of prostitutes was decreasing, the average proportion of prostitutes per brothel actually dropped from 10.7 in 1875 to a low of 5.1 in 1901. Although this figure rose to 7 by the end of the decade, it never regained its previous high from the period immediately after unification.[21] Thus a rather stable number of brothels housed a decreasing number of prostitutes, resulting in a dispersion rather than a concentration of those inscribed on police lists. From this point of view, regulation was a failure in disrupting the mobility of prostitutes to favor surveillance.

While isolated prostitutes hampered police efficiency, "clandestine prostitutes"—those who eluded registration—caused authorities the greatest concern. As Bolis warned, "Clandestine prostitution is, in a word, an unregulated vice which propagates uncontrollable physical and moral corruption. Instead, registered prostitution is a vice which is restrained by the regulation laws in order to protect public health."[22] Estimates of clandestine prostitution varied widely, but both critics and supporters of regulation agreed that a large number of prostitutes escaped the discipline of registration and examination. The abolitionist Tommasoli charged in 1899 that police lists included only one-sixth to one-tenth of all prostitutes.[23] Critical of the regulation system, this source might be suspected of overestimating its inefficiency. Bureaucrats working within the system and with a stake in its perpetuation, however, offered similarly dismal figures. Gamberini counted, on the average, slightly more clandestine than registered prostitutes for the years 1863–1886 in Bologna.[24] During the same period, Achille Breda, director of the sifilicomio of Padua, estimated that no more than three-fifths of all prostitutes in his city were registered with police, a calculation echoed by the prefect of Turin for his provincial capital in 1886.[25] In 1897, in the same report that boasted the increase of regulated brothels in Rome, the questore admitted to the minister of the interior that probably 400 clandestine brothels remained undetected.[26] Two years later the provincial doctor of Rome confirmed this state of affairs, claiming that officials knew of at least 700 clandestine prostitutes beyond the 164 who were registered.[27] Most estimates tended to bear out the words of the commission of 1885 that "the most honest conclusion is to say that it is not possible to come up with an exact figure. Nevertheless, it appears without doubt that the number of clandestine prostitutes must greatly exceed the number of those inscribed."[28]

While calculations of clandestine prostitution varied, observers agreed that illegal practice began to increase in the 1890s, an expansion that continued until World War I.[29] During the first twenty-five years of unity, indicators pointed to a rather steady proportion of registered and clandestine prostitutes. As noted earlier, the totals of registered prostitutes increased until the early 1880s, signifying the success of police in encouraging compli-

105

ance with the law. In Bologna, arrest figures for clandestine prostitution oscillated widely during this period but showed, if anything, a tendency to decrease rather than increase.[30] In the
1890s, however, both the prefect and the provincial doctor of Bologna began to complain about the problem of clandestine prostitution, a preoccupation shared by administrators in the other
eight major cities.[31] Bolognese officials blamed the articles of
the Nicotera Regulation, which allowed only the registration of
places, rather than persons, by police. Reports from other
provinces also criticized the law, although the prefect of Palermo acknowledged that the worsening economic situation of
the 1890s was most responsible for the expansion of clandestine prostitution.[32]

In two major addresses to international medical conferences at
the turn of the century, Director of Public Health Santoliquido
declared that broad social and economic conditions, and not the
law, accounted for the declining proportion of prostitutes registered with police. He could cite no specific statistics on clandestine prostitution, since those furnished by police were, in his
words, "too vague and general to be taken into serious consideration."[33] Yet, he insisted:

> I am saying something which is well known and unanimously
> admitted by specialists: that in all countries, the relation be-
> tween clandestine prostitution and regulated prostitution is
> undergoing a modification which accelerates each day—
> the progressive augmentation of the first and the diminu-
> tion of the second. In other words, to the decrease of tol-
> erated houses and registered prostitutes corresponds an
> enormous increase of clandestine prostitution, in the most
> various forms.[34]

Noting that "this tendency [is] constant and uniform, in all countries and under all systems," Santoliquido dismissed complaints
about the Nicotera legislation as a specific cause of the Italian situation.[35] Instead he argued that the closed houses constituted "a
form of commerce which tends to disappear because it is becoming unproductive."[36] More women were now practicing prostitution on a part-time basis to supplement their income from other

sources. Even those who remained in the profession full-time wanted to set their own prices and avoid handing over the major part of their earnings to a madam. Thus during the fifty years after unification, the organization of the trade changed from one dominated by state-controlled brothels to one characterized by individual, illegal entrepreneurship.

Social Profile of Prostitution

The decline of the closed house and the proliferation of clandestine practice provides the context for a closer examination of the social profile of prostitutes as a group. When possible, I draw distinctions between registered and clandestine prostitutes as I analyze such characteristics as age, civil status, education, birthplace, and former profession. Of course the documentation for this profile, for both Bologna and Italy as a whole, is much more extensive and complete for the former than the latter. Comparing registered prostitutes with Italian women in general shows whether there were significant differences between the lives of "normal" and "deviant" women.

The age of registered prostitutes tended to cluster around the years of the early twenties. Under the Cavour law, the largest percentage of prostitutes fell into the category of 21–25 years old, followed by that of 16–20 years, and finally 26–30. Only 10–15 percent of all prostitutes exceeded the age of thirty.[37] Gamberini confirmed this pattern for Bologna (Table 4.3), reporting that, on the average, 40 percent of those inscribed on police lists were 21–25; 27 percent were 16–20; 20 percent were 26–30; and only 13 percent were over 30 years of age.[38] The southern cities of Naples and Palermo offered the only significant modification of this pattern, being characterized by a larger group of prostitutes under 21; this group equaled or slightly exceeded that between 21 and 25.[39] In both northern and southern communes, prostitutes were heavily overrepresented in the age categories from 16 to 30. While only 26 percent of all women in general fell into this age range during the years 1861–1881, it characterized 87 percent of the registered prostitutes of Bologna and 82 percent for Italy as a

Table 4.3. *Age of Registered Prostitutes in Bologna*

Year	16–20	21–25	26–30	Over 30
1863	45	33	16	6
1864	28	44	17	11
1865	38	36	18	8
1866	29	43	20	8
1867	26	48	18	8
1868	22	47	23	8
1869	28	41	22	9
1870	28	40	23	9
1871	26	36	26	12
1872	28	36	26	10
1873	24	41	24	10
1874	28	40	22	10
1875	26	43	19	12
1876	28	37	21	14
1877	29	38	17	16
1878	29	37	20	14
1879	25	42	15	18
1880	25	39	17	19
1881	32	34	16	18
1882	25	39	19	17
1883	28	37	17	17
1884	19	44	18	19
1885	16	40	20	23
Average	27	40	20	13

SOURCE: Pietro Gamberini, *Rapporto politico-amministrativo-clinico della prostituzione di Bologna* (Bologna: Gamberini e Parmeggiani, 1864–1886).

NOTE: The numbers in the four columns are percentages and do not always add up to 100 because of rounding.

whole.[40] There was much less difference between the ages of prostitutes and other women who worked outside the home, however, since the latter were also mostly young adults.[41]

The average age of prostitutes appears to remain constant after 1881, but statistics are not strictly comparable because of the legal redefinition of the age of minority. Under the Crispi and Nicotera laws, police could register only women who had reached the age of 21 rather than 16. Thus women seemed to be entering prostitution at a later age simply because the second largest category, those 16–20, was dropped from official registration statistics. Other sources, such as criminal anthropological treatises and admittance records at venereal disease clinics, however, confirm that many women under 21 continued to practice prostitution.[42]

Rather than diminishing real prostitution, the higher legal age of minority simply increased the number of clandestine prostitutes. Even under the Cavour Regulation, clandestine prostitutes were apt to be young. According to the questore of Bologna in 1868, clandestine prostitution was most widespread "among young girls under the age of sixteen, who abandon themselves with disgraceful ease to a depraved life because of want, natural laziness and bad education, or because they find themselves, at that age, immune from the severity of the law."[43] The director of the Health Office of the same city claimed that a large part of these girls could no longer count on the financial support of their parents, "many of whom were not reluctant to thrust their daughters into such a shameful life."[44] Whatever the causes, prostitution attracted a large number of teenage girls, a phenomenon that frightened administrators. Doctors believed that these unregistered minors posed a special menace to health: they were much sought after, had many contacts per day with clients, were ignorant of the prevention and diagnosis of venereal disease, and were most likely to be in the early, and therefore the most contagious, stages of syphilis.[45] In the 1890s southern doctors, such as Tommasoli and Ravicini, argued that prostitution of minors was most extensive in their region of the country; Ravacini estimated that almost one-half of all prostitutes in Sicily were under 21.[46] In Naples and Palermo authorities arrested girls as young as 10 and 11 for prostitution.[47]

Clandestine prostitution involved more than just minors too young to be legally registered. Many women slipped frequently between registered and illegal practice. Furthermore, the 1890s witnessed a growing contingent of part-time prostitutes: women who supplemented their income by practicing prostitution after working hours or when work was scarce. Some wives of lower- or lower-middle-class men also pursued the profession while their husbands were absent at work.[48] These women vigorously resisted registration because such a procedure would have inter-

rupted their normal patterns of employment and self-identifica-
tion. In conclusion, clandestine prostitutes tended to be younger
than registered women but not exclusively minors.

As might be expected from the youth of prostitutes, a higher
percentage were single than among the female population in general. For the nation as a whole, 82 percent of all registered prostitutes were single; 13 percent, married; and 5 percent, widowed.[49]
In Bologna, Gamberini found an even larger proportion of unmarried prostitutes, their quantity steadily rising from 83 percent
in 1863 to 99 percent in 1886 (Table 4.4). Congruently, married
prostitutes dropped from 14 percent to 1 percent, while widows
decreased slightly from 3 percent to less than 1 percent.[50] In
contrast, during this period, the largest group of Italian women
over 15 were married, although the percentage was lower for
Bologna than the nation in general. Only 43 percent of Bolognese women were married as opposed to 54 percent for the kingdom; yet even the figure from Bologna clearly outstripped that
for prostitutes.[51]

That the civil status of prostitutes was partly a function of age
is confirmed by a more precise comparison with women between
15 and 35, the age range of most prostitutes. In this case, the proportion of married women drops over 10 percent, to 44 percent
for the nation and 31 percent for Bologna.[52] In other words, the
majority of women between 15 and 35 years of age were single,
whether or not they were prostitutes. As Carlo Cipolla, a demographic historian, has pointed out, the average age of women at
first marriage was 24 in 1871 and remained stable until 1951.[53]
Thus it was the rule, rather than the exception, for women in the
two largest age categories of prostitutes, 21–25 and 16–20, to be
single. Yet the exceptionally low rate of marriage for prostitutes
underlines their isolation from the nuclear family and the absence
of any financial or emotional support from husbands.

Few data exist on the civil status of clandestine prostitutes.[54]
Administrators suggested various conflicting hypotheses as to
their marital situation. Those who blamed clandestine prostitution on minors also characterized it as dominated by single
women. Others claimed instead that married women were those
who most carefully avoided the notoriety of police registration, especially if they practiced the trade without the knowledge or con-

Table 4.4. *Civil Status of Registered Prostitutes in Bologna*

Year	Single	Married	Widowed
1863	83	14	3
1864	83	14	3
1865	88	9	3
1866	88	10	2
1867	89	9	1
1868	89	7	4
1869	90	8	2
1870	91	8	1
1871	90	7	3
1872	91	6	2
1873	92	7	2
1874	91	7	2
1875	91	7	2
1876	92	5	2
1877	91	7	2
1878	94	5	1
1879	94	4	2
1880	95	4	1
1881	93	6	1
1882	94	3	3
1883	97	2	1
1884	98	1	1
1885	99	1	1
1886	99	1	0
Average	92	6	2

SOURCE: Pietro Gamberini, *Rapporto politico-amministrativo-clinico della prostituzione di Bologna* (Bologna: Gamberini e Parmeggiani, 1864–1887).

NOTE: The numbers in the three columns are percentages and do not always add up to 100 because of rounding.

sent of their husbands. In fact, police may have avoided registering married women because they were not autonomous but under the legal tutelage and control of their husbands. Bolis advised that married prostitutes be registered only in "very serious cases" and mothers only in "quite exceptional cases."[55] He explained that, for the latter, registration would only bring a greater evil, that of providing "a bad example for their children, who will be

Table 4.5. *Education of Registered Prostitutes in Nine Communes, 1875*

	Percentage illiterate	
	Prostitutes	All women
Bologna	78	40
Florence	64	38
Genoa	57	37
Milan	63	24
Naples	95	62
Palermo	100	68
Rome	86	40
Turin	55	22
Venice	74	44
Kingdom	84	70

SOURCES: Parlamento, Camera dei Deputati, *Atti Parlamenti*, Documenti, sessione 1876–1877 (Rome: Camera dei Deputati, 1877), n. 146, pp. 16–21; Direzione Generale della Statistica, *Censimento della popolazione del Regno d'Italia al 31 dicembre 1881*, (Rome: Bodoniana and Botta, 1883).

scandalized that their mother practices prostitution with the tolerance of the state authorities."[56] This ambivalence toward the registration of married women partially accounts for their relative absence from police lists but does not counter the fact that the overwhelming number of prostitutes were single.

While women in pre–World War I Italy were decidedly less educated than men, regulated prostitutes ranked even lower than women as a group. The illiteracy rate for women in general, exceeding by 10–15 points that for the male population, dropped from 81 percent in 1861 to 70 percent in 1881.[57] Figures available for prostitutes show a similar diminution but starting at a higher level: from 88 percent in 1868 to 83 percent in 1875 to 74 percent in 1881.[58] Thus prostitutes were less educated than women in general, but the gap between the two was smaller than that between women and men. It was only during the first decade of the twentieth century that the majority of women could read and, maybe, write.

For both prostitutes and women in general, illiteracy rates varied widely from city to city (Table 4.5). In 1875, for example, the figures for the two groups show a similar pattern, being highest in the southern communes of Naples and Palermo and lowest in Turin, Milan, Genoa, and Florence, with Rome, Bologna, and Venice falling in between. The rates of illiteracy ranged from 22 percent (Turin) to a high of 68 percent (Palmero) for women in general and 55 percent (Turin) to 100 percent (Palermo) for registered prostitutes.[59] Prostitutes, then, were at a greater disadvantage when compared with women of the same city rather than with the female population of the kingdom. Of this population, urban women were most likely to read and write. Thus in 1875 there was a sliding scale of illiteracy, from prostitutes at the top, with 84 percent illiteracy, to women in general with 70 percent, to women of the nine major cities with 42 percent. The rural origins of many prostitutes partially explain the large difference between their level of education and that of urban women. The disparity reflected the lack of schools and failure to enforce compulsory education in the countryside from which many prostitutes migrated.[60] It also meant that rural migrants were at a distinct disadvantage when competing with urban women for jobs.

Official records contain no data and few speculations as to the educational status of clandestine prostitutes. The minors who had left home early to practice prostitution would most likely have exhibited a rate of illiteracy equal to, or higher than, registered prostitutes. On the other hand, police believed that quite a few literate, middle-class women—especially teachers—supplemented their income with part-time prostitution. Female teachers received notoriously low salaries, often less than those of working-class women. According to authorities, education was a double-edged sword, for reading as well as ignorance could lead to vice. As Gamberini warned, those prostitutes who could read limited their material to "novels, immoral books and similar literature which certainly does not encourage virtue."[61] He added that reading could not counteract the other motives for prostitution and could be of possible use only if "surveillance and wisdom" determined the choice of books.[62] In short, "literacy does not provide and can not provide a hard enough armor for resisting the strong arrows of all the arts of seduction."[63] This antipathy toward the education of women sprang partially from the economic and intellectual independence it promised them. Geared to com-

113

Table 4.6. *Birthplace of Registered Prostitutes
in Nine Communes, 1875*

| | Percentage from: | | |
	Same province	Another Italian province	Foreign country
Bologna	23	68	9
Florence	24	62	14
Genoa	15	77	8
Milan	38	50	12
Naples	41	56	3
Palermo	75	25	—
Rome	49	47	4
Turin	42	51	7
Venice	27	44	29
Kingdom	50	45	5

SOURCE: Parlamento, Camera dei Deputati, *Atti Parlamenti*, Documenti, sessione 1876–1877, (Rome: Camera dei Deputati, 1877), n. 146, pp. 14–21.

bating female automony, the regulation laws were therefore directed at all women who transgressed their prescribed role, whether educated or illiterate.

Unlike much of the Italian population, prostitutes did not always work in the city of their birth (Table 4.6). Gozzoli noted that "in the large cities, most of the pupils of Venus are not from the locality, but come from other Italian provinces and from France, England, Spain, and especially Austria and Germany. And it is easy to understand why: they prefer to practice their shameful profession far from their family and friends."[64] In statistical terms, the commission report of 1877 confirmed Gozzoli's judgment, establishing that only 50 percent of all registered prostitutes resided in the province of their birth. Even this 50 percent was not totally stable, for it included those who had migrated from the countryside to a larger commune within the same province, usually the capital. Looking only at the nine major cities, the number of prostitutes born in the province where they were registered drops even further, to 37 percent. Of the remainder, 53 percent came from other Italian provinces, while 10 percent

Table 4.7. *Birthplace of Registered Prostitutes in Bologna*

	Province of Bologna	Northern Italy	Central Italy	Southern Italy	Foreign
1865	30	62	3	—	4
1866	25	68	1	—	6
1867	25	66	1	—	9
1868	26	65	1	—	8
1869	29	60	2	—	8
1870	20	67	3	1	8
1871	26	62	2	1	9
1872	25	61	4	—	10
1873	20	65	4	1	10
1874	20	63	6	1	10
1875	19[a]	62	6	2	12
1876	20	59	8	1	11
1877	19	59	6	2	14
1878	19	55	8	2	16
1879	16	52	6	3	22
1880	16	56	5	2	20
1881	17	58	5	1	18
1882	15	52	5	3	26
1883	16	54	6	1	24
1884	16	51	7	3	23
1885	16	51	7	1	26
Average	21	59	5	1	14

SOURCE: Pietro Gamberini, *Rapporto politico-amministrativo della prostituzione di Bologna* (Bologna: Gamberini e Parmeggiani, 1865–1885).

NOTE: The numbers in the five columns are percentages and do not always add up to 100 because of rounding.

[a]This figure does not match exactly that given by Gamberini in Table 4.6; the two statistics may come from different dates during the same year.

had immigrated from foreign countries such as Austria, Germany, and France.[65] As might be expected, foreign prostitutes tended to head for large, well-known cities located along major railway lines.

According to the statistics of Gamberini, registered prostitutes were increasingly apt to migrate away from their birthplace in the postunification period (Table 4.7); between 1865 and 1885 the percentage of prostitutes born and practicing their trade in Bologna dropped from 30 to 16 percent. In compensation, the proportion of foreigners on police lists rose from 4 percent to 26 percent during the same period. The proportion of migrants from other parts of northern Italy remained rather steady, while the numbers of women born in the central and southern regions expanded. Even in 1886, however, under 10 percent of all Bolognese prostitutes came from areas south of Florence, showing that within Italy women migrated rather short distances.[66] A report published by Francesco Poggiali, director of the Health Office of Naples, confirmed this pattern from the southern perspective. While only 50 percent of all Neapolitan prostitutes had been born in the same province, another 46 percent had come no further than from other communes of southern Italy and Sicily. Only 3 percent had been born north of Naples; 1 percent were foreign.[67] In general, registered prostitutes migrated frequently but for relatively short distances.

It is difficult to compare the mobility rates of registered prostitutes with those of either clandestine prostitutes or women as a whole. No statistics exist on the birthplace of women arrested for clandestine prostitution, but members of the commission of 1885 surmised that official figures underestimated the numbers of indigenous prostitutes in each city. In their opinion, naive and inexperienced girls from the countryside were more likely to be caught in police snares and registered than their more wily and worldly urban counterparts.[68] They believed that local women with stable residences typified those who worked outside the discipline of the closed houses. On the other hand, to remain clandestine, women had to stay on the move, making it likely that the unregistered were more mobile than the inscribed. Certainly, the easiest way to remove oneself from police lists was secretly to leave one city and set up shop in another. A prostitute previously restricted by police surveillance regained a certain autonomy once she took on the status of clandestinity.

Equally problematic is the task of ascertaining whether the mobility rates of prostitutes were typical of women in general because of the lack of demographic research on female migration in post–Risorgimento Italy. Unlike single men, who emigrated in large numbers to the Americas, single women seemed to have

moved much shorter distances within Italy. The few who emigrated by themselves traveled no further than to neighboring European nations like Switzerland, France, and Germany.[69] This
pattern of migration corresponded to that of prostitutes, who
tended to circulate only within their native regions, that is, the
North, Center, or South of Italy. As yet, migration from South to
North, typical of the period after World War II, was rare since
even the industrialization of cities like Turin and Milan proceeded
slowly and could not absorb workers from other parts of the
country. While the patterns of migration of prostitutes resembled
those of other single women, the rates were higher for the former
than the latter. Recent studies have tentatively argued that mobility rather than stability characterized the lives of the poor even
before the industrial revolution. Prostitutes, however, were apt to
change residence even more often to escape police detection.[70]

The former professions of prostitutes, before they entered the
closed houses, provide another indicator of the social distance between them and other lower-class women. This information must
be seen in the context of the general working patterns of women in
Italy. The proportion that worked was high but decreased from
47 percent in 1861 to 40 percent in 1881 to 29 percent in 1911.[71]
Looked at in another way, the percentage of the employed population that was female totaled 37.6 in 1881 but only 31.2 in
1911.[72] This decline characterized not only the population as a
whole, which was predominantly rural, but also that of the urban
areas. In Milan, the most rapidly industrializing large city, the
percentage of adult women (those over the age of ten) working
dropped from 54 percent in 1881 to 50.5 percent in 1901 to 42
percent in 1911.[73] This diminution in the percentage of active,
employed women in fact continued until the 1950s, when significant numbers of women again began to enter the work force.

The decline in the numbers of working women was linked to the
types of jobs they held in the Italian economy. Like men, most
women were employed in agriculture, which was increasingly unable to absorb the demographic growth in the rural areas. Between 1881 and 1911 women lost ground slightly to men in the rural sector, dropping from 35.9 to 32.7 percent of all agricultural
workers.[74] Urban women were highly concentrated in textiles,
garment making, and domestic service, in that order.[75] These

117

three categories, for example, employed three-fourths of the working women of Milan throughout the period from 1881 to 1911.[76] All highly feminized, the three trades nationally employed more women than men. Their size and structure underwent certain modifications, however, that explain, for the most part, the declining proportion of working women in the female population.

Textile manufacturing, the mainstay of Italian industrialization in the nineteenth century, never ceased to count more women than men among its employees between unification and World War I. In 1876 textiles employed 170,000 women as opposed to 45,000 men; thirty years later, women continued to make up 79 percent of all textile workers.[77] Yet, by the turn of the century, the textile industry was declining and heavier manufactures, like iron, steel, and machine tools, which employed few women, took its place.[78] Even those textile firms that kept afloat employed a decreasing number of women, for they shifted their manufacturing organization from one based on cottage industry to one based on larger, urban shops. In the process of concentration and mechanization, women often lost their jobs to men. Many married women, burdened with the burgeoning families of the nineteenth century, could not follow their jobs out of the house and into a factory.[79] With industrialization, then, a certain portion of the female population dropped out of the work force both because of job discrimination in mechanized trades and because of their inability to combine the domestic role with a full-time occupation outside the home. Similar problems afflicted women in the garment trades, while the demand for domestic servants also dropped in the early years of the twentieth century. Many middle-class families preferred privacy to the comforts of live-in servants, while women increasingly feared the bad influence of nursemaids and personally took over the upbringing of their children. In contrast, a small proportion of middle-class women were only just beginning to seek outside employment, mostly as teachers in the rapidly expanding national school system.

In every category of employment, women received a meager financial return. As Majno Bronzini pointed out, "there are often cases in which the maximum salary for a woman is lower than the minimum salary for a man."[80] In fact, men's wages were roughly double those of women even when they performed the same task for an identical employer. For example, in the Lombard textile mills at the time of unification, men received 1.33–2.77 lire per day, while women made only 46–76 centesimi.[81] Homeworkers received less than shopworkers, and spinners less than weavers. Garment making, which was usually farmed out as a sweated industry, also paid poorly; in the 1870s shirtmakers made 50 centesimi per day while Venetian lacemakers received .60–1 lira by the end of the century.[82] Florentine straw workers made a ridiculously low 20–30 centesimi per day.[83] At the bottom of the wage scale for lower-class women were servants, whose small salaries partly reflected the fact that they received free room and board. In the ranks of the middle class, teachers received salaries of 100–250 lire per year which, calculated on a daily basis, put them behind many lower-class women.[84] Office work paid only 15 lire per month.[85]

Wages improved during the period so that by the eve of World War I women in textiles, for instance, made between 1 and 2 lire per day. Male wages had risen concurrently, however, so an income gap of 30–50 percent continued to divide the two sexes. Even 1–2 lire per day, however, could barely be considered a subsistence wage when bread cost an average of .47 lira per kilogram and pasta .71 lira per kilogram.[86] In the relatively fat years of the early twentieth century, families continued to spend over half their income on food.[87] A working woman could not usually live on her "starvation salary" alone, much less support other members of the family: parents, siblings, or children.[88]

Besides low wages, women suffered other handicaps as workers. First, a higher proportion of female than male workers were young—under 21. Because married women with children tended to withdraw temporarily from the work force, those women who did work clustered in the low age categories. Furthermore, boys went to school in greater numbers and for longer periods than girls, so that teenage girls flooded the labor market. In 1904 an inquiry by the Bureau of Labor found that 38.5 percent of all female workers were under the age of 20.[89] Figures for Milan show that, in 1881, 73 percent of all women between 15 and 20 years of age worked, as opposed to 56 percent of those between 21 and 60. While the latter statistic dropped to 48 percent by 1901, the proportion of employed women under 21 held steady. The female work force was growing younger. The pattern was reversed for men; in both 1881 and 1901 a higher percentage of males in the age category from 21 to 60 worked than in that of 15 to 20.[90] Since age as well as sex determined wage scales and top salaries came only after the age of 21, young women were doubly penalized.[91]

Young or old, women suffered wretched working conditions. Factories were dirty, noisy, hot, and dangerous and required long hours on the shop floor. Even by 1910, textile workers spent 10–11 hours daily on the job.[92] Most women, however, worked not in factories but at home, where they were often paid by the piece and charged for materials such as needles and thread.[93] Economic historian Stefano Merli found that the home weavers of Biella earned only 2–3 lire per week because it took them two days to pick up and return the goods to the manufacturers at Ivrea and Vercelli.[94] He concluded that "home work took every free hour from workers and left them with practically nothing more than the life of an animal which exhausts itself in physiological functions."[95] Unlike homeworkers, servants did not even have a private domicile but lived in that of their employer, for whom they were on call 24 hours a day. They received only a few hours free on Sundays and, if they wanted to continue in service, usually had to renounce marriage as incompatible with their live-in status.

The new middle-class professions treated women no better. In a report to the International Council of Women in 1899, Maria Montessori charged that the lives of the 36,000 female teachers in Italy were filled with "material hardship and intellectual starvation."[96] Paid a pittance, they often were expected to conduct classes of 80–120 students. Female office workers, like women in the factories, spent 10–12 hours a day on the job.[97] While hospital nurses officially worked 12 consecutive hours, the Bureau of Labor found that their shifts sometimes lasted up to 24.[98] Although women's hours did not exceed those of men, wives and mothers had the double responsibility of housework and child care in addition to wage-earning employment.

Instability and seasonality also characterized many female occupations. The Bureau of Labor reported in 1904 that, on the average, women worked only 261 days per year.[99] Thus women were not underpaid but underemployed. This necessitated scrambling for second jobs, sometimes in agriculture, or slipping even further below the subsistence level. In most occupations, pregnancy brought fines or dismissal.[100] Furthermore, economic crises affected women more than men. Louise Tilly found that, for Milan between 1881 and 1911, rates of male and female migration did not always coincide; in some periods, male movement into the city rose at the same time that female immigration fell. This suggests that "women's employment was more sensitive to depressed economy than that of skilled men. This follows from the relatively few areas in which women worked, mostly connected to consumer needs, particularly domestic service and clothing, which respond very quickly to poor general economic conditions."[101] As a result of low wages and the precariousness of employment, women made up a disproportionate part of the poor. According to a municipal report of 1903, 50 percent of all female-headed households in Milan lived in one room in contrast to only 36 percent of those headed by men.[102]

Against this dismal portrait of employment opportunities for women, the choice of prostitution as an alternative or supplemental source of income becomes understandable. But did prostitutes resemble other women in their work patterns before registration on police lists or were they in some ways deviant, and did they constitute an anomaly? Compared with the general female population, registered prostitutes were underrepresented in the categories of housewife and agricultural laborer. While up to 50 percent of Italian women reported themselves as housewives to census takers between 1861 and 1911, few prostitutes claimed that background. According to the report of the Nicotera commission, only 6 percent of all prostitutes inscribed on police lists in 1875 had formerly been housewives (Table 4.8).[103] In Bologna between 1863 and 1885, a similar proportion—7 percent, on the average—reported no previous occupation to police at the time of registration (Table 4.9).[104] Similarly, few prostitutes came from the rural occupations that employed one-fourth of the female population in general. The Nicotera commission gave the figure of 13 percent for all of Italy, but Bologna reported a lower average statistic of 6 percent.[105] Other available inquiries confirm this 6–13

Table 4.8. *Former Occupations of Registered Prostitutes, 1875*

	Number	Percentage
Domestic service	2,574	28
Garment making	2,097	23
Agriculture	1,151	13
Textiles	610	7
Housewifery	591	6
Miscellaneous	1,290	14
No occupation	785	9
Total	9,098	100

SOURCE: Parlamento, Camera dei Deputati, *Atti Parlamentari*, Documenti, sessione 1876–1877 (Rome: Camera dei Deputati, 1877), n. 146, p. 21.

percent range for the category of farm worker.[106] The fact that most registered prostitutes were single and poor partially explains why few of them had previously been housewives, a category that included those bourgeois and petty bourgeois women who lived on the income of their husbands. The urban residence of most prostitutes explains their relative absence from the category of agricultural worker. Many prostitutes, however, had been born in rural areas and grew up in a peasant family before taking up an urban occupation upon migration to the city.

While underrepresented in the categories of housewife and farm worker, prostitutes resembled other urban, working-class women in the pattern of their former occupations. Like their "normal" peers in the cities, prostitutes came from the ranks of the major, nonagricultural, female professions: textiles, garment making, and domestic service. According to common wisdom, the factory, which had made greatest inroads in the textile trades, corrupted young women and set them on the road to prostitution. As Merli points out, "The factory is considered the school of perversion and anarchy which dissolves both public and private morality. Numerous are the denunciations and complaints about this system which separates the young girl and the woman from the center of the family and about the incapacity of women workers for housework and their excessive vanity."[107] According to statistics, however, the textile trades ran a poor third to garment

Table 4.9. Former Occupations of Registered Prostitutes in Bologna

| | Agriculture | Manufacturing | | | Tertiary | | |
		Textiles	Garment making	Other	Servants	Other	None[a]
1863	8	13	31	1	38	1	8
1864	6	12	33	3	40	3	3
1865	6	11	31	3	42	4	4
1866	5	9	31	3	45	3	5
1867	9	8	26	2	45	4	6
1868	7	7	32	2	41	5	6
1869	7	7	28	3	44	5	7
1870	6	6	32	1	42	5	8
1871	5	4	37	2	44	3	6
1872	4	4	34	1	48	5	4
1873	5	4	35	1	47	3	5
1874	5	2	36	1	50	2	4
1875	4	5	34	—	49	3	5
1876	4	6	34	—	48	4	3
1877	4	6	32	1	49	2	6
1878	5	6	31	2	46	4	6
1879	5	5	29	1	46	5	9
1880	7	6	37	4	32	4	11
1881	4	6	27	2	44	4	14
1882	5	1	29	3	47	6	10
1883	3	5	35	2	40	3	12
1884	8	2	25	—	56	2	7
1885	8	3	30	—	57	1	1
Average	6	6	32	1	45	4	7

SOURCE: Pietro Gamberini, *Rapporto politico-amministrativo della prostituzione di Bologna* (Bologna: Gamberini e Parmeggiani, 1863–1885).

NOTE: Figures in the columns are percentages and do not always add across to 100 because of rounding.

[a]Mostly housewives.

making and domestic service as a source of prostitutes. In 1875 only 7 percent of all prostitutes across Italy claimed to have been employed in textiles compared with 23 percent in garment making and 28 percent in domestic service.[108] Gamberini's figures for Bologna confirm this picture: on the average, between 1863 and 1885, 6 percent of legal prostitutes had a background in textiles, while 32 percent had been garment workers and 45 percent servants.[109] Despite discriminatory wages and concentration in unskilled sectors, the textile trades lost few employees to prostitution. This was partly due to the concentration of mills in middle-sized towns rather than the large urban centers of prostitution. In the textile towns women often lived with their families while working and therefore suffered less isolation than urban migrants. In addition, factory work offered women relatively better salaries and steadier working conditions than alternative sectors, a situation that prevented most employees from having to supplement their income by practicing prostitution.

Instead, the garment trades and domestic service provided the two most steady sources of prostitutes. The garment worker, usually working at home and alone, had no economic cushion against periods when the demand for certain types of apparel dried up. This census category also included washer and ironing women, whose work was extremely menial, badly paid, and unorganized and depended on the constantly shifting needs of individual families. Equally precarious was the life of a servant, who most often was a new migrant from the countryside.[110] Offering room, board, and the illusion of still living with a family, domestic service was favored by rural parents for their migrant daughters. There was a peasant tradition of sending extra daughters to neighboring farm families to help with the housework. Urban employers, however, often differed greatly from those of the countryside—peasant or aristocratic—in their treatment of live-in maids; the bourgeoisie considered them employees, not daughters, and did not hesitate to dismiss them, especially in the case of pregnancy. Migration and domestic service, then, were correlated, and it is not coincidental that both constituted the recent experience of many registered prostitutes. Prostitution offered one alternative for unskilled and unemployed women, who had little opportunity to move into the more attractive factory jobs already monopolized by native, female residents of the city.

Suspicion of loose morality and prostitution also fell on middle- and lower-middle-class women who were moving into professions such as teaching and clerical work. In her social history of Italian women, Gloria Chianese has written that "the accusation of prostitution was also directed at those women who worked in the tertiary sector, an accusation which was formerly reserved for factory workers."[111] This was especially true of teachers, who often had to leave their families and hometowns to take up their assigned post. Living alone without the protection of a family connoted promiscuity. Although the low salaries of teachers gave them an economic incentive for prostitution, few inscribed themselves on police lists according to official statistics. More numerous were singers, models, actresses, and equestrians, who were also counted as middle-class but who may just as well have derived from lower-class backgrounds. In all, police registers included very few middle-class women, being made up overwhelmingly of female workers.

The professions, or former professions, of clandestine prostitutes did not differ greatly from those of registered prostitutes. According to the best statistics, those of Gamberini for Bologna, one-third to one-half of all clandestine prostitutes had been servants, with garment makers in second place. Housewives made up a slightly larger category than on the lists of legal prostitutes.[112] In 1900 Santoliquido also produced a detailed survey of the occupations of clandestine prostitutes, culled from registers found by police in unauthorized brothels.[113] The women listed in the registers exercised clandestine prostitution as a part-time profession to supplement their regular income. The hours of availability, included on the lists, indicated that servants worked in the brothels on their days off; textile and garment workers, in the evenings after the shops closed; housewives, during the day while their husbands were at work; farm girls, when they came to the city to sell flowers or pose as artists' models; and teachers, after school. Singers, actresses, dancers, and other entertainers made up the largest mass of wandering, illegal prostitutes. Santoliquido's report seemed to confirm that in fact women in every occupation sometimes found it necessary to take up prostitution, at least temporarily. While middle-class women—housewives as well as teachers and entertainers—were most successful in staying off police lists, lower-class women also did their best to evade registration. Clandestine prostitution was not the profession of a small group of deviant women but rather widespread, since economic fragility typified all sectors of female employment.

To round out the social profile of prostitutes, there is one final factor to consider that was, unfortunately, not always reported in government statistics: family background. According to one nineteenth-century writer on prostitution, Ettore Botti, most prostitutes came from broken homes and grew up without a father to protect their honor.[114] Statistics partially back him up. Few prostitutes seemed to have been illegitimate children, although common opinion held that immorality, like infectious disease, was passed down from generation to generation. Yet, according to Poggiali, 76 percent of all Neapolitan prostitutes in 1863 had lost at least one parent; 37 percent of these had lost both.[115] Gaetano Pini quoted similar figures for Milan in 1887, reporting that 74 percent of the prostitutes in the sifilicomio were orphans; 30 percent, of both parents.[116] Of course, during a period when life expectancy was markedly lower than today, it was normal for a good proportion of the population to lose before the age of twenty at least one parent.[117] Nevertheless, an excessively high percentage of prostitutes lacked at least one parent, a fact that lessened their economic security and forced them to support themselves at an early age.

Being an orphan may have had emotional as well as economic ramifications. Lacking sentimental ties to a strong family, adolescent girls may have sought male support to survive, both emotionally and financially, in the city. At least in northern Italy, traditional moral codes had often approved premarital sex between engaged members of a couple since it would soon be followed by the legalization of marriage.[118] This course of events, virtually guaranteed by the pressure of the girl's family and village opinion, did not always proceed smoothly in the city, which lacked the social control characteristic of a small community. Girls lacking a family, either because of migration or death of parents, were least likely to be able to exert the pressure on a fiancé necessary to insure marriage. At this point, especially in the case of pregnancy, prostitution offered a means of self-support for a woman deserted by her betrothed. The plausibility of this scenario is enhanced by available statistics on the "deflowering" of girls who later became registered prostitutes. In the majority of cases, prostitutes claimed that they had had their first sexual experience with men from their own class rather than with middle-class employers. Contrary to the commonly held notion of the time, these girls voluntarily entered into sexual relationships, although with the expectation of marriage.[119] A large proportion were teenagers trying to survive those years when pay was lowest and emotional insecurity highest.[120] In her study of British prostitution, Walkowitz suggests that this seeking of a sexual relationship, or even prostitution, was an expression of independence by women who had, because of broken families, escaped "the stranglehold of standard female socialization."[121] From this perspective, weak family ties could positively encourage the development of an independent female will, although the choice of prostitution, as Walkowitz points out, did not usually bring the expected profit and happiness.

The social profile of the prostitute that emerges from police files and the studies of experts thus does not duplicate that of women in general, but it closely resembles that of the female portion of the urban lower classes. The fact that economic necessity did not push middle- and upper-class women into prostitution explains, for the most part, their absence from police registers. All prostitutes, however, were not poor. As I explain in the next chapter, police specifically targeted lower-class women for arrest on charges of prostitution and ignored the licensing of brothels catering to the wealthy. In this way, the strategy of social control, as well as the economic needs of lower-class women, insured that the lists of the inscribed were rarely interclass.

Yet most prostitutes *were* poor and shared a variety of characteristics with other urban, female workers. Both groups went to work at a young age, usually in the midteens, and remained single until at least the midtwenties. Without the supplementary income of a husband, many had to migrate to find work. Because of low pay, seasonality, and the economic fragility of women's occupations, mobility typified the female worker's struggle to track down a succession of temporary jobs or combine two or more part-time occupations. High rates of illiteracy marked all poor women and abetted other types of discrimination that kept them in unskilled sectors with no hope of upward promotion. Like most other types of women's work, prostitution was organized on a preindustrial basis, either on the model of the street vendor (isolated streetwalker) or artisan shop (brothel).

Despite the overall likeness between the portraits of prostitutes and other lower-class, urban women, the former did exhibit some particularities. Prostitutes were likely to come from the most ill-paid, precarious occupations such as domestic service and to have received even less schooling than other women. They showed an extremely high rate of geographical mobility, with the majority leaving their native provinces after childhood. Not only over-whelmingly single but also frequently orphaned, prostitutes were more "autonomous" than the rest of the poor. Unskilled and un-educated, they lacked the economic and moral protection of a husband, family, or community. The difference between pros-titutes and their lower-class peers was only one of degree; the life of those who turned to prostitution was simply more isolated and precarious.

It can hardly be concluded, however, that prostitutes consti-tuted a "deviant" category juxtaposed to that of "normal" urban, working-class women. The two groups, in fact, overlapped. Large numbers of women moved on and off police lists each year, some-times alternating periods of prostitution with "honest" work or marriage. Prostitution, then, did not turn women into moral pari-ahs but simply represented one choice among the small range of unappealing jobs available. Combining part-time prostitution with regular employment to supplement an insufficient income became increasingly common as the nineteenth century came to a close and clandestine prostitution grew at the expense of the tolerated brothels. The closed houses required that a woman give over not only all of her work time, but also her personal identity, to prosti-tution. Lower-class women resisted this mechanism of labeling, preferring to retain the flexibility and opportunity to move in and out of prostitution at will. That the regulation system tried to erect barriers between prostitutes and "respectable" women does not deny the similarities in their social origins or the frequent overlapping of these two categories in the working-class world.

5

Prostitutes and Police: Surveillance

In 1907 Ottolenghi, the foremost theoretician of police profession-alization, predicted that the role of the PS would soon be trans-formed from one of "blind and harmful repression" to one of "rigorous but humane assistance, an activity of healthy moral hy-giene."[1] As a result of this evolution, he foresaw the formation of "a halo of sympathy around the Public Security forces such as will favor the encouragement and cooperation of the population in place of the present mistrust and opposition."[2] The problem of improving the image of the police had plagued every government since unification, and Ottolenghi's was only the latest of a string of similarly wishful proposals for change.[3] Relations were espe-cially strained between police and prostitutes, whose lives were subjected to the minute controls of the regulation system. Even when inscribed on police lists, and therefore legal, prostitutes were under the continuous surveillance of the "morals squads" to ensure their complete compliance with the statutes.

Through their powers of arrest, registration, and surveillance, the morals squads continued, and in a sense refined, the labeling function of the prostitution laws. None of the successive regula-tions defined the act of prostitution precisely, so the police were left with the task of interpretation. According to Article 17 of the Cavour law, "All women who notoriously practice prostitution are considered prostitutes."[4] The Crispi and Nicotera statutes echoed this vague and circular wording, although the object of definition was now not a person but a place. Both described a brothel as a place "where prostitution is habitually exercised."[5] Lacking a clear directive as to the definition of a prostitute or a brothel, police possessed wide discretionary powers in deciding which women to arrest and register. Police, therefore, constituted a vital link in the labeling process, mediating between the abstractions of the law and the masses of migrating, working women. At the microcosmic level of the street, PS agents offered a practical interpretation of the national statutes by the way in which they selected out those women who were to be subjected to them.

A central question then arises as to how closely the police followed the intentions of the molders of the regulation system in their everyday implementation of the law. How did the interaction between the state and prostitution function in practice through the intermediary agents of the PS? To clarify the role of the police, I turn first to the general organization and philosophy of the Division of Public Security, a bureaucracy about which little has been written for the pre—World War I period.[6] A powerful administration within the Ministry of the Interior, it was highly centralized and exercised a certain amount of independence both from other parts of the state bureaucracy and from the legislature. Second, I trace police interaction with prostitutes through the moments of arrest, registration, request for change of residence, and cancellation from the lists. Simultaneously, "from the bottom up," I trace the life cycle of the women who became enmeshed in the regulation system. As police surveillance shaped their lives, conversely their resistance to registration circumscribed the effectiveness of Italy's prostitution policy.

The Morals Squads

The polizia dei costumi, or morals squads, formed part of the PS, one of the several police forces in Italy after unification. Its older companion and sometimes rival, the royal *carabinieri*, took orders from the Ministry of War but performed civilian as well as military duties. In broad outline, the PS patrolled the cities while the carbinieri kept order in the countryside, but the latter was also entrusted with various urban duties, such as crime detection, that overlapped the role of the PS. In addition to these two major forces, the new state also established finance police, forest police, prison police, and municipal police.[7] Despite this confusing multiplication of police, however, the duty of enforcing the prostitution laws was clear: it fell only on the PS. In towns too small to boast a PS office, the mayor himself was entrusted with overseeing the implementation of the law.

Established in Piedmont in 1852, the Division of Public Security was a relatively new body whose organization and philosophy were still being formed during the early decades of unity. A relatively small force in the nineteenth century, it numbered about 5,000 men in 1895 (compared with 25,000 carabinieri).[8] Unlike the police of other nations captained by military officers or political appointees, the Italian force was unique in being "equipped and officered on military lines but directed, as far as its police functions are concerned, by a corps of trained civilians."[9] Two distinct echelons existed, then, within the PS: the middle-class, well-educated functionaries and the lower-class uniformed guards. The guards made up the bulk of each morals squad, which was directed by a functionary.

Both functionaries and guards received orders directly from Rome, which oversaw the enforcement of the penal code, PS laws, and special statutes like that on prostitution, all national in nature. In theory the prefect constituted the link between the Director of the PS in Rome and the provincial personnel, so that on paper the lines of command and power appeared very direct and even authoritarian.[10] All orders, in the form of "circulars," were to be passed down through the prefect, who in turn collected answers and statistical information from the lower authorities. Yet the clear role of the prefect as the enforcer of national policy from above was vitiated in two ways. First, as an outgrowth of the liberal spirit of the Risorgimento, the prefect also came to be seen as the conduit of local grievances to higher administrators in Rome. In the case of prostitution, for example, he directly received complaints from local residents about the manner in which the PS was enforcing the regulation laws. Second, unlike the Napoleonic system in France, the Italian prefect was not the exclusive channel of communication between the central and peripheral authorities. The questore, the provincial police commissioner, sometimes bypassed the prefect to contact directly his superiors in the Ministry of the Interior. Compared with the British, American, or German administrative system, the Italian was highly centralized, but these limitations on the control of the prefect mitigated in practice the authoritarian model adopted from France.

Local moral squads worked most closely with the questore rather than the prefect. Located in the provincial capitals, the questore was responsible for relaying the circulars issued by the prefect to local police and for collecting statistics on prostitution, which were then relayed to the Ministry of the Interior through the prefect. Until 1888 the morals squads worked out of the Health Office, which constituted the lowest link on the administrative chain originating from the Division of Public Security in the Ministry of the Interior and running through the prefect and questore. The locus of registration and examination, the Health Offices were headed by a PS functionary and staffed by guards of various ranks as well as a doctor.[11] In the case of Bologna, the early director of the Health Office was Delegate Biondini, who held his post for many years and provided continuity for a shifting staff of uniformed agents. During its twenty-eight years of existence, the Bologna Health Office could boast on the average only 5–8 PS personnel.[12]

After 1888 and the closing of the Health Offices with the passage of the Crispi Regulation, the morals squads became special units located in the *questura*, the office of the questore. Their size expanded little in those years despite the increase in urban population and the perceived growth in clandestine prostitution. In response to a special questionnaire issued by the PS administration in 1897, questori reported that Rome devoted 20 agents to the surveillance of prostitution; Naples, 11; Bologna, 7; Venice, 4; Palermo, 4; Turin, 4; Milan, 4; Florence, 3; and Genoa, 3.[13] Several noted that "mobile units" of regular city guards supplemented the work of the tiny morals squads yet added that the rapid turnover in personnel on the mobile units decreased their acquaintance with specific neighborhoods and therefore their effectiveness in ferreting out clandestine brothels.[14]

The guards assigned to the morals squads were, according to law, to be chosen from "among those men most distinguished for energy, good conduct, and honesty."[15] Only men of unquestionable morality could be trusted to resist the temptations offered by the corrupt world of prostitution. Furthermore, frequent accusations by private citizens and the press of collusion between the police and prostitutes—or more often, madams—made administrators in Rome especially sensitive to the problem of assigning the appropriate agents to the "delicate" work of disciplining morality. National bureaucrats encouraged good behavior by their local subordinates through regular financial bonuses. During his tenure as head of the Bologna Health Office, Biondini periodically suggested to the questore the names of those men who deserved special rewards, and the questore passed the names on to his superiors.[16] When the budget permitted, the upper administration routinely approved these requests, which were graduated according to recipient's rank, length of service, and the quality of service. Upon the recommendation of the questore of Bologna, Biondini himself also received periodic words of praise from Rome for his unfailing "zeal" as director of the Health Office.[17]

As good work elicited reward, immoral behavior could bring penalty. In 1866 the Bolognese guard Rosati spent twelve hours in the *sala di disciplina* (disciplinary cell) as punishment for "having permitted himself to maintain a shameful and intimate relationship with a prostitute."[18] In addition, he was ordered to break off this sexual affair under threat of more rigorous measures, while the highest ranking uniformed agent on the morals squad, Vice-Brigadier Neri, was told to investigate his peers to unmask any "similar relations" between prostitutes and police. Neri himself, however, came under criticism several years later in 1868. Biondini, while admitting that Neri had "useful qualities," reported to the questore that, "on the other hand, his impetuous character and his irritating and uncouth traits elicit complaints which, although put forth by a vile group [prostitutes], are often just and with foundation."[19] In the same letter, Biondini highly praised a third guard, Gardegni, for "continuing proofs of probity and discretion."[20] Within a year, however, Gardegni was under suspi-

133

cion for having been found at the house of a prostitute, Enrica Stanzani, several times in one evening. As Biondini drily remarked, prostitutes did not require that much surveillance. Although Gardegni defended himself by claiming that he had only been trying to collect taxes as required by law, Biondini pointed out that taxes were never collected at night. As a result of this incident as well as other "serious and strong suspicions" of fraternizing with prostitutes, Gardegni was transferred from duty in the Health Office.[21]

As illustrated by the experience of Bologna, finding qualified and honest guards for the morals squads was not easy. Many police, even if dutiful at the beginning of their assignment, became corrupted or excessively repressive after several years of service. Questori sometimes sought married men in the hope that they might be less apt "to be entrapped by some Prostitute."[22] This was not easy, however, because the laws regulating the forces allowed for marriage only after ten years of duty and with special permission from Rome. Most members of the morals squads, then, were single. As a result, the continuous transfer of agents from the squads for disciplinary reasons caused a high rate of turnover among the personnel dedicated to enforcing the prostitution laws. The almost totalitarian aim of total knowledge and control of prostitutes by police as envisioned by regulationist theorists and administrators was undercut by the variability of enforcement at the local level. Through their lack of discipline, many city guards demonstrated little conviction of the necessity or efficacy of the policy of regulation.

One explanation for the unwillingness or inability of lower ranking guards to enforce efficiently the laws on prostitution may lie in their minimal education and training compared with their superiors. Access to the upper administrative ranks required a university degree and successful competition in civil service examinations. Middle or upper class, these functionaries began their careers at the lowest rank of delegate and were promoted, according to merit and experience, to the posts of assistant commissioner, commissioner, questore, and perhaps, the central division in Rome. After 1903 the Ministry of the Interior also stipulated that aspiring functionaries attend courses at the newly founded police institute in Rome, the School of Scientific Policing. The school aimed to replace intuition with science in police work; instead of acting on hunches, the PS officer would now be familiar with the rational and efficient methodologies of modern investigation. To this purpose, the curriculum included courses on the new tool of fingerprinting as well as photography, laboratory analysis, and the drawing up of exhaustive criminal dossiers.[23]

In contrast, the uniformed guards had usually received little schooling before enrolling in the PS. A large social cleavage existed between them and the functionaries to whom they were strictly subordinated. Coming from the urban and rural working classes, they were sometimes barely literate and often spoke in dialect rather than Italian. In the first decades of the twentieth century, guards began to receive six months of training, but it focused on fundamentals such as arithmetic, the Italian language, and ethics rather than specific techniques of policing. As the instruction also ignored the social background of student guards and their problems adapting to the force, it tended to produce, in the words of one critic, "a machine rather than a man . . . a narrow visioned official who does not appreciate properly either his position or his duties."[24] Only a few select guards were given the opportunity to take a course at the School of Scientific Policing, which, if passed, allowed them to join the ranks of the delegates. But this procedure was only a small breach in the otherwise firm stratification between the administrative and uniformed ranks of the PS, a stratification duplicated in the Health Offices and morals squads.

Not only technical innovations but also the development of criminology as a new "scientific" field of study influenced the training of functionaries. In addition to fingerprinting, photography, and laboratory analysis, students at the School of Scientific Policing heard "a series of remarkable lectures . . . on the motives and methods of criminals."[25] The author of these lectures was Ottolenghi, the director of the school and a former student of Cesare Lombroso. Internationally known as the father of "positivist" criminology, Lombroso had begun to challenge the "classical" school of penology with the publication in 1876 of the book *L'uomo delinquente* (*Criminal Man*). In this work, he rejected the enlightenment tenet that delinquents act out of free will and therefore deserve retribution equal to the severity of the crime.

135

Instead, he held that material factors, especially biological inheritance, caused individuals to break the law. Pushed by physical forces outside their control, criminals could not logically be held responsible for their acts. They were, however, dangerous to society so that punishment could not be dispensed with. Length of sentences would correspond, however, not to the type of crime committed but to the degree of *pericolosità* (dangerousness) of each delinquent.

A corollary to the rejection of the doctrine of free will was, as Lombroso put it, "the . . . proposition . . . that we ought to study not so much the abstract crime as the criminal."[26] Complaining that classical penologists spent too much time theorizing at their desks, Lombroso began to gather empirical data on criminals in prisons, hospitals, and insane asylums: thus, the denomination of positivist criminology as criminal anthropology. Instead of dealing with varieties of crime as ideal categories, he focused on the criminal as an object that could be observed, measured, and experimented on. Since the etiology of crime lay in the interplay of material factors, environmental as well as inherited, the criminologist could hope scientifically to isolate and understand each one. Punishment could then be tailored to suit the unique physical constitution and social background of individual criminals. Rather than an equation between crime and punishment, the positivist wished to construct an equation between the delinquent and his treatment.

Although criminal anthropologists focused on physical measurements, they believed that external physiognomy reflected internal moral character. As Lombroso remarked in *Criminal Man*, "The ability to discriminate between right and wrong, which is the highest attribute of civilized humanity, is notably lacking in physically and psychically stunted organisms."[27] Thus in any individual a direct correlation existed between the number of physical malformations, or "anomalies," and the degree of deviancy. Anomalies could be found on almost any part of the body and included such traits as prehensile feet, cheek pouches, flattened noses, excessively long arms, and extra teeth. According to Lombroso, the coexistence of four or five anomalies marked an individual as a *delinquente nato* (born criminal), a man doomed from birth to psychological aberrations and moral irresponsibility.

136

Having inherited a propensity for crime, born criminals could hope for no modification of their antisocial natures, even from positive environmental influences.

Lombroso utilized a type of social Darwinism to explain the appearance and significance of physical anomalies. To him, anomalies represented atavistic throwbacks to earlier stages of evolution. The similarities he claimed to find between the skull of a notorious Italian criminal, Villella, and those of lower types of primates, rodents, and birds initially inspired him to link delinquency with degeneracy: "At the sight of that skull—I seemed to see all at once, standing out clearly illuminated as in a vast plain under a flaming sky, the problem of the nature of the criminal who reproduces in civilized times characteristics not only of primitive savages, but of still lower types as far back as carnivora."[28] Constructing an evolutionary hierarchy, Lombroso distinguished among categories of criminals, banishing the born delinquent to the lower rungs of the ladder while placing those less physically deformed—the criminoloids, criminals from passion, and occasional criminals—closer to the top. Environment played a large part in explaining the behavior of these last three categories, whose members might be salvaged by appropriate measures of reform and reeducation.

With barely any modification, Ottolenghi adopted Lombroso's theories as the basis for his courses at the school. Calling Lombroso "our venerable master," he prided himself on putting into practice not only the ideas but the methodologies of criminal anthropology.[29] For example, classwork included the physical and psychological examination of actual suspects after arrest. In fact, the school was located in the main prison of Rome, Regina Coeli, so that the human experimental material would be close at hand. By using the prison as a "clinic of criminology," Ottolenghi looked forward to "the day in which every functionary will know how to examine a suspect," for close observation constituted the first step toward the ultimate goal of a police officer: the complete knowledge of the suspect.[30] This training was to benefit guards as well as functionaries, for the latter had the duty "to inculcate in the agents, by example and by word, these principles which will radically transform the method of struggle against the human products of degeneration, intoxication, and the proletariat and will

137

serve to tame these ferocious human animals, the so-called beasts of the penal code."[31] Thus, while only administrators attended courses in criminal anthropology at the school, they were to pass down its scientific tenets to their uniformed subordinates.

Prostitution held an important place in the iconography of deviance as outlined by positivists. Lombroso considered it the female equivalent of male crime, remarking that "the primitive woman was rarely a murderess, but she was always a prostitute."[32] Primarily sexual, female deviancy reproduced the nature of women as it had been during earlier stages of evolution before they had acquired the modesty and frigidity typical of nineteenth-century civilization. The sexual promiscuity of prostitutes, so contrary to the character of normal women, posed as grave a danger to society as male crime: "The physical and moral characteristics of the delinquent belong equally to the prostitute and [there is] great sympathy between the two classes. Both phenomena spring from idleness, misery, and especially from alcoholism. Both are connected, likewise, with certain organic and hereditary tendencies."[33] It followed, therefore, that society had the right to defend itself equally from both phenomena.

Like criminals, many women were labeled by Lombroso as *prostitute nate* (born prostitutes). As one of his colleagues wrote, "The born prostitute has always existed, exists, and will always exist and everywhere seems to exhibit the same fundamental traits."[34] According to supposedly scientific tests, these traits included insensitivity to pain, lower (masculine) voices, and more irregular fingerprints than normal women.[35] Ottolenghi was one of the leaders in research on deviant women, publishing a book in 1896 the title of which translates as *The Sensitivity of Women*.[36] Using electrodes taped onto the hands of women, he found all of his female subjects to be less sensitive to pain than men, but deviant women and prostitutes to be the most insensitive. Other researchers did not limit their shock experiments to the hands but also tested more delicate parts of the body including the tongue, nose, forehead, thighs, stomach, breasts, even clitoris. Almost invariably, the experiments revealed "defective sensitivity in female prostitutes when compared with honest women."[37] Positivist criminologists interpreted these results as simply another indicator of the atavistic nature of prostitutes: like their intellect, moral conscience, and psyche, even their tactile sense was underdeveloped.

Personality traits such as immorality, vanity, laziness, and stupidity accompanied the biological inferiority of prostitutes according to positivists like Ottolenghi.[38] In fact, the character of the prostitute represented the negation of the normal woman, who was assumed to be pious, maternal, sexually passionless, and physically weak. Criminal anthropologists, therefore, typed prostitutes as virile and compared them to "primitive" women: "We only have to remember that virility was one of the special features of the savage woman . . . we have the portraits of Red Indian and Negro beauties, whom it is difficult to recognize for women, so huge are their jaws and cheekbones, so hard and coarse their features."[39] Most tellingly, the lack of maternal affection in the female prostitute was a sign that she could not be "more than half a woman."[40] While in the "ordinary run of mothers the sexual instinct is in abeyance," the exaggerated sensuality of prostitutes destroyed "the spirit of self-abnegation inseparable from the maternal function."[41]

While claiming to have put criminology on a scientific basis, positivists simply perpetuated many of the traditional prejudices about prostitutes. Lombroso's comparison of male criminals and prostitutes echoed uncannily the words of Bolis quoted in the introduction to this study. According to both writers, female deviance tended to manifest itself in sexual excess, that is, prostitution. Nor had the list of major personality traits—immorality, laziness, improvidence, vanity, and disorderliness—undergone great modification since Bolis's book on the dangerous classes. Furthermore, both Bolis and Lombroso located the etiology of prostitution within the nature of each individual "fallen" woman. It is true that Bolis's references to the "vicious" nature of the prostitute lack the scientific trappings found in positivist writings; Bolis was repeating a common-sense stereotype, while his successors claimed to have established an objective category of the "born prostitute." But the "scientific" experiments of criminal anthropologists never fundamentally challenged the nineteenth-century image of the prostitute, a fact that underscores the subjectivity permeating positivist research. Lombroso and his colleagues proved what they had set out to prove: that a large proportion of prostitutes had inherited both physical and moral inferiority and therefore required police discipline.

Positivist criminologists agreed with regulationists that this discipline should take the form of registration on police lists rather than the imprisonment applied to male criminals. As Guglielmo Ferrero, Lombroso's son-in-law and collaborator, wrote:

> Certainly, it is not exact to say that prostitution and criminality are the same in all respects; it cannot be otherwise because prostitution, far from being a harm to society like criminality, is, alas, very often an advantage because, given the present difficulty of contracting marriage at an early age, without prostitution in which all the extra energy of the male genetic instinct finds an outlet, an enormous number of young men would be thrown into desperation from the inability to satisfy such a keen need.[42]

In a cruder manner, Lombroso similarly defended the necessity of prostitution for society when he argued that "it is especially necessary to make sexual intercourse accessible to all dissolute-minded young men."[43] Like regulationists, positivist criminologists saw prostitution as a sexual safety valve for the natural male sexual drive and, therefore, as not eradicable. They feared, however, the disruptive potential of clandestine prostitutes, whom Lombroso considered "the most harmful sort" because their degenerate natures escaped any sort of discipline.[44] Instead, registration and surveillance segregated the atavistic "born prostitute" from the rest of society while guaranteeing her availability to meet male needs.

Parallel to his analysis of male criminals was Lombroso's admission that many prostitutes fell into the category of "occasional" practitioners of the trade. For Lombroso, occasional did not mean part time, but a condition determined by environment rather than heredity. These women could and should be reformed. As a preventive measure for occasional prostitution, he suggested that women, more than men, needed the control and guidance of the family. Claiming that a higher percentage of female than male foundlings and orphans became delinquent, Lombroso explained that "this is, however, quite natural. A woman, being weaker and more passionate than a man, has more

140

need of the support and restraint of the family to keep her in the right way, from which she is more easily turned than a man, on account of the slippery path of prostitution that is always open to her."[45] For many female orphans, he counseled that prostitution "is checked only by the intervention of an early marriage."[46] He also advanced maternity as a "moral antidote" to crime and prostitution, while admitting that its beneficial effects were usually only temporary.[47] Finally, although generally hostile, as a materialist, to religion, he suggested that young occasional prostitutes be sent to convents, where, because of women's "great susceptibility to suggestion," they could be led to substitute religion for sex.[48] In this analysis of occasional prostitutes, Lombroso again repeated nineteenth-century stereotypes about women, emphasizing their weakness, susceptibility, domesticity, and piety. His theories offered little hope to abolitionist feminists that science would disprove old prejudices and come to the aid of their cause.

It would be wrong to represent Lombroso's criminal anthropology as the single uncontested school of criminology in Italy. Besides the residual defenders of classical penology, lodged in the legal profession, a third group of "sociological" criminologists put forth theories that traced the etiology of all crime to the environment. For example, Botti, in his book on female delinquency in Naples, reproduced the thesis of Napoleone Colajanni that poverty caused both prostitution and the physical manifestations noted by Lombroso, that is, organic degeneration.[49] But Ottolenghi taught at the school only the ideas of Lombroso, not Botti, and the former therefore shaped police mentality. By 1914 over 1,200 functionaries had graduated from the four-month training given at the school as well as 55 select carabinieri.[50] The school, then, provided the link between the dominant group of Italian criminologists, the positivists, and the practical enforcement activities of the PS. The *savoir* of criminal anthropology penetrated and reinforced the *pouvoir* of the morals police charged with the surveillance of prostitituion.

The approval given by criminal anthropologists for the regulation system goes a long way in explaining its continued popularity within the PS during the pre–World War I period. While regulation was being challenged, often successfully, in other Western nations, Italy held firm in its commitment to a system widely sup-

141

ported by police. Of course, like any bureaucracy, the police wanted to defend and perpetuate a system that gave them extensive discretionary powers; centralized administrations are slow to change. Yet, as becomes clearer in the next chapter, police did lose part of their domain of control to the innovative doctors of the Division of Public Health. Holding on to old ideas did not assure retention of power. For police, however, regulation was not simply an old idea, but one that had received new legitimization by positivist criminologists, making it possible to defend it not as an ideological preference but as scientific necessity.

Surveillance

The morals police shaped the lives of registered prostitutes through a series of moments of interaction prescribed by law: inscription on police lists, arrest, inspection of brothels, request for transfer of residence, and cancellation from lists. At these points, the PS tried to formalize and systematize an activity that for most lower-class women was fluid and temporary rather than a lifetime career. Unemployed and homeless, female migrants drifted into prostitution, often after a relationship with men of their own class. Never clearly choosing prostitution as a profession, these women took advantage of the possibility of supporting themselves with its earnings in the hope of then contracting marriage or finding "honest" work. Registration made public a status many of them did not consider basic to their identity but which became, as a consequence, harder to shed. To a great extent, the widespread resistance of prostitutes to police was a resistance to the rigidification of their status that lessened their opportunity to move on later to a new job or to combine prostitution with the role of wife and mother. The constant surveillance of the morals squads promised to mold their lives into a cycle that was much more formal and predictable than that of other poor women who moved continuously among occupations, and perhaps cities, in order to make ends meet.

Prostitutes first came in contact with police at the moment of inscription on official lists, which then obligated them to obey the multiplicity of restrictions contained in the law. Registration

142

could proceed in two ways. Police preferred that women present themselves spontaneously for registration, either at one of the 264 Health Offices before 1888 or at the questura after that date.[51] According to one expert on prostitution, Mario Licciardelli Galatioto, the majority of women complied with the police, considering the Health Office equivalent to "an agency where jobs are given out."[52] He went on to argue that they were willing to give up their liberty and pay taxes because "the physical punishment of their evil lives, the fear of death, and the lack of financial support outweigh their pride and moral suffering."[53] Gamberini's statistics for Bologna (Table 5.1) seemed to confirm the words of Licciardelli Galatioto: from 1864 to 1886, voluntary registration did constitute the majority—69 percent—of all registrations.[54] Foreign prostitutes were especially punctual in their appearance at the Health Office upon their arrival in a new city. Most came from other regulationist states, like Germany, Austria, and France, and were familiar with the procedure. Furthermore, foreigners had little hope of disguising themselves as local citizens and therefore provided easy targets for arrest. They probably preferred to regularize and legalize their residency through inscription on the police lists.

In theory, police did not grant all requests for voluntary registration. The law forbid the registration of minors—those girls under sixteen before 1888 and under twenty-one afterward—who were to be returned to their parents or sent to a reformatory. In spite of this legal stipulation, police, especially in the South, were often charged with closing their eyes to the registration of minors who lied about their age in order to work in the case chiuse. Public Security functionaries gave some credence to these charges by the form of their defense: they pointed to the lack of alternatives if the family refused to take back a daughter and if, as was often the case, no local reformatory existed. In this situation, failure to inscribe a minor on the lists would only swell the ranks of clandestine prostitution. Even women of legal age faced lectures by police agents on the moral and physical dangers of prostitution and the grave implications of registration. These warnings, however, seemed to be rather routine and intended to satisfy abolitionist critics rather than really discouraging registration. At the time of registration, women underwent vaginal examination and,

143

Table 5.1. *Registered Prostitutes in Bologna*

Year	Number registered on January 1	New Registrations during year			Total registered
		Total number	Percentage voluntary	Percentage forced	
1864	185	224	60	40	409
1865	198	199	71	29	397
1866	192	204	79	21	396
1867	188	180	67	33	368
1868	200	135	53	47	335
1869	154	155	57	43	309
1870	159	167	63	37	326
1871	161	159	46	54	320
1872	163	138	62	38	301
1873	165	179	65	35	344
1874	182	175	69	31	357
1875	165	195	62	38	360
1876	164	130	73	27	294
1877	142	144	64	36	286
1878	138	148	66	34	286
1879	142	149	64	36	291
1880	132	140	65	35	272
1881	135	209	74	26	344
1882	139	173	64	36	312
1883	141	210	68	32	351
1884	146	200	78	22	346
1885	142	191	79	21	333
1886	134	175	78	22	309
Average	159	173	69	31	332

SOURCE: Pietro Gamberini, *Rapporto politico-amministrativo clinico della prostituzione di Bologna* (Bologna: Gamberini e Parmeggiani, 1864–1886).

until 1888, were assigned a special *libretto* (passport) in which future medical checks were to be noted. The libretto was to be carried at all times and be available for inspection by any PS agent in lieu of the normal documents of identification, which were retained by the Health Office. After 1888 the madam of each brothel was responsible for keeping a list of all employees and the dates and results of their examinations. In both cases, police noted the addresses and biographical data of all prostitutes to aid further surveillance.

More controversial was the second method of registration:

iscrizione d'ufficio, or registration by order of the morals police. According to abolitionists, overzealous agents picked up innocent girls and forced them into prostitution by inscribing them arbitrarily on official lists. This procedure, which was believed to ruin the "honor of families" as well as that of the unjustly registered daughter, constituted one of the major focuses of every legislative commission inquiry.[55] Even if the girl had prostituted herself, abolitionists like Mammoli charged that police prevented repentance by proceeding with immediate registration. He claimed that a hundred or even a thousand prostitutes in the tolerated brothels would say: "After the first time, I could have returned to being an honest woman, if the police had not forced me to be examined, registered, licensed, and closed in these jails of vice, precluding any possibility of finding work or rehabilitation."[56] Abolitionists argued that these girls would have voluntarily returned to their families had the morals squads not intervened and, by registration, regularized and fixed their status as prostitutes.

The preoccupation of police with the problem of clandestine prostitution seems to confirm the impression that morals squads acted aggressively and unscrupulously to root out any woman hiding from their gaze. Correspondence from questori to their superiors contained an unending chorus of warnings about the threat of unauthorized brothels and complaints about restrictions on their powers of arrest. This chorus increased after 1891 when their discretionary acts of registration came under increasing supervision. According to the Nicotera law, which forbade the registration of "persons," streetwalkers could only be arrested and fined up to fifty lire or jailed for a maximum of five days. Incarceration for ten days was restricted to "the most serious cases."[57] These penalties, considered light by police, now came under court review, a process intended to make impossible the abusive arrest of prostitutes. In practice, the transfer of sentencing from the PS administration, as under the Cavour statute, to the *pretore*, the judge of the minor courts, hardly put a leash on police. As the highest court, the Corte di Cassazione, ruled in 1893, "the exercise of prostitution as verified by a police statement of arrest is a material fact in which one must have faith until proven to the contrary."[58] Experience confirmed that judges almost inevitably convicted women arrested by police for soliciting.[59]

In the case of "places," which could be registered, residents now had the right of appeal, although the process, unlike the judicial review of personal arrests, was not automatic. Complaints were heard by a special commission made up of the prefect, the mayor, and the pretore, which, after hearing testimony from both parties, decided the case by majority vote.[60] Being long and complicated, the new mechanism of self-defense was little used by prostitutes and madams.[61] Furthermore, rather than registering clandestine brothels, police tended to order their closure since few met with all the stipulations of the law as to proper location and sanitation. Police complained that, after they closed a clandestine house, prostitutes usually disappeared, moving their practice somewhere else, rather than modifying the establishment to comply with the law.[62] Frustrated by the safeguards on civil liberty contained in the Nicotera law, PS functionaries called for the return to the registration of persons rather than places.

In spite of police laments about the problem of clandestine prostitution, they did manage to make a large number of iscrizioni d'ufficio. Superiors encouraged the morals squads to increase continually their quota of forced registration, basing the periodic bonuses in pay on their zeal as well as their morality. In 1871 Biondini requested extra recompense for the guards in the Bolognese Health Office not only for good conduct but also "for their special efforts which have led to the discovery of many clandestine prostitutes and their sharp-sighted surveillance on prostitution in general."[63] The 31 percent of all registrations in Bologna that were at the order of police is not a negligible number. The figure for Bologna approaches that for Italy as a whole, which, in 1875, was 36 percent.[64] Several cities, like Naples and Palermo, showed significantly higher proportions of coerced inscription on official lists, 73 and 68 percent respectively. The great diversity in statistics among cities demonstrates that registration rates reflected the level of local police activity rather than the amount of "real" prostitution. When and where the morals squads wanted to increase the numbers on their lists, they had the power to do so.

Even after 1891, the registration of brothels by police order did not decrease uniformly among the major cities. It is true that several cities reported the opening of very few new brothels, explaining that the procedure was now legally too complex. For example, Milan, Turin, and Venice reported to the Ministry of the Interior no authorizations of new brothels for most of 1897.[65] Yet, Palermo, Rome, and Naples counted 58, 30, and 26 new houses respectively during the same period. Since at least 50 percent of these were registered by order of police, it is clear that the PS retained sufficient authority to license brothels if it so wished. Further proof of the continuing power of police over prostitutes can be found in the high number of arrests for soliciting. While these arrests resulted in fines and imprisonment rather than registration, they indicated that police had not decreased their surveillance over lower-class women. Agents in Rome and Naples each claimed to have arrested, in six months alone, over one thousand women, several times the number of legally registered prostitutes.[66] Thus, police control over prostitution did not cease with the Nicotera Regulation but tended to be exerted more in the form of repeated arrests than inscription on official lists.

In their hunt for clandestine prostitutes, police often arrested women on very slim evidence. Typical of many other cases was that of Elena Righi, arrested in Bologna on Via Galliera "because she was found to be without the prescribed internal passport as well as unemployed and lacking any means of support."[67] The statement of arrest offered no more specific proof of prostitution; police assumed that any woman without an "honest" job was a prostitute and consequently released immediately any woman who could prove she was working. Eugenia Rigoni, for example, convinced the police that she had been employed regularly as a servant during her three-month sojourn in Bologna. Having held jobs in a brothel, with a family, and with a lawyer, she was now working as a domestic for the madam of a brothel located on Via delle Ocche. She was released to resume her job.[68]

The place and time of apprehension by police could increase the suspicion of streetwalking. Agents picked up Ines Mirandola in a dancehall where they assumed no respectable woman would be found.[69] Clotilde Scuri drew the attention of police by the proximity of her apartment to the barracks of military trainees. Their commander had noticed Scuri "standing almost continuously at the window overlooking the before-mentioned rooms and attempting, whenever possible, to start a conversation with the already mentioned students, who are all very young. She not only excites their imaginations and keeps them in a state of semicretinism, but also distracts them from their studies, resulting in serious damage to their education and their health."[70] Armed with this complaint, police arrested Scuri although they lacked proof of any physical contact between her and the trainees.

Women alone in the evenings on city streets also came under immediate suspicion. Morals police arrested Maddelena Beninsegni and Virginia Fiorelli in the courtyard of the Town Hall, at 1:45 AM, because "they could give no plausible justification for being at that place at that hour."[71] Nor did the time have to be so late to attract the attention of police. Officers pursued Erminia Saffi because, besides looking foreign, she was alone on the streets at 8:30 PM.[72] After they grabbed her by the arm, a gentleman who claimed to be the director of the local paper, *Il Resto di Carlino*, intervened to protect her and threatened to denounce their actions in his paper. The group then proceeded to the house of a "count" for whom Saffi worked and who spoke up in her favor. In this case, the questore disciplined the PS guards with several days arrest for improper conduct. The punishment, however, followed only from the fact that respectable men of a high social rank had stepped in to protect Saffi. Ordinarily, no penalty fell on morals police for arresting women without any concrete evidence of wrongdoing.

Even when agents caught women in more compromising situations, their statements of arrest generally failed to advance adequate proof of prostitution. Angiolina Bassini, for example, "was surprised in bed with Giuseppe Frangarelli" in a lodging house by PS guards.[73] Bassini denied the charge of prostitution, saying that she had a job in a restaurant but no place to sleep, so had accompanied Frangarelli to the lodging house, "where I passed the night with him."[74] Police arrested another woman, Letizia Angiolini, for being found in a furniture store owned by "a known procuress," Claudia Venturoli.[75] Discovered hiding under a bed, Angiolini defended herself by saying that she was embarrassed to be seen by strangers since she was "wearing only a housedress."[76] These examples illustrate that any woman engaged in extramarital sexual activity or found in the company of "immoral" companions was assumed to be corrupt. Only rarely, as in the case of Paolina

Pancerasi, is PS evidence convincing. According to the arresting officer, Panceresi was soliciting on Via Castiglione and invited him to go with her into a doorway. The policeman may have been lying, as Panceresi later claimed, but at least he built a plausible case for arrest.[77]

While frequent and often arbitrary, arrest for clandestine prostitution did not always lead to registration. Instead, police employed several diverse strategies for managing women brought to the Health Office or questura. Abolitionists, therefore, correctly criticized police for arresting women without adequate evidence but overstated their case when they claimed that inscription on the lists and entrance into the closed houses inevitably followed. Over the more than twenty years for which Gamberini kept statistics for Bologna, the Health Office registered only one-third of those picked up for clandestine prostitution (Table 5.2).[78] Police were especially hesitant to register the young, even if they had reached the age of majority and were legally eligible. Instead, the periodic reports of the Bolognese Health Office boasted of the large number of young girls who, after arrest, were returned to their families. According to the director, their conduct resulted from "inexperience" rather than irreversible depravity, so that there was hope for reform.[79] The dossiers of many of these youths show a repeated consignment to their families, who promised to guarantee their future behavior. If a girl was not a local resident, the questore would write to his counterpart in her town of birth and make inquiries about her past conduct, judicial record, and whether her relatives were willing to take her back.[80] Sometimes parents aggressively defended their daughters' reputations, as in the case of Adele Salvanini, whose father assured police of her "praiseworthy conduct" and begged that she not be registered, an action "which could hurt a young girl who aspires to an honest marriage."[81] Having been returned twice already to her parents and, even worse, having insulted the director of the Health Office, Salvanini did not escape inscription on police lists. Antonietta Antinore was more fortunate. After being summoned to the Health Office on charges of clandestine prostitution and given a vaginal examination, she was released. The director of the Health Office wrote that "before setting her free, I sternly warned her to change her behavior, making her understand that if there

149

Table 5.2. *Women Arrested for Clandestine Prostitution in Bologna*

| | | Result of arrest (in percentage) | | |
	Arrested	Registered	Sifilicomio	Warned and freed
1864	266	34	21	45
1865	190	31	20	49
1866	202	21	20	59
1867	257	23	15	62
1868	277	23	19	58
1869	338	19	19	62
1870	172	36	19	45
1871	194	44	18	38
1872	137	38	25	37
1873	163	39	14	47
1874	266	21	14	65
1875	262	29	10	61
1876	80	44	16	40
1877	139	38	22	40
1878	105	48	15	37
1879	149	36	12	52
1880	165	30	20	50
1881	109	50	7	43
1882	146	42	9	49
1883	167	24	22	54
1884	146	28	17	55
1885	146	27	19	54
1886	144	27	13	60
Average	183	33	17	50

SOURCE: Pietro Gamberini, *Rapporto politico-amministrativo clinico della prostituzione di Bologna* (Bologna: Gamberini e Parmeggiani, 1864–1886).

were further complaints about her conduct, she would be registered as a tolerated prostitute without delay." She was then consigned to her father, "who formally promised to pay more heed to her education."[82]

In some instances, relatives refused to take back girls they considered irredeemable. The two brothers of Anna Caneppari, for example, claimed that they had done everything "in order to put

150

their sister on the right path" and were now ready to "abandon her to her fate."[83] Their motives may have been economic, actually, since few avenues of employment lay open to Caneppari. Without the support of her family, she was sent immediately to a closed house. Adalisa Fornasari, at age eleven, was too young to be inscribed on official lists. Police periodically arrested her for soliciting men under the guise of selling flowers and returned her to her mother. Although requested to prevent her daughter from "leading such a sad life," her mother, according to authorities, liked the money that she made from prostitution.[84] Upon reaching the legal age, Fornasari most likely would join the ranks of the registered.

Police were more likely to register older women than teenagers, "because these had already given themselves to vice and immorality for a long time."[85] Even those with past records sometimes eluded registration if they could produce a friend who would swear to take care of them financially. The Health Office of Bologna released Angia Mastellini with only a warning after she claimed to be supported by Gaetano Parvignani, a resident of the same city.[86] In the case of migrants, morals police often "repatriated" them rather than inscribe nonnatives on Bolognese police lists. Arrested after eleven days residence in Bologna, Clotilda Peruzzi was given a *"foglia di via"* (administrative order to leave the commune) and sent back to her hometown, Modena. An unemployed cleaning woman, she claimed to receive money from her fiancé stationed in the regiment at Parma.[87] Police gave little credence to her explanation.

Even educated women risked arrest and repatriation if found unemployed. Picked up by morals agents for lacking money and identification, Amelia Cortes said she had been in Bologna for two weeks looking for a position as a teacher. In response to the questore of Bologna, the mayor of her hometown telegraphed that Cortes had always exhibited "good behavior and her family is of sufficient means."[88] In addition, a gentleman named Masi, of Bologna, had promised to find her a teaching position and support her in the meantime. Despite these proofs of upright character and local patronage, police cut off Cortes's search for a job in Bologna and repatriated her. While not as serious as registration, repatriation constituted an annoying weapon by which police

151

could harass migrant women without judicial review. Through use of the foglia di via, police attempted to check the movement of anyone considered dangerous to order and morality, a category that encompassed all unemployed and unprotected women on city streets.

Despite their reputation for having close ties with the underworld, prostitutes faced relatively few arrests for crimes against the penal code compared with arrests for infractions of the prostitution statutes. While the latter resulted in a few days detention in a local prison (*carcere giudiziaria*), longer sentences and transfer to one of the few national prisons for women (*casa di pena*) followed conviction for more serious crimes. According to government statistics for 1906, which broke down convictions by profession, prostitutes were more likely to be condemned for penal offenses than other categories of women. Nevertheless, the total number of prostitutes sentenced—529—fell far below the thousands convicted each year for soliciting and represented only 1.85 percent of the total female prison population.[89] Courts in fact convicted the largest number of prostitutes for "threatening" and "resisting" police, usually verbally rather than physically.[90] Bolognese records document at the local level this tendency of prostitutes to defend and assert themselves against the PS through vocal mockery and threats. In 1885 Rosalia Costantini was arrested for drunkenness and for directing "verbal insults" at city guards.[91] Clementina Sarnieri also shouted menacing things at police and aggravated her case by waving an illegal knife at them.[92] Other crimes committed by prostitutes included theft, pandering, and outraging common decency. The fact that convictions for insulting and resisting public authorities outdistanced those for indecency and procurement, both intimately connected to the profession, signaled the high level of tension between prostitutes and the PS. Prostitutes viewed police as agents of a repressive regulation system, not as members of a modern civil service intent on defending their rights as citizens.

Surveillance over prostitutes continued once they were legally registered and settled into the closed houses. Brothels tended to be clustered together, facilitating police control, which involved setting the hours of opening and closing, checking the sanitation, collecting the registers, and punishing disorderly behavior. In Bologna, for example, the tolerated houses were grouped in several neighborhoods including those around the market in Piazza 8 Agosto, the university, and directly inside the wall at the Castiglione gate. None were located in the close vicinity of the main square, Piazza Maggiore.[93] A remarkable stability over time characterized these establishments so that police had the opportunity to become very familiar with each brothel and its personnel. According to a tax list of 1885, 86 percent of the closed houses dated back to the 1860s, 6 percent to the 1870s, while none had been recently opened in the 1880s.[94] Most of them were small, averaging three employees each. "Isolated" prostitutes, on the other hand, posed a greater obstacle to police discipline, being scattered throughout the city. After 1888 the job of the morals squads became more difficult as the number of the traditional houses slowly decreased, only to be supplanted by clandestine establishments or short-lived brothels registered at police insistence but quickly closed.[95]

In the tolerated brothels, madams, aided by the enclosed nature of the houses, could either help or hinder the proper implementation of the law. An ambivalent figure, the madam both exploited her employees and shielded them from the police. Authorities minced no words in accusing brothel managers of the former type of conduct. According to Bolis, "The following is a just and reasonable distinction: the prostitute is often the victim of seduction, of poverty, and of hunger; the madam, instead, is a vile and loathsome being who speculates on the dishonor of others for her base self-interest and culpable greediness."[96] A circular from the director of the PS advised police to "intervene directly" between the two parties to guarantee the financial independence of employees.[97] But regulationists such as Castiglione warned that "there is a filthy league organized among brothel managers" who wish to perpetuate a "servile chain of debts" by trading prostitutes from house to house without releasing them from paying sums owed to the former employer.[98] In his book on Naples, De Blasio reproduced several pages of a brothel register that juxtaposed the debt of a prostitute, Nanninna (80 lire) with the actual cost of the items purchased (20 lire).[99] These exorbitant prices madams charged for clothes and toilet articles left some prostitutes in perpetual debt.

153

Periodically, prostitutes ran away illegally from brothels to escape intolerable working conditions. In 1881, for example, three women turned up at the Health Office of Bologna "without the official permission [to transfer into the city] and in secret because of the continued ill-treatment they had received from the madam" of a brothel in nearby Imola.[100] Although imprisoned for three days as punishment for leaving Imola without permission, the three were allowed to stay and register in the closed houses of Bologna. Such instances of exploitation by madams created a climate of distrust within the tolerated houses and necessitated frequent police intervention to mediate disputes between employers and employees.

Madams, however, could also play the role of female protector in the face of police harassment. Although in a position of authority, most were former prostitutes and shared the subculture's negative view of the police. In 1865 Ester Laurenti lodged a complaint with the questore of Bologna against the director of the Health Office, Faccioli, on behalf of two employees. According to the deposition of the first, eighteen-year-old Teresa Felicini, Faccioli called her into his office and "began fondling me, putting his hands on my breasts while he made me sit down beside him. Then he told me that I had always been attractive to him; he stood up, came closer to me, unfastened his trousers, took out his member, and wanted to force me to hold it."[101] When she refused, saying she was "ashamed for him," he asked her to keep her voice down and finally let her go.[102] The second prostitute had an equally incriminating tale. Faccioli, although defended by Gamberini for "the dignified and firm way in which he runs his office," lost his job to Biondini after further complaints about his conduct.[103] Madams, then, could form a front of female solidarity with prostitutes, a fact that softened police discipline and vitiated the need for protection from male pimps. Except in parts of the South, where the Camorra and Mafia already controlled rings of prostitutes, it was primarily women who ran the closed houses and organized the subculture of clandestine prostitution.

As part of their duty to oversee the tolerated brothels, morals squads had to check out complaints from "honest" neighbors. If unsatisfied with police response, these residents often went over the head of the questore to the prefect or even the director of the

PS in Rome. Some letters were short and anonymous, like that received by the Bolognese questura in 1886 denouncing a noisy brothel and signed "one who wants to sleep at night."[104] Others were more lengthy and critical like that of seventy-four residents around Porta d'Azeglio to the prefect of Bologna. As "peaceful citizens," they claimed that the registered brothels in nearby streets did not comply with the stipulations on hygiene and morality contained in the Cavour law: "Many prostitutes station themselves continually on the public streets, soliciting passersby in the most licentious manner and with obscene words. Walking around in clothes which are downright sickening, they exhibit themselves both at the doors and the windows, which lack those blinds which are prescribed in other cities to protect public morality."[105] Similar complaints came from all the nine major cities to the minister in Rome. In a letter from Florence inhabitants of Via dei Federighi worried that the sight of nearby brothels would have a corrupting effect on their children. Written in 1914 the letter asked rhetorically, "Why have we gone to take civilization to Africa when our own house lacks it?"[106] If properly registered, brothels tended to survive such complaints. Police investigated and gave warnings but were loathe to close an establishment legally under their control.[107] Unlike clandestine prostitutes, who received immediate retribution, legal brothels received rather lenient treatment from police, who wished to perpetuate an arrangement that made surveillance easier.

These letters of complaint about prostitutes do not represent all segments of public opinion, especially that of the lower classes. In Bologna five neighbors sent a petition to police denying a story in the newspaper *Il Resto di Carlino* claiming that "many inhabitants of Via Centotrecento are objecting because a goddess of Aphrodite shows herself too often at the entrance of her house and causes all kind of scandal."[108] While they admitted that a prostitute lived in the vicinity, no one would censure her. And, although brothels clustered in certain streets, they were always interspersed with the houses of other poor residents. The criminologist Alfredo Niceforo described one street in Rome room by room; his directory revealed a mixture of poor families, unmarried couples, and prostitutes.[109] While his conclusion was one of disgust, one could also interpret this intermingling as a sign that the lower classes accepted prostitution as a necessary, although perhaps temporary, phase for young, unemployed women. In residential patterns and sexual comportment, no strict line existed between "normal" and "deviant" woman. "Honest" acquaintances frequently volunteered to take moral and financial responsibility for prostitutes to help them get off police lists. Although the paucity of direct evidence makes any conclusion hypothetical, the middle classes seemed overwhelmingly hostile to the prostitute, while the lower classes were more divided in their judgment and often offered her support rather than disdain.

Besides arrest, registration, and surveillance of closed houses, police came into contact with prostitutes at the moment of residential transfer, either within the city or, more commonly, among cities. Before 1888 and the liberalization of the law, prostitutes were required to get permission from the Health Office before moving or even absenting themselves from their brothel for more than three days. Failure to observe this article of the Cavour statute resulted in arrest. Police almost automatically granted requests for transfer, so that a rapid turnover characterized the personnel of most houses.[110] The rare exceptions involved women who wanted to move their practice from a closed house to their own homes, that is, change their status to that of "isolated" prostitute. Police sometimes denied these requests, preferring that women remain in the organized brothels that were easier to control.[111] In the majority of cases, prostitutes simply informed the PS of their destination, promising to check in immediately at the Health Office of the new town and register themselves. Through this process, an average of 44 percent of the prostitutes inscribed on Bolognese lists left the city every year between 1863 and 1886.[112] About one-half of these women moved on to another nearby town in Reggio-Emilia, following the railroad either east to Ancona or west toward Milan. Of the rest, over 40 percent set out to cities in other northern provinces, while only a few chose a destination in central or southern Italy.[113] This remarkable mobility contradicted the common image of the closed house as a prison from which there was no escape. Bologna was not exceptional, for the commission report of 1885 established that over one-half of the registered prostitutes in Italy changed address every year.[114]

Although prostitutes were theoretically committed to reinscribing on their arrival in a new city, many failed to do so. In 1875, for example, 6,756 prostitutes got permission to leave one city, but only 4,841 showed up at the Health Office at their destination to request a new libretto.[115] Thus 28 percent effectively slipped through the cracks of the system and freed themselves from police surveillance. Bolis was well aware of prostitutes' aversion to registration: "If the prostitute, by her nature, tries in every way to escape from the inconvenient surveillance which curbs her excesses and limits her freedom, it is easy to imagine that no one would spontaneously appeal for this hateful control."[116] He added that, even if arrested by police, few prostitutes cooperated by signing a declaration of registration because they "attribute much importance to this formality; by signing the papers, they consider themselves tied forever."[117] Through this technique of transfer without reinscription, many women managed to change their status from registered to clandestine; rearrest by the morals squads could bring renewed registration, which again could be erased by transfer. The boundary, then, between the two categories of legal and clandestine prostitution was not rigid but porous and forever shifting. Prostitutes used their "shrewdness" and ingenuity to exploit the loopholes in the law and escape surveillance.[118] By such resistance prostitutes managed to cripple a system that in theory promised to envelop them in discipline.

Because prostitutes moved so frequently, police received innumerable requests for information from families who had lost contact with female members in the profession. In 1886 the subprefect of Comacchio wrote to the questore of Bologna to inquire about Maria Zannini, since "her poor father" had not heard from her for several months.[119] Police found her, duly registered, in a brothel on Via delle Ocche, having come from Rome only a month ago. Similarly, Lucia Sanceson of Vicenza asked police to track down her daughter, a prostitute who practiced in Bologna under the name of Linda Viale.[120] Old and sick, the mother requested that the Health Office grant Viale several days leave to visit her. Finding Viale in the sifilicomio, police promised to send her to Vicenza as soon as she recovered. Husbands also used police when searching for wives who had deserted them. Domenico Dall'Ara of Rimini requested that Bologna police order his wife,

Table 5.3. *Strategies for Getting Off Police Registers in Bologna*

	Number of registered prostitutes[a]	Percentage		
		Legally canceled	Died	Disappeared illegally
1863	391	5	1	50
1864	409	8	1	42
1865	397	8	3	40
1866	396	10	2	40
1867	368	10	1	35
1868	335	10	2	42
1869	309	9	1	38
1870	326	9	2	40
1871	320	13	2	33
1872	301	15	—	30
1873	344	8	1	38
1874	357	7	1	46
1875	360	9	—	46
1876	294	7	—	44
1877	286	5	1	46
1878	286	6	1	43
1879	291	9	—	45
1880	272	4	—	47
1881	344	5	1	60
1882	312	7	—	46
1883	351	7	—	50
1884	346	10	—	49
1885	333	8	—	52
1886	309	12	—	43
Average	335	8	1	44

SOURCE: Pietro Gamberini, *Rapporto politico-amministrativo clinico della prostituzione di Bologna* (Bologna: Gamberini e Parmeggiani, 1863–1886).

[a]Total of all names that appeared on registration lists during the year.

Olimpia Giannini, back to his house. After interviewing Giannini, the madam of a closed house, PS agents informed the questore that "she firmly refused to return to her husband, not intending to be subjected to renewed ill-treatment."[121] In this case, police displayed no disposition to send her back. By providing such information, the PS thus carried out, in addition to its repressive function, a public service both for prostitutes and their relatives. In a society that as yet lacked mass communication by telephone, the poor were thrown back on the police, who provided the only network spread throughout the nation and equipped to find missing persons.[122] The lower classes took advantage of this service despite their traditional hostility to the PS. The large volume of letters requesting assistance from police attests to the fact that a good part of the day-to-day work of the morals squads lay in gathering information, not for surveillance, but for prostitutes' families.

Finally, prostitutes came into contact with police when they appealed for cancellation from official registers. Unlike permission to transfer residence, cancellation was not granted easily. The Health Office in Bologna released an average of only 8 percent from its lists each year (Table 5.3).[123] Even if cancellation was granted, a law aimed at detecting recidivism required that women undergo vaginal examinations for three successive months.[124] Getting off the lists, therefore, proceeded by stages under the mistrustful eyes of police. Besides death, which of course brought automatic cancellation, police considered appeals on the following grounds: marriage, sickness, entrance into a reformatory, initiation of an "honest" job, or the guarantee of support by a respectable citizen.

Of these various justifications for annulling registration, several almost inevitably met with success. Death compelled elimination from lists but accounted for only about 11 percent of the cancellations in Bologna (Table 5.4).[125] Poggiali reported roughly the same figure for Naples (Table 5.5).[126] Contrary to one popular belief, most women did not remain imprisoned in houses until weakened by venereal disease to the point of death. A significant number did request cancellation because of ill health, however, often following years of registration. If armed with a doctor's certificate, these prostitutes usually gained a favorable judgment from police. In Bologna, the Health Office freed Angela Barni, forty years of age, because her doctor wrote that she needed a long cure and complete rest for both cardiac and pelvic disease.[127] Even younger women, like Enrica Ancarani, aged thirty-

Table 5.4. *Reasons for Cancellation in Bologna*

	Guarantee or job[a]	Disease	Death	Marriage	Reformatory
1864	65	—	13	11	11
1865	51	—	30	14	5
1866	77	—	20	—	3
1867	90	—	10	—	—
1868	69	14	17	—	—
1869	73	15	12	—	—
1870	52	20	24	4	—
1871	39	37	17	7	—
1872	68	21	3	8	—
1873	65	15	12	—	8
1874	38	33	12	17	—
1875	76	8	4	12	—
1876	61	33	—	—	6
1877	64	21	15	—	—
1878	60	20	20	—	—
1879	74	21	—	—	5
1880	33	44	11	11	—
1881	26	58	11	—	5
1882	71	24	5	—	—
1883	89	11	—	—	—
1884	75	6	—	—	19
1885	86	—	—	—	14
Average	64	18	11	4	3

SOURCE: Pietro Gamberini, *Rapporto politico-amministrativo clinico della prostituzione di Bologna* (Bologna: Gamberini e Parmeggiani, 1864–1885).

NOTE: The numbers in the five columns are percentages and do not always add across to 100 because of rounding.

[a]Guarantee signifies that a family member, friend, or patron has agreed to guarantee financial support to a prostitute. Unfortunately, Gamberini lumped this group together with those who left the lists to take up a new, "honest" job.

one, were dropped from lists upon presentation of a doctor's certification; she was suffering from "profound tuberculosis and fever which are causing her progressively to lose weight."[128] Police refused requests, however, if sick women could not explain how they would support themselves in the future or if they continued flagrantly to solicit on city streets.[129]

Table 5.5. *Reasons for Cancellation in Naples, 1863*

	Number	Percentage
Guaranteed support by family, friend, patron	67	32
"Honest" job	25	12
Disease	54	26
Death	22	11
Reformatory	14	7
Marriage	6	3
Other	19	9
Total	207	100

SOURCE: Francesco Poggiali, *Manuale del funzionario di pubblica sicurezza pel servizio degli uffici sanitarii del Regno d'Italia* (Naples: Libreria Nazionale Scolastica, 1868), app., pp. 1–2.

While police readily approved cancellation for consignment to a reformatory, few registered prostitutes chose this route out of the system. Antonia Tortorelli of Bologna represented less than 3 percent of her peers when she successfully got off the lists to enter the home of the Buon Pastore.[130] Gamberini lamented this situation but believed that "not a few prostitutes would willingly abandon their disgraceful life and take up again the role of an honest woman if they knew that such charitable refuges existed."[131] He added, however, that despite its good intentions, the home of the Buon Pastore drove away repentant prostitutes by requiring an immediate transition from "their former life of orgy and passion" to a strict religious existence governed by rigid rules.[132] Indeed, Bolognese records include cases of prostitutes, like eighteen-year-old Giulia Zanasi, who could not adapt to the life of the Buon Pastore and were expelled "for bad conduct and serving as an evil example to others."[133] Police, who tended to be anticlerical, continually complained that all the reformatories were private and religious and called on the government to appropriate the money to found public, secular institutions. There is little evidence, though, that PS agents actively encouraged the redemption of those already registered; the young might be saved, but the habitual prostitute could not, in their view, be expected to change her

161

natural inclination toward a depraved life. As one regulationist advised, "Do not think about restoring modesty to those who have lost it, but try to make sure that those who have it do not lose it."[134]

Police were more selective about granting cancellation to those who claimed to have found a protector or an alternative job. Marriage always brought elimination from lists as well as exemption from the three further months of surveillance because it was thought to automatically normalize a woman's sexual status and guarantee her financial support. Yet few women left the lists directly to contract marriage. More often, patrons, friends, or lovers accompanied prostitutes to the Health Office to sign a declaration that they would guarantee the woman's livelihood and moral comportment. For example, Roberto Landini of Bologna promised to look after Filomena Jancovich, a twenty-year-old prostitute from Trieste, "in order to deliver her from her present unfortunate condition of life."[135] Director of a newspaper, *La Settimana*, Landini impressed police with his reliability. Patrons did not have to come from the middle or upper classes, though, for police consigned women to mechanics, butchers, and other members of the working classes as long as they had a record of good conduct and made a steady wage.[136] Paolo Betti, a varnisher from Bologna, made only 1.75 lire per day, but police approved his request to take over the support of Virginia Andalo after investigating his morality.[137] They gave a negative judgment to Tomaso Spagni, however, since he had an arrest record and could not be trusted to oversee the behavior of his charge, Cristina Colli.[138]

Likewise, police were suspicious of women who expressed the desire to find respectable work; good intentions would not secure cancellation from registers; only proof of having found a definite job would do. Most women returned to their original occupation, domestic service, since they remained unskilled and ineligible for craft or industrial trades. Some prostitutes, especially the elderly, became maids in brothels, where their former reputations were no hindrance to employment.[139] Others found families willing to hire a prostitute as a servant and, concurrently, watch over her comportment. Clotilde Birchner wanted to hire Carlotta Vigatti, a registered prostitute, to take care of her children so that she could assume a wage-paying job in a factory. The Health Office found Birchner to be "a person of good conduct" who would provide Vigatti with "a stable place of recovery."[140] Police also allowed Enrica Piccinini to take a job as a maid to the Sarti family, because its members were "honest persons who are incapable of abetting immorality."[141] The fact that prostitutes who switched occupations usually ended up in domestic service demonstrates that life in the closed houses did not provide a path to social mobility or financial independence.

This review of the moments of "interaction" between police and prostitutes reveals a certain disjuncture between the theory and practice of regulation. On the one hand, the system did succeed, as its framers had intended, in restricting the freedom of prostitutes. They were deprived of the right of privacy of domicile since their houses, that is, brothels, were always subject to police search. Concurrently, police compiled extensive dossiers on each registered woman, similar to those for criminals, even if she had not broken the law. Every detail of her life was open to public gaze. Denied the protection and respect due other citizens, prostitutes were, as abolitionists correctly charged, second-class citizens. Since cancellation was not granted easily, inscription became a status that perpetuated itself and hindered women from changing their lives. Even after 1888, when registration and cancellation applied to brothels rather than persons, the notoriety of having worked in a closed house significantly reduced the possibilities of finding alternative employment.

On the other hand, several factors undercut the oppressive, static, and all-encompassing nature of the regulation system as envisioned by the law, especially that of Cavour. In practice, police did not act with blind repression but tried to make distinctions, sometimes misguided, between different categories of women. Anyone who could return to her family was generally exempt from registration and likely to receive cancellation. Furthermore, police generosity with their permission to transfer residence contradicted the principle of enclosure underpinning the law. More important than certain leniencies in PS behavior was the rebellion against the system by prostitutes, who exploited every opportunity to remove themselves from police registers. Escape from the closed houses, both legal and illegal, was widespread and prevented the regulation system from functioning efficiently and effectively.

While the closed houses were not airtight, the threat of registration constituted a powerful mechanism of harassment potentially applicable to every lower-class woman. All unprotected, female poor were exposed to the intimidation of possible arrest and repatriation if they stepped outside the bounds of the proper female role. The prostitution laws became a weapon against the entire mass of migrating, unemployed, and homeless women who lived at the edge of subsistence because police tended to label them all as prostitutes and had the power to impose sanctions on them accordingly. The class nature of registration is clear from the unwillingness of police to register mistresses, courtesans, and other categories of higher class prostitutes. As the provincial doctor of Florence candidly reported to the prefect in 1896, the registered houses were located only in the most poor and crowded neighborhoods, whereas it was commonly known that there were other places in the city "where prostitution is notoriously exercised."[142] Protected by upper-class clientele or located near respectable hotels and wealthy shops, these establishments escaped police discipline. Statistics verify that the largest proportion of brothels were of the third, that is, lowest and cheapest, category.[143] Only poor women, then, were the targets of the regulation system, whose tentacles touched the lives of prostitutes and nonprostitutes alike.

In conclusion, regulation as enforced by the police only partially fulfilled the intent of those who framed the law. The morals squads were never able to erect a clear barrier between prostitutes and "respectable" women through enclosure, surveillance, and discipline. The precariousness and low pay characteristic of women's work made the state's task of identifying and separating moral and immoral women impossible. Middle-class notions of appropriate sexual behavior could not be forced on the large numbers of women whose economic survival depended on temporary, part-time, or permanent prostitution. Despite such failures in the system, administrators in the Division of Public Security never seriously considered alternative approaches. This intransigent defense of regulation prevented any amelioration of the relationship between police and prostitute during the fifty years before World War I.

6

Prostitutes and Doctors: Examination

On September 20, 1886 the director of the Bolognese Health Office requested permission from the questore to submit twenty-one-year-old Emma Ballarini to a vaginal examination. A native of Bologna, Ballarini had been deserted by her husband, the proprietor of a cafe, and left with their three-year-old child. Within the previous two years she had been repatriated from nearby Faenza and Forlì, where she had perhaps been looking for work. The questore immediately granted Health Office personnel permission to examine Ballarini, whom they claimed was a clandestine prostitute and had venereal disease. But upon examination, doctors pronounced Ballarini healthy. Nevertheless, the PS functionary who headed the office warned her to change her immoral behavior and find a job. She was told to report back to the Health Office within eight days or she would be automatically registered as a prostitute.[1]

Ballarini was not alone in being forced to undergo vaginal examination based on suspicion of venereal disease. Public Security guards also picked up Racchela Garagnomi on the same charges, although they offered no specific proof; the statement of arrest simply declared that she had no permanent residence or occupation. Twenty-five years old, Garagnomi explained that she had been in Bologna only three days, "where she had come to have a certain Luigi di Budrio agree to marry her."[2] Arrested by agents of the morals squad while talking to an old man, Garagnomi was told to report to the Health Office the next morning. Upon complying, she was given a health check but, like Ballarini, found without symptoms of venereal disease. Imprisoned nonetheless for clandestine prostitution, she was escorted after three days back to her village by a local carabiniere. Her search for her fiancé was ended.

As the experiences of Ballarini and Garagnomi illustrate, authorities could subject any autonomous, lower-class woman to the humiliation of a vaginal examination without proof that she was a prostitute, much less diseased. Police lacked any method of distinguishing a healthy from a sick woman, yet their routine assertions that certain women were spreading infection were accepted as fact by the questore. It is noteworthy that until 1888 the morals police and the questore, not physicians, decided which women would be examined. Clearly, the vaginal check was not only a medical but also a disciplinary tool used to intimidate lower-class women into finding some means of support and getting off the streets, even if that meant repatriation to another commune. Unconcerned that the vaginal examinations turned up so many healthy women, police continued to presume that all arrested women were prostitutes. Ballarini, for example, was warned about her future behavior and threatened with registration although physicians failed to find the expected sign of immorality: venereal disease. Thus the vaginal examination alone served as a mechanism to label its subjects dangerous and deserving of further surveillance even if it produced no evidence of illicit sexual behavior.

During the first decades of unity, doctors in the Ministry of the Interior defended this widespread submission of women to the vaginal examination as necessary to prevent an epidemic of venereal disease throughout the new Italian kingdom. In the 1880s, however, doctors began to split with the police, gradually coming to reject the regulation system embodied in the Cavour law, both because it proved medically inefficacious and because it left health personnel subordinate to the dictates of police. Government doctors came to favor instead a system of voluntary preventive venereal disease care for the entire civilian population including prostitutes. I explore in this chapter the changing relationship between doctors and prostitutes against this background of public health reform, first explaining the structure of the Division of Public Health and the state of medical knowledge about venereal disease before World War I, then following, as with the police in the last chapter, the moments of interaction between physicians and prostitutes that took place in the Health Offices, sifilicomi, outpatient dispensaries, and special hospital wards for venereal disease. I conclude the chapter with an evaluation of the effectiveness of the Italian police in limiting the diffusion of venereal disease.

The Doctors of *Sifilografia*

Doctors charged with the prevention and treatment of venereal disease formed part of a larger public health bureaucracy that took shape only slowly in the early decades of unity. As in most other matters, Piedmontese health policy, enshrined in a law of November 20, 1859, became that of the kingdom, and its outlines underwent little modification until 1888.[3] On paper, the early health bureaucracy looked rather centralized since decision making rested with the minister of the interior, who passed his orders down through the prefects and subprefects to local mayors. Alongside this administrative hierarchy existed one of appointed, advisory committees: the Consiglio Superiore di Sanità (High Council of Health) in Rome, provincial councils, and district councils. In practice, however, health service varied widely across the nation, for most matters were left to communal discretion and depended on local funding. Thus the cities in the former Austrian territory, which had boasted the most advanced health legislation, provided free assistance to the poor by a team of *medici condotti* (municipal doctors), whereas towns in southern Italy often lacked the services of any public health officer. Unlike the police, who were centralized and disciplined under the minister of the interior immediately after unification, doctors had a harder time gaining a secure place in the public administration.

The public health law of December 22, 1888 finally gave the

medical bureaucracy a shape closely resembling that of the PS. A director of public health was established alongside the director of public security, both subordinate to the minister of the interior. While each director theoretically worked through the prefect to implement local policy, the legislation created a new official, the *medico provinciale* (provincial doctor), who had jurisdiction over the same territory as the prefect. Like his PS counterpart, the *questore*, the provincial doctor often bypassed the prefect in reporting to his superiors in the division at Rome. He was responsible for overseeing implementation of national directives at the local level and certifying that communal health codes corresponded to national guidelines. According to these guidelines, every commune, or group of communes, had to hire a municipal doctor to treat the poor and provide, for a fee, services otherwise unavailable to the wealthy.[4] By the 1890s over half of the physicians in Italy were in the employ of the state rather than in private practice.[5] Despite this great expansion in personnel, the health bureaucracy remained relatively decentralized because funding of most services remained with the communes and provinces.

The immediate attention given by Cavour to the cure of syphilis becomes especially striking in the context of this rather slow and uneven development of the Italian health system. But medical opinion of the period warned that "of all the infectious diseases, syphilis causes the greatest damage, at least to the present generation. Besides being extremely contagious, it extends its poison from father to son and is one of the principal causes of the decay of the human species."[6] This attitude became only more pronounced as the century drew to a close and the fear of racial degeneration swept across Europe. In Italy the defeat at Adowa in 1896 fueled fright about the effects hereditary diseases like syphilis might have on the fiber of the nation. Syphilis also figured prominently in the writings of criminal anthropologists, as a major source of the atavisms of the "born criminal."

The battle of the Public Health Division against venereal disease went through two phases, each marked by a different set of personnel and different types of institutions. Before 1888 and the passage of the Crispi Regulation, teams of *medici visitatori* (examining doctors) carried out biweekly vaginal checks of registered prostitutes at the Health Offices or in the closed houses. Signifi-

cantly, this medical personnel was subordinate to the PS functionary who captained the Health Office, showing the secondary
place public health took to public order. Despite genuine concern
with the health of the military, framers of the Cavour Regulation
considered the instruments of the police—force and repression
—to be equally suitable for the control of disease. This reliance
on physical intimidation likewise characterized the second medical arena of the early period, the sifilicomio, which resembled a
prison more than a hospital. While medical authority predominated in this institution, it was not completely independent of the
PS, who were charged with forcibly admitting sick prostitutes and
pursuing and rearresting any woman who escaped before the end
of treatment. Within the sifilicomio, the *medico ordinario* (head
doctor), sometimes with the aid of an assistant, examined patients
daily, prescribed the appropriate medicines, and decided when
patients were well enough to be released.[7]

Not until 1888 did the state doctors gain autonomy from the PS
and, therefore, an increasingly important role in the administration of policy concerning prostitution and venereal disease. In
that year, the Crispi law, later copied in the Nicotera law, replaced the Health Offices and sifilicomi with outpatient dispensaries and special hospital wards, respectively. In the first, *medici
dei dispensari* (dispensary doctors) diagnosed and cured noninfec-
tious cases of venereal disease, while in the second, *medici delle
sale celtiche* (ward doctors) cared for patients requiring hospitalization and quarantine. In a revolutionary reversal of medical
strategy, both of the new institutions began to consider the entire
civilian population, rather than just prostitutes, to be their legitimate constituency. For the first time in most cities, men and "respectable" women had access to free and public care for venereal
disease. The examination of prostitutes in the registered brothels
continued, but each madam chose her own *medico fiduciario*
(confidential doctor) for the task and was held responsible by police for keeping her house free of disease. She could also provide
for the private cure of her employees in the brothel rather than
the hospital ward if she could guarantee the isolation of the contagious woman. The state did go on employing "examining doctors,"
but only for the purpose of making unannounced visits to brothels
to double-check the work of the confidential doctors.

171

Despite this elaborate system, health care personnel often lacked the training necessary to make it function effectively. Although Italy boasted a long and respected tradition of medical education, specialized courses in *dermosifilopatia*, or the study of skin and venereal diseases, were not so readily available. The number of universities with a chair in this field did increase as the nineteenth century progressed, from 1 in the 1850s to, 5 in the 1870s, to 17 by the turn of the century.[8] Even in 1900, though, specialists studying at these 17 universities received far too few hours of lessons, according to Tommasoli, and nonspecialists often graduated without any knowledge of the etiology and treatment of venereal disease.[9] Some professors, like Celso Pellizzari of Siena, tried to offset these deficiencies by emphasizing the practical education available in the few clinics attached to university hospitals. As he wrote in 1884, "I believe that few words are needed to make it understood that, if medical lessons should be practical and empirical, this necessity is especially obvious in the case of skin and venereal diseases, for which it is first necessary to educate the eye."[10] Concluding that, for students, "direct examination must take precedence over any other type of research," he admitted that it was often difficult to convince "honest" women to undergo vaginal checks for educational purposes.[11] He resorted to borrowing prostitutes from the local sifilicomio since these women, by fact of their immoral profession, abdicated any right to privacy.[12] In this way, the regulation laws provided specialists in venereal disease with human material for observation; progress in this "delicate" area of medicine depended on the forced hospitalization of prostitutes in the prisonlike sifilicomi. Doctors, therefore, had a stake in perpetuating a system that assured them a constant supply of diseased bodies for clinical experimentation.

In an attempt to guarantee the competency of its personnel, the Ministry of the Interior published successive guidelines for the hiring of doctors responsible for implementing the laws on prostitution and venereal disease. A decree of 1864 established the requirements for becoming an examining doctor, which included a university degree in medicine or surgery and evidence of some specialized knowledge of venereal disease.[13] Candidates could demonstrate special expertise either by previous experience in the field or by an examination. Most specialists preferred the latter and agreed with Gamberini, who desired that "the nomination of these physicians depend on a practical examination, presided over by experts in the cure of venereal disease, who are the only persons able to judge the knowledge of those being tested."[14] Certification of the examining doctors did not solve all problems of lack of expertise in the Health Offices. In 1869 the minister issued a circular forbidding assistant doctors and students from carrying out checks on prostitutes in the absence of the examining doctor, a practice still common in some communes. He argued that, "otherwise, the guarantee of competition, capacity, and personal morality, which we have given to this delicate service, will prove useless."[15] Obviously, legal requirements of competency were not always translated into practice.

After 1888 similar guidelines applied to physicians directing the dispensaries and hospital wards for venereal disease as well as to the examining doctors who made unannounced checks on brothels. According to law, "the examination consists of a clinical test performed on two patients, and it is aimed at ascertaining whether the candidate is capable of forming a just diagnosis of venereal and syphilitic diseases in their various manifestations."[16] Progress in the quality of education, number of teaching clinics, and strictness of government competitions for posts in the public health bureaucracy contributed to the development in Italy of a dedicated core of experts in the diagnosis and treatment of venereal diseases. Their abundant publications and active involvement in national and international medical congresses attested to their commitment to advance a relatively new field of medical research.

Yet general practitioners continued to exhibit a troubling lack of knowledge about venereal disease. This group included the confidential doctors employed, after 1888, by madams to examine their employees. According to Tommasoli, some of these physicians showed up at the closed houses without a microscope or speculum to certify the health of residents.[17] Lacking these instruments, they could look for only exterior lesions of syphilis; gonorrhea escaped detection altogether. Since the law required that shades be drawn at all times in brothels, examinations sometimes took place in rooms with weak or no artificial lighting, making exact diagnosis unlikely.[18] In the face of such unprofessional procedures, the Italian Society for Dermatology and Syphilography voted in 1911 to require the routine testing of all doctors claiming to be specialists in their field, such as the confidential doctors.[19] The director of public health, however, paid little heed to their recommendation.

In addition to the personnel of the Public Health Division, military doctors played a role in the enforcement of prostitution laws. Sometimes the prefect called on physicians attached to a regiment in the province to carry out a surprise examination of tolerated brothels in the vicinity.[20] More often, military doctors, upon detecting an increase in venereal disease in the weekly check of soldiers, encouraged their superior officer to complain to civil authorities. Already in June 1860 immediately following the annexation of Emilia-Romagna to Piedmont, the commander of the Bologna regiment claimed that the high number of men with syphilis was overburdening the military infirmary.[21] These cries of alarm occurred periodically, as in 1879, when the commander asked the prefect "to take whatever measures you think are appropriate in order to alleviate as much as possible the cause of these diseases."[22] Again in 1885 he warned the questore that "for some time we have noted, with deplorable frequency, cases of venereal infection among the soldiers of this garrison."[23] This pattern of army interference in the administration of the regulation system illustrates that the health of the military continued to take precedence over the rights of prostitutes. Although civilians, prostitutes had to submit to unannounced inspection by military physicians. In 1873 the commander even went as far as to order "strict military surveillance" over brothels frequented by soldiers, thus subordinating prostitutes to military discipline as well as that of the civilian police.[24]

In response to complaints from the army about rising rates of venereal disease, the Health Office in Bologna usually ordered special unannounced checks of all closed houses and redoubled efforts to apprehend clandestine prostitutes. In line with instructions issued by the Piedmontese minister of war in 1857 and extended to the kingdom in 1861, military hospitals were to notify the Health Office of not only the number of soldiers with syphilis but also the names and addresses of the prostitutes who had infected them.[25] This strategy, however, failed to aid doctors in

174

pinpointing the sources of contagion. As Gamberini remarked in 1867, the reports from the military hospitals rarely included prostitutes' names or addresses, only vague descriptive terms such as "tall, blond, thin, fat, dark, and the like."[26] Even when a name did appear on a report, public health doctors often found the alleged carrier of infection to be healthy.[27] For example, an army official charged that one of his men had come down with a case of venereal disease, "and he asserts that he got the infection in a brothel on Via Falcone n. 9 from a tall woman with black hair."[28] But the regular check carried out subsequently by the examining doctor found all residents at that address, as well as a brothel next door, to be healthy. Sometimes the desire to protect the identity of a clandestine prostitute explained the imprecision of a soldier's information; he might not wish to contribute to the arrest and registration of a servant, for example, who practiced prostitution part-time.[29] In other instances, the high rate of mobility of those inscribed on official lists made it likely that they would no longer be at the same address. One public health physician exhibited irritation at the constant criticism by the military, declaring that the examining doctors were competent and that any epidemic of venereal disease in the army could come only from clandestine prostitutes, whose detection lay within the purview of police.[30]

Regulationist doctors generally agreed that soldiers contributed to the spread of venereal disease but sympathized with their sexual needs.[31] Like prostitutes, men in the lower ranks of the military were subjected to routine checks and forced cure if infected. During the first few decades of unification, officers penalized subordinates who contracted venereal disease by lowering their pay, restricting their leaves, or simply refusing to pay them the usual hospital visit.[32] Gamberini criticized the reprimanding and shaming of ill soldiers, calling this practice "barbarous":

> I say barbarous because one cannot ask that a man damned to bachelorhood observe a monastic chastity. . . . I repeat barbarous because the instinctive, passionate nature of men is often compelled to quench its thirst at naturally impure fountains, the only ones which are generally granted to the militia, which does not always have and cannot have the

175

means to draw water at the good springs and therefore cannot and must not suffer the consequences of a disease caught involuntarily.[33]

Instead, he recommended that commanders use "kindness" and "persuasion" to encourage soldiers to reveal the identity of "those shameless priestesses of Venus" who had given them the infection.[34] Zampa went so far as to argue that the weekly examinations should be abolished since they constituted "a new and gratuitous offense" to the "liberty and dignity" of the troops.[35]

While Zampa's argument failed to change military policy, it was accepted among regulationists for civilian men. Bolis echoed his words when he called the examination of men "ineffectual, unjust, and contrary to the principle of liberty."[36] This mixture of pragmatism and principle ran through the comments of others who were horrified that a practice routinely required of prostitutes be asked of their male clients. Sormani explained why the examination of men would yield little practical benefit: "A sick man can spread contagion to only a few women; but a sick woman can make herself fatal to many dozen men. A sick man will usually tend to seek treatment immediately; a woman, on the other hand, will not."[37] Surveillance over the health of men was also illegal since, as Castiglione pointed out, the state had no right to sequester "an independent citizen" but instead had to rely on "counseling, teaching, and offering the means of cure."[38] A few voices recommended that customers undergo inspection by madams upon entering a brothel; one ingeniously suggested that each man's integrity and honor be protected by hanging a curtain that would reveal only his genitals during the examination.[39] Regulationists, however, hesitated to advocate the inspection of any groups of civilian men besides prisoners, vagabonds, and perhaps, laborers employed by the state.[40]

Throughout the debate over who would be subjected to health examinations, physicians revealed both sex and class prejudices that undercut their claims to be acting on scientific precepts. Most obviously, they identified a female group—prostitutes—as the primary carrier of venereal disease and therefore rightly subject to state regulation. The abolitionist doctor Bertani pointed out the hypocrisy of this sexist strategy in the following characterization of regulation: "The ideal of this school is legislation by whose force no healthy man would come in contact with a sick woman without, however, taking care of the opposite: that no healthy woman come in contact with a sick man."[41] Besides sexism, class prejudice pervaded the philosophy of the public health bureaucracy. In the military, the one male group routinely subject to examination, officers were exempt.[42] All the other male groups for whom inspection was suggested, such as criminals and vagabonds, were poor and, because of their dependency on the state, considered to have forfeited their personal liberty, as had soldiers. Behind the rhetoric of controlling venereal disease lay the more fundamental purpose of regulation, which was to discipline the dangerous classes. While doctors were genuinely preoccupied with public health, they tended to associate disease only with the poor and powerless and to envision their mission as the protection of the middle and upper classes from pollution.[43]

The promise of regulationist doctors to limit the diffusion of venereal disease by examining prostitutes becomes even more suspect in light of the primitive stage of medical knowledge before World War I. Yet few physicians admitted their incapacity to correctly diagnose and effectively cure patients with the three venereal diseases: syphilis, gonorrhea, and chancroid. As early as 1848 Gamberini, although noting the protean forms of venereal disease, gave confident assurances as to the efficacy of modern, scientific treatment. He suggested that "the patient must not let himself be blinded by appearances, suspicions, and fears, but . . . must get off that dangerous side street in order to take the road of positivism and the most reasoned rationalism."[44] By 1867 he declared that "the clinical study of syphilis has today reached such a high degree of positivism that no therapeutic errors can be tolerated."[45] The history of medicine, however, belies his words, for at midcentury knowledge about venereal disease was rudimentary. As the denomination of this branch of medicine as "dermosifilopatia" shows, these diseases were traditionally diagnosed and treated like skin infections. Diagnosis was based on the identification of a group of symptoms, either on the exterior skin or internal mucous membrane of the vagina. Doctors also looked at mucus secretions from the vagina, but there was much dispute about the significance of any alterations perceived.[46] Since venereal

177

sores resembled other types of less dangerous lesions of the skin, diagnosis could never be exact.

Debates about the most fundamental characteristics of venereal disease raged throughout the nineteenth century. In a pamphlet published in 1848, Gamberini felt compelled to rebut the theory of the "spontaneous" generation of syphilis. According to this hypothesis, "Dirt held for a long time in the reproductive organs . . . can become one of the elements contributing to venereal virus. If two individuals in this condition take too much sexual pleasure . . . in *an infinity of cases* they will develop syphilitic symptoms *according to the literal sense of the word syphilis*, or the inevitable effects of an impure love."[47] Claiming never to have encountered this "infinity of cases," Gamberini answered that

> it is time to abandon utopias and to observe the facts for what they are and persuade ourselves that a disease which is communicated through direct or indirect contact, which always maintains its original expression and qualities, which is transmitted to a certain extent by artificial innoculation and which is transfused from parents to children . . . testifies to the existence of a contagious virus.[48]

By the time of Italian unification, Gamberini's opinion held sway among specialists, although debate continued as to whether children could "inherit" syphilis from both the father and the mother.

Gamberini proved less prescient when he chose sides in the argument between "unicists" and "dualists." According to the unicists, who included most Italian doctors in the early nineteenth century, the same virus produced the "hard ulcers" of syphilis and the "soft ulcers" of gonorrhea and chancroid "depending on the special or idiosyncratic conditions of the contaminated individual."[49] In the 1830s Philippe Ricord of France challenged this theory by innoculating 667 prisoners with gonorrhea. When none developed syphilis, he declared the two diseases separate.[50] Although the historian of medicine Enrico Rasori later wrote that "Ricord could be considered the founder of the modern school for the cure of venereal diseases," dualism was not immediately accepted by many physicians such as Gamberini.[51] In 1848 the Bolognese doctor rejected the separation of syphilis and gonorrhea and asked, "What are the reasons which give Ricord the right to proclaim the [hard] ulcer the real and exclusive type of syphilis?"[52] Twenty years later, he specifically rebutted Ricord's experiment by developing his own hypothesis, "which emerges from my persistent and convinced belief in the unity of the virus": the soft ulcers of gonorrhea did not develop into the hard ulcers of syphilis because the former acted like a vaccination against the latter.[53] By the 1880s the majority of the Italian medical profession, including Gamberini, had been converted to dualism; but a lag of almost fifty years had occurred between Ricord's experiment and the general acceptance of his theory, a lag that highlights the sometimes slow absorption of new medical advances by physicians.

"Syphilization," another theory proved incorrect by time, was also popular among some Italian doctors. Its major proponent, Sperino, father of the Cavour law, explained syphilization as "the injection of a considerable number of [syphilific] ulcers into the organism but not to the point of saturation; these ulcers should prevent and cure syphilis."[54] Not lacking logic, his hypothesis rested on an analogy with smallpox, one of the few diseases that could be successfully prevented before the development of bacteriology in the late nineteenth century. A number of doctors in several countries heroically offered themselves as subjects for the testing of syphilization. In Italy Pellizzari carried out such an experiment, which Rasori later wrote was "memorable for us Italians" and involved three young doctors.[55] "For the love of science," they voluntarily underwent injections.[56] Only one subject contracted the disease, perhaps because the blood had cooled and coagulated before the innoculation, according to Rasori. Although such tests killed most enthusiasm for syphilization, the specialist Giuseppe Fermini reported in 1912 that research continued in the hope of finding a vaccine that would not infect its recipients.[57]

Despite such disagreements among doctors, the development of the new field of bacteriology in the late nineteenth century finally allowed a more precise identification of the three types of infection. Although hospitals did not yet officially separate skin and venereal disease care, it became apparent that the latter were internal rather than merely surface infections and were probably carried by a type of bacteria in the bloodstream or lymphatic system. Autopsies showed, for example, that syphilis in the third stage could attack bones, the brain, and other internal organs.[58] Thus began a search for the microbes responsible for syphilis, gonorrhea, and chancroid. Not until the bacteria had been discovered could doctors be certain that the three patterns of symptoms associated with these names actually described unique diseases.

Very early in the first period of fundamental bacteriological studies from 1878 to 1887, Albert Neisser isolated the gonococcus organism as the bacteria causing gonorrhea in both men and women. Five years later, in 1884, Hans Gram developed the "Gram stain" to test for the presence of gonococcus in human tissue.[59] While gonorrhea was recognized as contagious, it was believed initially to do no more than temporary harm to the outer tissues at the place of infection. For this reason, the sifilicomi and the clinics and wards that replaced them sometimes turned away gonorrhea patients, and most commissions of the 1880s advised that the state not support the cure of such an insignificant disease. Medical attention focused on syphilis not only because of its "hereditary" nature but also because it was understood to attack internal organs and the nervous system. When Augosto Ducrey discovered *Hemophilus ducrey*, the causative agent for chancroid, in 1889, this disease was also characterized as fairly benign. By the late 1890s, however, doctors began to realize that gonorrhea, while not "hereditary," could cause sterility, urinary complications, skin and eye infections, and other "constitutional" problems.[60] Alarm even arose over chancroid because it could destroy parts of the genitals. Therefore, while syphilis continued to dominate medical attention, doctors by the early twentieth century were increasingly recommending hospital treatment for all types of infectious venereal disease.

Although doctors realized that a microbe existed in the case of syphilis, it took years of research to isolate it. Based on clinical observation, physicians had already identified the three stages of the infection and their symptoms: a "hard" ulcer, at the place of initial contact, in the primary stage; multiple lesions in the secondary; and various types of physical and mental degeneration, sometimes decades later, in the tertiary. Not until 1905 did Fritz

Schaudinn discover the causative bacteria, *Treponema pallidum.* In 1907 August Paul von Wassermann created a giant breakthrough in diagnosis by developing a blood test based on recent advances in complement fixation.[61] While the test was not foolproof, the head of the national medical research laboratory in Rome concluded that "the Wassermann reaction, if interpreted prudently and in concordance with other data, is of very great importance."[62] He recommended its use and applauded the director of prisons in Turin for requesting funds to establish a laboratory to give such tests to inmates. Fermini also pronounced the discovery helpful, adding that its drawbacks would soon be overcome by the daily progress in the techniques of blood testing.[63]

While researchers made great strides in the diagnosis of all three types of venereal disease before World War I, they did not discover effective cures. From the earliest known cases of syphilis in the fifteenth century until the development of penicillin in the mid-1940s, doctors relied most heavily on mercury for the treatment of syphilis. Until the early nineteenth century this treatment often proved more painful and deadly than the disease itself. After being rubbed with mercury or inhaling its fumes, patients were purged, sweated, and drained of blood by leeches. Since it was thought that the evil humor surfaced mainly in the mouth, patients were urged to salivate at least six liters of liquid each day. As the mouth became poisoned from this process, it "was transformed into one gangrenous ulcer, out of which, together with saliva, often fell teeth, and even the jaws, the tongue, the lips, and the pharnyx, eaten away by the necrotic process."[64]

During the nineteenth century, physicians abandoned purging, bleeding, and vomiting for simple and controlled doses of mercury. In addition to ointments and vapor baths, treatment began to rely on mercury shots and pills.[65] Gamberini displayed great confidence in the curative effects of mercury, calling it "the sovereign antivenereal medicine which has no equal."[66] Specialists also began to prescribe potassium iodide, although it never replaced mercury as the major drug for syphilis.[67] In 1912 Fermini was still praising mercury and potassium iodide as "the really heroic drugs against syphilitic infection; they bring successes which it seems crazy to hope for."[68] He blamed any "accidents" to patients on irregular or excessive dosage and added, "From these

181

errors originate the fear of mercury and the prejudices of those who accuse it of remaining in the blood and corroding bones and teeth."[69] In fact, patients were right to worry, for mercury was never a very effective cure, while potassium iodide simply stimulated resistance to the bacteria. Doctors could not always distinguish cases of real cure from simple remission. Finally, as a poison, mercury could cause damage, and sometimes death, to those undergoing treatment.

Not until 1910 did there appear to be a major advance in medication. Paul Erlich and his assistant Sahachiro Hata formulated a drug to attack the syphilis microbe. Known as 606 or Salvarsan, its active ingredient was arsenic. With this wonder drug, most doctors expected syphilis to become a disease of the past. But as the health inspector of Florence pointed out in 1911, enthusiasm was already dying down a year after its discovery.[70] Fermini substantiated this in 1912 when he reported that many doctors had abandoned 606.[71] Not only was the drug hard to administer; like mercury, it could cause unwanted side effects or even prove fatal.

Treatment for gonorrhea and chancroid were less harmful than mercury and Salvarsan, but equally ineffective. For gonorrhea in men, the flushing out of the urethra with potassium permanganate, silver compounds, or mild antiseptics sometimes worked in the early stages, since the fragile bacteria died instantly in open air. Since lesions in the vagina could not similarly be disinfected, even in 1938 a doctor declared that "the treatment of gonorrhea in the female hardly deserves the name of treatment."[72] For chancroid, cleanliness and heat proved as good as other treatments, which included iodoform, balsam, alcohol, and ether. From lists of medicines ordered by dispensaries, it appears that Italian doctors relied most heavily on potassium iodide, potassium permanganate, mercury compounds, and silver nitrate as well as antiseptics such as Ichthyol to cure the three venereal diseases.[73] In 1898 the director of one dispensary in Palermo requested a few additional drugs, including compounds of zinc and bismuth, the latter of which became quite popular in the 1920s as a cure for syphilis.[74] But too much bismuth, like mercury and arsenic, could harm a patient.

In short, before World War I, correct diagnosis of venereal disease was possible only in the later years, and effective cure was nonexistent. And yet, the protection of public health continued to provide the major rationale for the perpetuation of the system of regulated prostitution. What is the explanation for this contradiction between the limited knowledge available to physicians and their extensive power of examination of prostitutes? First, from their own point of view, specialists were making great strides in the understanding of venereal disease during the decades following unification. After centuries of ignorance and confusion among the diseases, doctors had learned to distinguish between the three, first on the basis of symptoms; later, bacteriology. In addition, researchers had established how the infections were transmitted and the three stages, as well as the "hereditary" nature, of syphilis. Treatment was still primitive, but few patients seemed to die from mercury, arsenic, or bismuth poisoning while at the sifilicomi or state hospitals. Active in international conferences and writing for the many newly established medical journals, Italian physicians were proud of their contributions to the field of venereal disease studies. As Rasori triumphantly proclaimed as early as 1886, "Finally today the study of syphilis occupies a deservedly acquired place among the most important branches of Medical knowledge."[75]

Despite such progress in the field, a few doctors, such as the abolitionist Pellizzari, realized that "the last word has not been said" on the diagnosis and cure of venereal disease.[76] The fact that the state ignored the limitations of medical science in its defense of regulation revealed that the primary aim of the system was the maintenance not of health but of order. The perceived need to discipline the growing numbers of autonomous, migrating women outweighed any doubts about the effectiveness of regulation in decreasing the rates of infection. Furthermore, specialists downplayed the lacunae in their knowledge in order to legitimate medicine as a profession. Obsessed with stamping out charlatanry, folk medicine, and witchcraft, they exaggerated their claims to expertise and projected an image of themselves as the sole depositories of true, scientific information about the body. As one doctor wrote, "The great part of the public is incapable of judging if those who offer to treat and cure their diseases are at the height of contemporary science; in other words, they are incapable of distinguishing a real doctor from a mere quack or charlatan."[77] Finally, state physicians desired to impress not just the public, but also administrators in Rome, with their expertise. They considered the PS their major rival for control over the implementation of prostitution policy and sought to undercut the dominant role of police as established in the Cavour law.

Examination

As progress occurred in the diagnosis of venereal disease, public health administrators modified their prophylactic strategy from one focused on prostitutes to one concerned with the entire civilian population. Codified in the Crispi and Nicotera regulations as well as the public health law of 1905, this shift in philosophy from regulation to a limited medical abolition was never unanimously accepted by specialists. As a minority of abolitionist doctors, such as Bertani, had opposed the legislation on prostitution before 1888, regulationist voices continued to be heard within the medical community after that date. But the majority of experts in venereal disease approved the new laws, which enlarged the demographic pool from which their patients were drawn, supplied clinics with new human material for research, and broadened the arena of state intervention in the health of the nation. To look more closely at the interaction between public health physicians and prostitutes, then, one must consider the two very different groups of institutions: the pre-1888 Health Offices and sifilicomi, where force defined their relationship, and the post-1888 dispensaries and hospital wards for voluntary cure of venereal disease. As a corollary to the new approach to treatment, physicians modified their way of labeling prostitutes: as simply one of the several groups that might spread infection instead of its primary source. In turn, the quality of the relationship between doctors and prostitutes improved in contrast to the increasing resistance of prostitutes to police.

In the Health Offices, established by the Cavour Regulation, the examining doctors were subordinate to a PS functionary who acted as director. In 1870, 196 communes boasted a Health Office, a number that rose to 256 by 1883.[78] The majority employed only one examining doctor, usually on a part-time basis, because of the low number of registered prostitutes in the smaller towns.[79] In the larger cities several doctors, sometimes under the coordination of a health inspector, performed the routine examinations of prostitutes as well as the unannounced visits to brothels. Bologna, for example, began with four doctors on the roster of the Health Office in 1860 and dropped to three in 1868; the minister of the interior decided that Bologna did not need four physicians "in light of the good functioning of the office."[80] In addition, Gamberini served as health inspector for Emilia as well as chief doctor at the sifilicomio of San Orsola.[81]

According to the Cavour statute, examining doctors were to "use the utmost diligence, exactitude, and delicacy in fulfilling their duties in order to avoid any harm to public health.[82] In Bologna both the questore and the health inspector, Gamberini, repeatedly praised the physicians of the Health Office for exhibiting just such qualities. Upon promulgation of the Cavour law in 1860, the prefect had chosen Enrico Marchesini, Pietro Zurla, Giulio Borzaghi, and Pasquale Saragoni as the first examining doctors of Bologna because he found all four to be endowed with "scientific capacity, philanthropic spirit, disinterested and exemplary honesty, and energy."[83] In 1864 they were reappointed after the director of the Health Office reported that the four physicians "continue to carry out their duties with the usual skill and praiseworthy zeal."[84] Three years later, the questore requested that Gamberini and the examining doctors receive financial bonuses for their extra efforts to protect health "during the troop movements and the threatening invasion of cholera."[85] Clearly, the fear of contagion from the bodies of prostitutes was not limited to venereal disease. Having examined prostitutes four, rather than the usual two, times per week, the Health Office was credited with preventing the outbreak of even one case of cholera in the closed houses or the nearby garrison. Continually reappointed for successive three-year terms, the health staff of the Bologna office provided long-term continuity broken only by the deaths of Zurla and Marchesini. On the eve of the promulgation of the Crispi Regulation in 1888, Borzaghi and Saragoni were still examining the city's prostitutes with the help of a newly appointed colleague,

Camillo Moglia.[86] Turnover was thus much less among the health staff than among the PS staff, a fact that seems to indicate a lower level of corruption and incompetence.

Other indicators, however, point to weaknesses in the health service provided by the examining doctors. For example, an unannounced examination of the registered prostitutes of Bologna in 1877 found 12 of them infected and yet still working. The director of the Health Office expressed surprise that so many cases of disease had escaped the attention of the regular examining doctors, who, he claimed, carried out their jobs "with precision."[87] Perhaps the oversight was due to the excessive number of vaginal examinations each doctor was required to perform daily. For Italy as a whole, each examining physician in 1870 had, on the average, 72 appointments per week with the inscribed.[88] Since small towns had few registered brothels, doctors in large cities actually handled a greater number of appointments. In Bologna each member of the health staff carried out 100 examinations a week during the entire period of the Cavour Regulation.[89] According to Bertani, the results of understaffing were disastrous for public health, as is clear from his description of the procedures in one Health Office:

> The examination in this dispensary was carried out with extraordinary speed. The doctor, having withdrawn the speculum from one [patient], had hardly rubbed it on a sponge full of oil before he applied it to another. After about fifty examinations, the sponge was loaded with mucus and blood, but the doctor continued unperturbed. And with the same speed he proceeded to examine the mouth, inserting a metal spatula which he wiped on his apron during the instant when it passed from one mouth to another.[90]

In these conditions doctors spread infection rather than reduced it. Voicing similar criticisms, a prefect wrote to the Nicotera commission that, "once appointed to the Health Offices, the best doctors become, within a few months, the worst."[91]

Intermittently, prostitutes themselves complained to police authorities in Bologna about maltreatment by public health doctors. In 1881 Gamberini drew a reprimand from the questore after he lanced a genital tumor he had discovered during the routine examination of a prostitute named Elvira Bones. Bones screamed for "ten minutes," letting out "a continuous stream of complaint and cry of desperation which would elicit sentiments of pity even in the hardest hearts."[92] Upon being warned that the Health Office was not a theater for operations, Gamberini replied that he had drained the tumor out of humanity and never expected that the act would be painted "in such black colors."[93] Four years later, two prostitutes charged that Dr. Marchesini had left "lacerations" on their genitals to the point of "ruining the uterus" of one.[94] Defending his subordinate, Gamberini explained that "it can happen to any surgeon that, by chance, the insertion of the speculum may in some cases cause very mild damage."[95] He added that he hoped no penalty would fall on Marchesini, "whose capacity and zeal have always made him a distinguished examining health doctor."[96]

Direct complaints against physicians were much more rare, however, than against their PS colleagues in the Health Offices. Yet prostitutes put up indirect resistance to the government's prophylactic program by failing to cooperate with examining doctors. As Gamberini complained, "Prostitutes are very well versed in subterfuge and the art of escape; when it comes to deception, they are supported to the end by their companions."[97] Health personnel documented the various ruses registered prostitutes used to avoid examination: claiming falsely to be menstruating, changing their names to escape identification, or simply refusing to appear for regular appointments.[98] Even when ill with venereal disease, prostitutes sought to hide their condition by douching to flush away abnormal-looking mucus. In exceptional cases, women like forty-eight-year-old Luigia Carbone of Bologna did voluntarily seek cure at the Health Office.[99] But, like Carbone, these few were generally older women with a long history of illness and perhaps little hope of survival. Younger prostitutes blithely ignored any symptoms of venereal disease and adamantly resisted being sent to the sifilicomio. This behavior surprised and angered regulationist physicians, who believed that their expertise served the best interest of prostitutes as well as society in general. Why were prostitutes so shortsighted?

Underlying the apparently irrational behavior of the prostitute was the general suspicion of doctors that infused the lower classes of nineteenth-century Italy and is still evident in rural areas today. Having only recently established their credentials with the upper and middle classes, physicians had yet to gain the confidence of the illiterate and poorly educated, who were unacquainted with the theoretical principles of modern medicine and frightened by the mysterious terminology of specialists.[100] In light of the slow progress of medical research, which established the germ theory and the need for antiseptics only in the last decades of the nineteenth century, the distrust of urban workers and rural peasants for "that upstart, the book-trained physician" was not surprising.[101] Treatment did not necessarily lead to good health but just as often worsened the condition of the patient. Furthermore, the doctors entrusted with providing medical care to the poor—the municipal doctors and, in the case of prostitutes, the examining doctors—were paid by the state and perceived by local communities as intruders similar to the carabiniere or the PS agent. Such feelings were not limited to the South, as this account of the reaction of Florentines to physicians sent to stem a cholera epidemic illustrates:

> As for the physicians, provided for them at the public expense, they look upon them with horror, and it is dangerous for them even to walk the streets. About a week since Dr.C, on his way to visit a patient, excited a veritable tumult. "Give it to him, give it to him," was cried out from the infuriated crowd. "He is one of the doctors paid by the municipality to poison the poor people.[102]

Years of foreign, authoritarian rule had planted among the popular classes a fear of all state functionaries, and the public health physician did not escape this opprobrium.

Peasants and urban workers, often recent migrants from the countryside, put their faith in traditional healers rather than in representatives of the modern medical profession. Often women rather than men, these "witches," as they were called by doctors, practiced an art handed down from previous generations.[103] Their prescriptions combined herbal recipes, which were sometimes efficacious, with ritual gestures and words that gave comfort to the patient.[104] Folk remedies for venereal disease ranged from the magical to the moderately effective. Included in the former category was, as Bolis defined it, "an abominable prejudice, unfortunately widespread among the lowest classes of society, who believe that contact with a female child or a young virgin can free a sick man from venereal disease."[105] For women, De Blasio described a Neapolitan cure that involved the application of threads from men's clothing to the syphilitic lesion.[106] Female healers—often old, retired prostitutes—also prescribed various drinks composed of herbs and weeds and solutions made of urine, wine, vinegar, lemon juice, or ammonia.[107] While specialists dismissed these medicines as useless, Gamberini did admit that the "simple and frequent ablutions" prostitutes habitually gave themselves to "remove the contaminating material" were quite useful in combating disease.[108] He recommended that all prostitutes wash with a solution of calcium chloride immediately after sexual intercourse.[109] Popular remedies also included lotions of mercury and potassium not dissimilar from those prescribed by professional physicians.[110] Despite the dubious value of most of these treatments, prostitutes tended to trust female healers, who were not only of the same sex and class but often of the same profession and therefore thought to harbor special wisdom gained from experience.[111]

Besides a generalized suspicion of doctors, prostitutes had particular reasons for resenting those of the Health Offices. Carrying out their duties in what was essentially a police station, examining doctors became identified with the PS agents who ordered the initial health checks for the newly inscribed prostitutes and routinely arrested any woman who missed her scheduled appointment. The fact that some Health Offices, like the first one in Bologna, were attached directly to prisons only strengthened their image as institutions of repression.[112] Furthermore, the attitudes of doctors toward prostitutes were hardly more positive than those of police. At the National Medical Congress in Rome in 1870, Castiglione expressed "profound disgust" when he had to report on "the moral and social conditions of that degraded part of the sex which we are used to calling gentle."[113] He argued that regulation should apply to prostitutes, and not their clients, since the behavior of the former was "immoral in itself" as well as a source of infection.[114] Doctors charged that prostitutes, "from ignorance, criminal inertia, and brutishness," showed no "tendency to have themselves cured."[115] Significantly, criticism on this account was directed mainly at poor women, whom one expert called "the most *prostitute* part of all prostitutes."[116] Labeling prostitutes as immoral and irresponsible, examining physicians shared the regulationist view that the state had to use force against prostitutes in order to protect public health. Understandably, this patronizing and authoritarian posture did not elicit respect and cooperation from their patients.

Prostitutes especially detested the vaginal examinations that concretely symbolized their subjugation to doctors and, in turn, the state. Middle-class feminists denounced the procedure as a type of rape that invaded women's privacy. In an age when many women hesitated to consult any type of male doctor, regulationists lamented that modesty prevented many "respectable" women from seeking treatment for venereal disease.[117] They discounted these refined sentiments in the case of those inscribed on police lists, explaining that "by the very nature of their work, prostitutes cannot feel, during the examination to which they are subjected, all of that shame which some [i.e., abolitionists] would like to see."[118] Yet, as Gamberini observed, prostitutes displayed an "aversion . . . even to the idea of submitting themselves to a health examination" and continually sought out new places to exercise their "dirty profession" in order to avoid the discipline of doctors.[119] While modesty cannot be discounted, prostitutes probably resented the vaginal examination more as a depersonalizing ritual that branded them as deviant. That the checks were not confined to the sick is evidenced by statistics from Bologna; over a twenty-four-year period, more than 50 percent of the women arrested for clandestine prostitution were neither registered nor found infected.[120] For those arrested but released, the submission to the vaginal examination lacked any medical justification but served instead as a warning against further involvement in activities unbecoming to their sex. From the point of view of the prostitute, then, no clear link existed between examination and good health but only between examination and harassment by the state. Since any woman arrested by police could be ordered to undergo a vaginal check, regardless of her state of health, it came to mark the passage in status from normal to deviant.[121] For the minority found to be sick, the next step was admission to the sifilicomio.

Until 1888 the sifilicomi provided care for both registered and clandestine prostitutes with venereal disease. Dating sometimes from the period before unification, the sifilicomi were systematized and put under state supervision by a ministerial decree of September 2, 1871 that complemented the Cavour law. At this time, there were 18 such institutions in the kingdom, a number that rose to 28 in 1884 and then dropped to 25 by the date of their formal abolition with the promulgation of the Crispi statute.[122] All nine major cities had their own sifilicomio with the exception of Venice, where, as one doctor put it, the law of 1871 remained "a dead letter."[123]

Most of the sifilicomi offered treatment only to prostitutes, as stipulated in Article 1 of the statute of 1871, but homogeneity was also lacking in this regard.[124] A few admitted "honest" women and children, while one, San Lazzaro in Turin, was exceptional in treating both sexes.[125] Theoretically, men and nonprostitute women could simply apply to their local hospital for cure, but many of these, run as opere pie, forbade the treatment of "immoral" diseases in their charters. Regulationists railed against this traditional, exclusory practice and charged that "the prejudice of refusing treatment to patients with venereal infections is a medieval remnant from the time when those sick with venereal disease were either not accepted or were required to link penance, like flogging, with their cure."[126] Lacking the political will to confront the church over the issue, the state instead began to establish special clinics for venereal disease connected to the universities and open to men and women. Pellizzari, for example, opened a model clinic in Siena with two "clean and well-ventilated" rooms, one for each sex, as well as smaller, individual rooms for the isolation of special patients such as adolescents who might be corrupted by association with adults.[127] Before 1888, though, such facilities for the civilian population were rare since only prostitutes, and secondarily soldiers, were believed responsible for the spread of venereal disease.

While prostitutes might be considered fortunate in having access to treatment, the sifilicomi resembled not so much hospitals as prisons. As one director admitted, no woman who was free and wealthy would ever seek entrance into his sifilicomio, which was nicknamed by the public the *ergastolo*, or "life sentence

191

prison."[128] Such a characterization was not without foundation, for many such institutions, like the one mentioned above, were in fact annexed to prisons; in communes lacking a sifilicomio, prostitutes were cured in prison infirmaries.[129] The experience of Bologna points up the ambiguous distinction between the sifilicomio and the prison. At the time of unification a sifilicomio attached to the prison of San Ludovico routinely provided medical care for prostitutes. After Gamberini was made health inspector of Emilia and complained that the prison facilities "were not appropriate to the requirements of good health," he began moving the seriously ill patients to the Hospital of San Orsola.[130] With the approval of the questore, who agreed that prostitutes should not be treated like prisoners, San Orsola took over the hospitalization of all women in 1861.[131] Even in the venereal disease ward at San Orsola, however, doctors kept prostitutes separated from other women "for reasons of morality."[132] Bolis explained that "this caution is indispensable for impeding a fatal moral contagion since unfortunately it happens many times that these hospices take in a woman who has simply gone astray and restore her to society a prostitute."[133] In effect, the special section for prostitutes became a new sifilicomio. The medical director of the sifilicomio of Padua, Breda, echoed this need for "numerous separations" among patients of different sexes, ages, and "social positions."[134]

Other features of the sifilicomi reinforced this identification with the prison. Unlike hospitals characterized by accessibility, the law of 1871 recommended that "the public sifilicomi be established whenever possible in isolated buildings outside the center of the city and in rarely frequented places."[135] The nonmedical administrators were to be chosen "preferably from among the employees of the prisons," and when possible the director of the local prisons would also serve as head of the sifilicomio.[136] Eight articles of the statute defined the duties of the gatekeeper, whose importance derived from the need to keep extraneous people out and patients in.[137] Clearly, visitors were not encouraged as in regular hospitals, and patients needed the permission of the director even to write letters to friends and relatives.[138] As these rules imply, neither admittance nor release was voluntary but always carried out under the armed guard of a PS agent. Bolis recommended that "both when entering and leaving the sifilicomio, prostitutes be driven in a closed carriage so that they do not cause spectacle or scandal."[139] No patient could leave without the "pertinent permission slip"; if she escaped, she was returned by police, using force if necessary.[140]

According to the law of 1871, the sifilicomi were to provide a clean, disciplined environment of work and reading to counter the previous immoral habits of the patients. The regulationist Sormani explained that "instead of being schools of immorality, the sifilicomi could become places not only of physical but also moral healing; the inmates would receive an education and initiation into work which would prepare and facilitate their redemption."[141] With this aim, the law stipulated that inmates make their beds each morning and take turns helping the servants perform their "lowly duties."[142] After the daily visit by the resident physician, they were to "occupy themselves in their own rooms with some type of work or service to the Establishment like preparing cord, bandages, and the like. They can also occupy themselves with their own work or with reading moral and educational books."[143] This orderly, disciplined atmosphere was to be reinforced with cleanliness and good care. Accordingly, the law contained minute instructions as to the quantity and quality of food, clothing, bedding, and linens for each patient.

In reality, however, prostitues experienced very different conditions. According to the commission report of 1885, the directors of a number of sifilicomi complained about the squalid physical state of their institutions. In Genoa only 8 unusable wool blankets were available for over 60 patients. At the "ergastolo" of Turin, "the food is served to the inmates in messtins without knives and forks. There is no dining room, and they have to eat while sitting on stools at the foot of their beds."[144] The situation at Foggia was even worse; the director lamented that his institution lacked "baths, facilities for vaginal douching, a dining room, a recreation area; nor are there separate rooms for women giving birth, for mothers with children, for visitors, for hanging clothes, for bathing and combing one's hair, for work, and for a more rational discipline; this multiplicity of things has given these places the reputation of being prisons for women."[145] As a result of unfit buildings, crowding, and dirt, diseases such as typhoid and rheumatic fever spread through various establishments, often killing more patients than did syphilis.[146] After visiting the sifilicomio at Naples, the nurse and feminist Jessie White Mario described it as "an institution worse than the evil which it claims to cure."[147]

Even organized work, which was considered the linchpin of moral reform, was lacking. Milan provided the only exception; there Gaetano Pini ran a model institution that employed its patients in needlework, sewing, and knitting. Yet Pini complained that he was not able to train the sick for other types of work beyond these customary female activities, since he was dealing with "women who are unaccustomed to paying close attention, unwilling to practice, disinclined to learn, and uninterested in earnings that require patience and toil."[148] Pini's experience seems to indicate that prostitutes undergoing cure harbored little desire to work or at least rebelled against the presumption that they should labor while in a hospital. It is also true, however, that by providing no opportunity, except in the case of Milan, for patients to learn new skills or even receive an elementary education, the sifilicomi completely failed in their aim of reform. Thus internment only served the negative purpose of quarantining a specific group considered too irresponsible to cure itself while completely neglecting any genuine effort to reintegrate these women into society. As the director of the institution at Lecce reported, "Of the many women who have been confined in this sifilicomio over many years, *not one*, as far as I know, has withdrawn from her depraved profession."[149]

Instead, Gozzoli reported, prostitutes recovering from venereal disease were undisciplined, lazy, and carried on "obscene conversations" to wile away the time.[150] After several visits to San Orsola, Bolis also claimed to have witnessed "disgusting scenes" and added that "although, due to my position, I have already had to confront profound immorality and shameful secrets, I must confess that the faces of these victims of debauchery are more repulsive than one could imagine."[151] Both Gozzoli and Bolis loudly denounced lesbian relationships among patients, which they asserted were widespread and which the former ascribed to "both satiety and the lack of men."[152] Quite a few directors reported to the commission of 1885 a problem with lesbianism in their sifilicomi; in Palermo, the practice even involved one of the nurses, who was "notorious" for "having indecent relations with the inmates."[153] It is difficult to judge the accuracy of these accounts since regulationists assumed that prostitutes, as sexual deviants, were prone to all sorts of excesses, heterosexual or homosexual. On the other hand, lesbianism may have offered one of the few pleasures and sources of affection available in the unpleasant, segregated world of the sifilicomio.

Patients fomented other less ambiguous disturbances like the food riot at San Orsola in 1875. According to the report sent to the questore, "The prostitutes, protesting the bad quality of the food and the way in which it was distributed, created an uproar by breaking plates, glasses, and windows."[154] In response, the authorities arrested twelve women and sent them to the prison infirmary of San Ludovico to continue their recovery. An investigation of the food, ordered by the minister of the interior, found the menu matched that of other hospital patients: broth and bread in the morning; soup, meat, bread, and wine at lunch; and broth and bread at night. The director of the Health Office, who was conducting the investigation, suggested two alternative explanations for the riot. First, maybe those women who were "young and of strong constitution" really were hungry since venereal disease "does not paralyze the desire to eat, but allows the sick person to consume as much as the healthy one."[155] Second, perhaps the food was just a pretext for fomenting disorder, though he failed to surmise what the real grievance might have been. He added that tumults in the sifilicomio were almost always caused by "the insufficiency or unsanitary condition of the food," implying that such incidents occurred with a certain frequency.[156] Insubordination by patients was not limited to Bologna, for other physicians such as Pellizzari of Pisa lamented that, "in a word, the sifilicomio seems to be a hell, and I feel like I am in an insane asylum."[157]

The fact that few inmates were actually bedridden may partly explain the high level of disorder in the sifilicomi. According to Gamberini's statistics for 1879–1888, only 17 percent, on the average, of all prostitutes in San Orsola had syphilis.[158] Cartenio Pini reported a slightly lower average of 12 percent for the years 1869–1884 in Florence. As Table 6.1 indicates, rates of syphilis ranged between 8 and 18 percent during that period.[159] For the

Table 6.1. *Rates of Syphilis for Prostitutes in the Sifilicomio of Florence*

	All patients	Number with syphilis	Percentage with syphilis
1869	424	56	13
1870	508	62	12
1871	556	89	16
1872	523	75	14
1873	439	50	11
1874	372	49	13
1875	347	42	12
1876	303	39	13
1877	241	30	12
1878	229	23	10
1879	231	25	11
1880	224	29	13
1881	199	35	18
1882	155	14	9
1883	250	34	14
1884	307	25	8
Average	332	42	12

SOURCE: Cartenio Pini, *Dati statistici dall'anno 1869 al 1887 sulle visite mediche nelle malattie venereo-sifilitiche in relazione alla questione igienica* (Florence: Monnier, 1887).

kingdom as a whole, the commission of 1885 computed a figure of 15 percent.[160] The majority of patients—who had gonorrhea, chancroid, or mild cases of syphilis—needed treatment but not hospitalization. The small number of deaths in the sifilicomi may have reinforced the notion among prostitutes that they were not very sick. For the nation as a whole, less than 1 percent of all inmates died while hospitalized, a figure that corresponds to those available for Bologna and Rome.[161] These statistics on types of disease and rates of death do not prove that prostitutes received high-quality treatment given the known gaps in medical knowledge of the period. Many cases of disease were certainly misdiagnosed. Yet they do suggest that prostitutes probably perceived their illnesses to be mild, which would have increased their resentment at being forcibly admitted to the sifilicomi.

Furthermore, patients tended to be young, thus presumably rather robust and energetic. Over 41 percent of the women admitted to San Orsola were under the age of twenty-one as compared with 27 percent of the registered prostitutes.[162] The long hospital stays, thirty days on the average in Bologna and even higher for the kingdom as a whole, only compounded the boredom and restlessness of inmates. In fact, many were "recidivists," that is, women undergoing cure for more than the first time in the same year. San Orsola admitted 36 percent of its patients more than once, and 8 percent were hospitalized at least four times a year (Table 6.2).[163] This phenomenon was not unique to Bologna, for the number of patients admitted to the sifilicomi each year for Italy as a whole always outnumbered by far the total on police lists.[164] Bolis estimated that over one-fourth of all prostitutes were, at any one time, under cure, while Gozzoli suggested the slightly lower figure of one-fifth.[165] Even if they exaggerated, it is clear that registered prostitutes spent long and often frequent periods of their lives in sifilicomi.

Like the rest of the population, prostitutes distrusted any type of hospital. Especially before the adoption of antiseptics, the concentration of patients with different diseases in an enclosed space spread, rather than circumscribed, infection. Perhaps this is why a popular Italian proverb taught that one went to the hospital only to die.[166] Until at least the turn of the twentieth century, all classes preferred treatment at home in the comforting atmosphere of family and friends. To resort to institutional care was a sign of destitution.[167] Prostitutes, then, had a general adversion to hospitals that was only reinforced by the prisonlike conditions of the sifilicomi.

According to Pellizzari, prostitutes were not so much careless about their health as outraged at the restriction on their freedom imposed by hospitalization. An abolitionist who tried to run his sifilicomio as humanely and efficiently as possible, he finally concluded that the tumultuous atmosphere within was a "willed disorder" on the part of "women . . . who consider themselves to be prisoners":

The only concern of a prostitute in the sifilicomio is to get out as soon as possible and to deceive the doctor. She pays no at-

Table 6.2. *Yearly Recidivism among Prostitutes
in the Sifilicomio of Bologna*

	Percentage of prostitutes admitted			
	Once	Twice	Three times	Four times or more
1864	69	18	6	7
1865	70	20	6	4
1866	69	18	7	6
1867	69	22	6	3
1868	63	20	7	10
1869	63	21	10	6
1870	62	19	12	7
1871	62	21	10	7
1872	64	19	12	5
1873	64	19	10	7
1874	70	10	10	10
1875	58	23	10	9
1876	60	16	10	14
1877	52	25	12	11
1878	61	20	9	10
1879	65	15	9	11
1880	67	20	7	6
1881	68	14	11	7
1882	62	25	8	5
1883	61	24	8	7
1884	66	15	9	10
1885	67	19	8	6
Average	64	19	9	8

SOURCE: Pietro Gamberini, *Rapporto politico-amministrativo clinico della prostituzione di Bologna* (Bologna: Gamberini e Parmeggiani, 1864–1885).

tention to her own health compared to her unbridled desire for liberty. And this feeling is so excessive in the prostitute that she loses, for the most part, or pretends to lose, all faith in the physician, whoever he be, because she considers him the last cog in that machine—which for her is an instrument of torture—that is made up of the surveillance on the brothel, the forced examination at the Health Office, and the coerced cure in the sifilicomio.[168]

Statistics of admissions to the sifilicomi seem to bear out Pellizzari. In scarcely more than ten years, the number of patients dropped over 50 percent, from 22,089 in 1875 to 10,425 in 1887.[169] Since rates of venereal disease did not drop correspondingly and the sifilicomi did not change their criteria and procedure for admission, it is plausible to hypothesize that prostitutes, just as they were increasingly resisting registration, were also eluding forced cure whenever possible.

Acts of protest in the sifilicomi brought punishment of various forms to their authors. Rather than simply releasing patients who objected to their treatment as in regular hospitals, sifilicomi submitted prostitutes to disciplinary measures copied from the prison. According to the law of 1871, directors could either deprive patients of part of their food (that is, put them on a bread-and-water diet) or lock them up in an isolated cell.[170] Such punishments could not exceed three days. In response to a request by the questore of Bologna for "a more precise definition of the limits of corporal punishment" for inmates who were "insubordinate, quarrelsome, and impertinent in words and deeds," the minister of the interior added the prohibition of visitors to the above list.[171] Although unnamed in official regulations, confinement in a straitjacket also ranked among the "severe chastisements" used by administrators; Bolis thought it necessary to keeping order in the sifilicomi.[172] Only Pellizzari suggested a less brutal solution to indiscipline but one also based on force: he refused to examine unruly patients to scare them into cooperation since, without treatment, they could neither be cured nor released.[173]

These severe failings prompted a radical change in the official approach to the prevention and cure of venereal disease, and the new philosophy was incorporated into the Crispi and Nicotera laws. Beginning in 1888 the High Council of Health "did not wish to limit prophylactic measures to prostitutes; rather, it considered all the sick as hotbeds of infection and desired that cure be vastly facilitated for all."[174] This new policy sprang not so much from idealism or abolitionist sentiment as from the recognition of "the minimal influence which regulated prostitution has on venereal and syphilitic contagion. . . . Today the aphorism no longer holds that regulated prostitution and venereal contagion exist in inverse proportion in the sense that an increase of one must coincide with

199

the diminution of the other and vice versa."[175] In short, rates of infection were often highest in provinces, such as Sicily, where the number of registered prostitutes was also rising. The new system that extended treatment to the entire population, then, "was not only in conformity with the principles of liberty and respect for the human personality, but also the most certain and efficacious means of prophylaxis."[176]

Since admittance was not voluntary, the staffs of the new dispensaries and hospital wards had to educate the public to recognize the symptoms of venereal disease and to take advantage of the available facilities without guilt or embarrassment. To this end, the dispensary of Bologna, once moved to its new location on Via Cartoleria in 1889, advertised its services "by means of signs posted at street corners throughout the City and through circulars to pharmacies, factories, and barracks."[177] In 1902 Santoliquido distributed to all prefects a poster drawn up by the Italian Committee of the International Society for Moral and Sanitary Prophylaxis. He instructed that they circulate the posters widely and hang them in dispensaries, brothels, hospitals, and factories. Intended to "instruct the public, with easy notions accessible to all, about the individual and collective dangers of venereal disease," the posters explained the symptoms, perils, and methods of transmission of the three infections.[178] The instructions were direct and factual, lacking emotional or moralistic overtones. Large cities received up to 9,000 copies, while smaller towns were sent at least 1,000. The project seemed to have been a success, since the Division of Public Health received numerous requests for additional posters.[179] Indeed, Dr. Pietro Ramazzotti pointed out the presence of these posters in his dispensary in Milan; in addition, he provided that "printed guidelines, written in a popular style, be given to all patients in order to limit the damage to each individual who is struck with the disease and to mitigate its sad effects."[180] The influx of sick to the dispensaries and hospital wards attests to at least partial success in this government campaign to raise public health consciousness among a population that had traditionally distrusted doctors and hospital care.

Registered prostitutes did not, however, fall fully into the purview of this new system of dispensaries and hospital wards but continued to be disciplined for the most part by the old guidelines. After 1888 biweekly examinations were still mandatory, although private fiduciary doctors, rather than public examining ones, carried them out. The latter checked the work of the former through unannounced visits to brothels, sometimes in response to complaints, most of which continued to come from the military (although, as Ramazzotti remarked, "The results of examinations given to prostitutes who had been designated by soldiers as a source of their contagion were, however, rarely positive).[181] During those years for which there are statistics, government physicians carried out 3,000–5,000 unannounced inspections, which, if evenly distributed across the kingdom, would have assured at least two per brothel.[182] But the frequency varied widely among cities; the health staff in Milan, under the direction of Ramazzotti, completed over 1,000 checks each year.[183] Furthermore, the law required that each registered prostitute submit not only to routine and unannounced examinations but also to treatment either in the new hospital wards or privately in her brothel; escape before recovery brought fine or arrest. Thus, the newly proclaimed principle of liberty applied mainly to those not on registration lists, including clandestine prostitutes. The reformed system, then, only alleviated, rather than eliminated, the discipline of the state over the health of the regulated prostitute. Alleviation meant provisions for private examination and cure as well as care in dispensaries and wards equal to that available to other civilian patients.

The new dispensaries for the cure of venereal disease were not as numerous as the Health Offices they replaced. Numbering 167 in 1889, they decreased to a low of 81 in 1903 and then rose again to over 100 by the end of the decade.[184] They were concentrated in the largest urban centers so that Naples boasted 10; Rome, 9; Milan, 5; and Palermo and Turin, 4 each. The smaller communes of Bologna, Florence, Venice, and Genoa had only 1.[185] Consolidation partially explained the initial drop in the numbers of dispensaries during the 1890s after special inspections of cities such as Naples and Palermo found some facilities almost totally unused.[186] The economic and budget crisis of that decade prompted the state to close down underused institutions. In addition, the process of transferring the major funding from the national gov-

Table 6.3. *Patients in the Dispensaries, Percentage by Sex*

	Women	Men
1889	22	78
1890	21	79
1891	22	78
1892	22	78
1893	22	78
1894	23	77
1895	24	76
1896	24	76
1897	25	75
1898	27	73
1899	26	74
1900	23	77
1901	24	76
1902	22	78
1903	23	77
1904	22	78
1905	23	77
1906	24	76
1907	25	75
1908	25	75
Average	23	77

SOURCE: Direzione Generale della Sanità Pubblica, *II Regolamento 27 luglio 1905, n. 487 e la profilassi delle malattie celtiche dal 1905 al 1908* (Rome: Manuzio, 1910), p. cxliii.

ernment to the communes, begun in the 1890s, forced the abandonment of dispensaries in the poorer communes. When the subsequent Health Statute of 1905 obliged all communes with a population exceeding 40,000 to support a dispensary, their numbers again rose.[187] The dispensaries fell into two categories: they were either "autonomous" establishments, often located in working-class neighborhoods, or outpatient clinics annexed to hospitals. In both, national guidelines required that treatment be provided free to all patients regardless of their economic status or the gravity of their disease.[188] Thus despite the municipalization of the dispensaries in fiscal terms, Rome maintained a certain control over

Table 6.4. *Occupation of Female Patients in the Dispensaries
(in percents)*

Occupation	1903	1904	1905	1906	1907	1908	Average
Prostitute	32.5	31.2	34.3	29.5	30.6	31.0	31.5
Housewife	30.7	35.6	38.1	38.0	40.2	41.3	37.3
Worker	12.9	12.0	10.7	14.4	12.0	12.7	12.5
Servant	10.5	10.7	8.0	8.8	9.0	6.3	8.9
Other	13.4	10.5	8.9	9.3	8.2	8.7	9.8

SOURCE: Direzione Generale della Sanità Pubblica, *Il Regolamento 27 luglio 1905, n. 487 e la profilassi delle malattie celtiche dal 1905 al 1908* (Rome: Manuzio, 1910), p. 84.

their functioning, which showed its continuing concern over the problem of venereal disease.

Because the new health philosophy guaranteed treatment for all citizens, the composition of the population examined in the dispensaries differed greatly from that examined in the Health Offices. Most striking, 77 percent of the patients were men (Table 6.3), a group that had never come under the purview of the old institutions.[189] For those years in which information is available, over half of the men were urban workers, followed by much smaller numbers of white-collar workers, farmers, liberal professionals, and students.[190] The male middle classes were not necessarily immune to venereal diseases, as these statistics might indicate, but probably sought private cure. Of the 23 percent of the patients who were women, slightly under one-third admitted to being prostitutes (Table 6.4).[191] This category was outnumbered only by housewives, some perhaps clandestine prostitutes, but most infected by their husbands. Urban workers and domestic servants followed at a distance. Rather than constituting the exclusive focus of examination as before 1888, prostitutes now made up under 10 percent of those receiving outpatient care. For both men and women in general, the patient population clustered around the age group of 21–25.[192] This was also true for prostitutes, reflecting the age structure of inscription lists.

The experience of being a patient at the dispensaries differed widely from that at the Health Offices. Physically, the buildings were cleaner and better equipped than their predecessors, and, therefore, more inviting. In his report of 1907 on one of the Milanese dispensaries, its director, Ramazzotti, proudly published a floorplan showing twelve rooms as well as photographs of the modern furnishings in several of these. He was especially pleased with the newly installed telephone, "which has proved extremely useful for quick communication, when needed, with the Provincial Health Office; with pharmacies; with colleagues who specialize in eye and throat diseases, in regard to patients being treated for common illnesses; with colleagues who live in the countryside; and, when required, with the municipal office of surveillance, etc."[193] He admitted that it had been a problem finding a landlord who would rent an office to receive the victims of venereal disease, but he was highly satisfied with the final site on Via Borromei. Administrators in Bologna faced similar resistance when, in 1888, they sought to move the new dispensary from Via Pratello, the street on which the prison of San Ludovico was located. Established originally in the quarters of the old Health Office, the dispensary was still identified with prostitutes rather than "as a place of free cure for all."[194] Finally, in August 1889, the questore notified his superiors that a new location had been found on Via Cartoleria.[195] While the transition from the Health Offices to the dispensaries was not always smooth, Santoliquido could report by 1899 that "the premises of the dispensaries are generally in satisfactory hygienic condition."[196]

New internal regulations sought further to comfort the prospective patient, who now had to be attracted voluntarily rather than admitted by force. To assure separation of the sexes, dispensaries provided two distinct waiting rooms and scheduled appointments for men and women in alternate hours or on alternate days. Ideally, doctors were to receive patients one at a time, although this was not always possible in the case of men, who flocked in great numbers to the dispensaries during the short breaks available from work.[197] To minimize embarrassment, physicians did not request the names of patients but simply assigned a number to each. Instead, admission forms recorded other types of information less personal but useful to the state for compiling statistics: the age, profession, sex, and disease of the patient as well as the dates of the first and last visits, the number of examinations, and

Table 6.5. *Diseases of Prostitutes in the Dispensaries*
(in percents)

	Gonorrhea	Chancroid	Syphilis	Other (non-venereal)
1903	28	27	31	14
1904	27	25	38	10
1905	21	26	38	15
1906	23	27	38	12
1907	24	28	38	10
1908	26	28	38	8
Average	25	27	37	11

SOURCES: Direzione Generale della Sanità Pubblica, *Malattie infettive e diffusive dall'anno 1901 al 1904 e profilassi delle malattie celtiche dal 1902 al 1904* (Rome: Manuzio, 1907), pp. 162, 166; idem, *II Regolamento 27 luglio 1905, n. 487 e la profilassi delle malattie celtiche dal 1905 al 1908* (Rome: Manuzio, 1910), pp. 70, 74, 78, 82.

the results of treatment.[198] Once diagnosed, the sick received prescriptions for medicine on which it was forbidden to write the name of the dispensary or the nature of the disease.[199] Through such precautions to protect anonymity, physicians hoped to encourage even those victims of venereal disease who were ashamed of their illness to seek treatment.

The dispensaries offered treatment for all three venereal diseases, although doctors advised hospitalization for the most serious cases. Nevertheless, 37 percent of the prostitutes who sought treatment at the dispensaries had syphilis, the most harmful of the three, as opposed to 27 percent with chancroid, 25 percent with gonorrhea, and 11 percent with non-venereal skin diseases (Table 6.5).[200] In fact, female patients in general showed higher rates of syphilis than men, who tended to have milder infections.[201] This difference, which also shows up in Ramazzotti's statistics for Milan, may be explained by the general reticence of woman to seek medical attention for "immoral" diseases unless very serious.[202] The fact that only 23 percent of the dispensary patients were female underscores the hesitation of women to seek treatment for venereal infection, perhaps because this treatment necessitated the embarrassing vaginal examination. Likewise, women were less able than men to detect gonorrhea since the symptomatic lesions were internal for the former and external for the latter. Statistics on length of treatment reinforce the hypothesis that female patients suffered graver illnesses than men. On the average, women made 11 visits to the dispensary before apparent cure, while men returned only 9 times.[203] The number of appointments per patient seemed to have ranged widely, though, among dispensaries, for Ramazzotti reported a much higher average—18—for patients at his dispensary in Milan.[204] Although he treated proportionately fewer cases of syphilis than the national average, he was sensitive to popular panic about the disease: "Very circumspect in announcing to our patients that they have syphilis, we always take care to support and encourage them in case they have exaggerated apprehensions and fears, assuring them of the efficacy of the treatment."[205] He added that for syphilis the cure required three to four years including "the required pauses" when the symptoms were in recession.[206]

All evidence points to a distinctly improved relationship between doctors and patients, including prostitutes, in the dispensaries compared with the Health Offices. According to a government report of 1895, in all the major cities "the diffidence of the public has disappeared and they flock to the dispensaries in ever greater numbers."[207] Official statistics support this observation: the number of patients treated rose from 51,948 in 1889 to a high of 86,215 in 1900, although it dropped back to 63,209 by 1908.[208] While administrators voiced concern in 1896 about the "relatively low number of women which have recourse to [the dispensaries]," the proportion of female patients did rise slightly from 22 to 25 percent of the total during the two decades after their establishment in 1888.[209] Among prostitutes, those who benefited most were the clandestine, since the inscribed were usually hospitalized or cured privately in their brothels. Thus by the 1900s between 3,000 and 4,000 clandestine prostitutes were voluntarily seeking cure in government dispensaries. At a time when registration rates had fallen to under 6,000, two-thirds that number of clandestine prostitutes were being cared for outside the regulation system. This is a noteworthy sign of the increasing trust the doctors were winning from hitherto hostile prostitutes.

Besides increased use, the calm atmosphere in the dispensaries also suggests that prostitutes' resistance to public health physicians was fading. In response to a nationwide survey conducted by the minister of the interior, provincial doctors reported that the dispensaries in all nine major cities functioned well.[210] They praised the medical directors of the dispensaries, such as Oliviero Benigni of Bologna, who "insures that the service is well run and who justly merits a word of commendation."[211] Raffaello Zampa, provincial doctor of Rome, even expressed surprise at the cooperative spirit of the prostitutes undergoing treatment, noting that "they are not generally among the most well-mannered and docile" when hospitalized.[212] The only sour note was sounded by a special inspector of Naples, who found that several dispensaries in that city did not live up to "standards of decorum and hygiene" and that the patients lacked any sense of "decency, order, and discipline."[213] But such criticism was rare compared with the more negative reports on the old Health Offices. By 1899 Santoliquido could write that "all [dispensaries] are characterized by order and discipline, and the diligence of the personnel is praiseworthy."[214]

The hospital wards for venereal disease never elicited the same unqualified admiration as their companion institutions, the dispensaries. But to both doctors and prostitutes, they were a decided improvement over the unpopular sifilicomi. Although the Health Offices closed immediately in 1888, the transfer of services from the sifilicomi to the wards proceeded more slowly since hospitalized patients could not be turned out onto the street until new facilities were built. Owing to budget problems in the 1890s and foot dragging by administrators loyal to the old Cavour law, the abolition of the sifilicomi was not completed until 1901.[215] Meanwhile, the number of new wards, which were annexed to communal hospitals, leaped from 45 in 1888 to 115 in 1901; after a slight drop during the next few years, the total finally reached 124 in 1908.[216] According to the High Council of Health, it was "indispensable . . . to multiply the venereal disease wards and to avoid their concentration in a few populous cities, to which it is not always easy to rush in order to request recovery in a hospital."[217] By the turn of the century, the council began favoring treatment in the wards, rather than the dispensaries, since it assured the total isolation of infectious patients. Only in 1912 was this policy reversed after rising costs forced administrators

Table 6.6. *Patients in the Hospital Wards, Percentage by Sex*

	Women	Men
1895	62	38
1896	65	35
1897	67	33
1898	70	30
1899	63	37
1900	63	37
1901	63	37
1902	63	37
1903	65	35
1904	59	41
1905	57	43
1906	53	47
1907	48	52
1908	46	54
Average	60	40

SOURCE: Direzione Generale della Sanità Pubblica, *Il Regolamento 27 luglio 1905, n. 487 e la profilassi delle malattie celtiche dal 1905 al 1908* (Rome: Manuzio, 1910), p. 150.

in Rome to limit hospitalization to the most highly contagious and, in the case of men, to those who really represented "a social danger."[218]

The quantity of patients requesting admittance—or in the case of registered prostitutes, those forcibly admitted—to the wards rose in seeming correlation with the growth of available beds. From 9,696 in 1895, their numbers increased to 12,745 in 1899, only to drop slightly over several years until a second spurt reached 15,102 in 1908.[219] Unlike the dispensaries, where men predominated, the majority of ward patients—60 percent—were women (Table 6.6).[220] Only slowly losing their identification with the hated sifilicomi, the wards did not at first attract large numbers of men. As the era of the Cavour law faded and the wards gained a more positive reputation, the proportion of male patients rose to over 50 percent by 1908. Unfortunately, administrators did not routinely collect detailed statistics on the professions of ward inmates as they did for those treated at the dispensaries. Only for 1899 do sources reveal the percentage of prostitutes in

Table 6.7. *Diseases Treated in the Hospital Wards*
(in percent)

	Gonorrhea	Chancroid	Syphilis	Other (non-venereal)
1905	37	28	30	5
1906	39	26	30	5
1907	38	27	30	5
1908	39	25	32	4
Average	38	26	31	5

SOURCE: Direzione Generale della Sanità Pubblica, *Il Regolamento 27 luglio 1905, n. 487 e la profilassi delle malattie celtiche dal 1905 al 1908* (Rome: Manuzio, 1910), p. clii.

relation to the total population hospitalized. Out of 12,745 patients in all the wards throughout the kingdom, 3,153, or one-fourth, were prostitutes; of the women, 39 percent were prostitutes.[221] If these figures were typical of other years, prostitutes were a much more significant and visible group in the wards than in the dispensaries. This high rate of hospitalization reflected a continuing attitude among administrators that prostitutes, unlike the rest of the population, invited and deserved internment and surveillance because of immorality and irresponsibility in spreading disease.

Although specific information on the state of health of prostitutes in the wards is lacking, statistics on the general patient population are useful since prostitutes formed such a large part (Table 6.7). Syphilis cases made up only 31 percent of the diseases treated; gonorrhea, 38 percent; chancroid, 26 percent; and non-venereal infections, 5 percent.[222] Thus the wards, although intended to take on the more severe cases, did not admit a higher rate of syphilitic patients than the dispensaries. Treatment averaged 24 days, at least a week less than in the old sifilicomi.[223] According to the doctors directing the wards, each year they released 68 percent of their patients in perfect health and another 20 percent after substantial improvement (Table 6.8). A meager .6 percent died while hospitalized.[224] It is interesting that while the proportion that died fell between 1895 and 1908, so did the percentage cured. In compensation, the group with "improved"

209

Table 6.8. *Condition of Patients in the Hospital Wards*

	Cured	Improved	Not Improved	Continuing in Treatment	Died
1895	69	19	4	7	.6
1896	71	17	3	8	.7
1897	73	15	3	8	.8
1898	73	15	3	8	.7
1899	75	14	3	7	.8
1900	74	14	4	7	.8
1901	70	18	4	8	.7
1902	65	24	3	7	.7
1903	67	21	4	7	.6
1904	66	22	4	7	.6
1905	61	28	3	7	.6
1906	60	29	4	7	.5
1907	61	29	4	6	.4
1908	62	28	4	6	.4
Average	68	20	4	7	.6

SOURCES: Ispettorato Generale della Sanità Pubblica, *Malattie infettive e diffusive e profilassi della sifilide e delle malattie veneree: Anno 1899* (Rome: Mantellate, 1901), p. 127; Direzione Generale della Sanità Pubblica, *Malattie infettive e diffusive dall'anno 1901 al 1904 e profilassi delle malattie celtiche dal 1902 al 1904* (Rome: Manuzio, 1907, p. lii; idem, *Il Regolamento 27 luglio 1905, n. 487 e la profilassi delle malattie celtiche dal 1905 al 1908* (Rome: Manuzio, 1910), p. clii, cliii.

NOTE: The numbers in the columns are percentages and do not add across to 100 because death rates were less than 1 percent.

health rose. Perhaps the introduction of the Wasserman test explains the decline in the cure rate, for with it doctors could better distinguish the absolute extinction of the syphilitic spirochete from simple remission. Even with the progress in diagnostic techniques, one must be wary of these optimistic statistics reported by physicians. Not all doctors used the new methods, and those who did often substituted mere observation for bacteriological testing when the case seemed clearcut. But it is clear that most prostitutes were not bedridden with severe syphilitic infections, remained less than a month, and rarely died while interned.

While the wards represented a great improvement over the sifilicomi, only part of the benefits accrued to prostitutes. Like the dispensaries, the wards offered anonymity to minimize embarrassment and to "remove the notion of a prison."[225] The Health Statute of 1905 prescribed that "the female patients who are recovering in the wards for venereal disease shall not be designated publicly in the hospice by their last names, but with their first names or another name and the number of their bed. In running the ward, the director must scrupulously avoid anything which might offend their sense of propriety and personal sensibilities."[226] Prostitutes profited little from these provisions for anonymity, though, since another article of the statute ordered that "in these health care institutions, [the director] will see to the separation of the prostitutes from the other women."[227] Correspondence from Bologna confirms that the director of the ward at San Orsola, Dr. Maiocchi, did indeed implement this provision "for reasons of discipline."[228] Consequently, in the new, liberalized wards, prostitutes did not escape being labeled as deviant and segregated from the "honest" women they might morally contaminate. The specter of the sifilicomio lingered.

Yet, in comparison to their predecessors, the wards elicited general applause from government reports. In response to the survey of the minister of the interior in 1896, the provincial doctors in eight of the nine major cities wrote that their local facilities functioned regularly under competent directors.[229] Only Palermo complained of a multitude of problems: inadequate equipment, unsatisfactory sanitation, and too few beds.[230] The last prompted doctors either to assign two prostitutes to one bed, which was unhygienic, or to turn away those in need of cure. As the number of wards multiplied, shortages of beds and the need to limit admissions no longer plagued administrators. Sick prostitutes could now enjoy treatment in a facility that was truly a hospital rather than a prison or a workhouse. While separated from other patients, prostitutes did not have to make their beds, assist the maids, or spin thread in order to imbibe the work ethic. No longer aiming at moral reform, the wards simply focused on curing the body. Did regulated prostitutes react any more favorably to hospitalization in the wards than they had to the sifilicomi?

One indicator of prostitutes' attitudes might be found in the comparison of how many requested private cure in their own brothels as opposed to admittance to the wards. According to

Ramazzotti, "Few in number are the women [prostitutes] who voluntarily or at the advice of a physician have recourse to the hospital for cure."[231] Statistics for 1899, the only year for which they are available, seem at first glance to contradict this statement. For Italy as a whole, 74 percent of those prostitutes diagnosed as having venereal disease by confidential doctors underwent cure in the wards rather than privately in their brothels.[232] Yet almost half were admitted by force so that, in fact, only 38 percent of the total number of prostitutes in hospitals had voluntarily requested inpatient care. Perhaps even more would have chosen home cure if police had been disposed to grant the necessary permission. But the PS in most communes, usually with the support of health authorities, tended to restrict the right of prostitutes to undergo private treatment since "one can have no faith in the promise of the sick that they will abstain from prostitution nor on the other hand is the PS able to exercise effective surveillance to this end."[233] Thus the high proportion of prostitutes undergoing cure in the wards was probably due as much to police pressure as voluntary request.[234]

The behavior of prostitutes in the wards also provides a clue to their opinion of the new system. The evidence is mixed and supports the conclusion of the director of public health after he had surveyed the reports of 1896 from all the provinces: "In general . . . where wards for venereal disease exist, they function well, although there are always some difficulties in maintaining discipline due to the special nature of the patients; all the same, there is no comparison with the insubordination which characterized the coercive cure in the ancient sifilicomi."[235] In short, complaints of misbehavior and rebellion continued but much less frequently.[236] For example, a long letter from the prefect of Florence to his superiors in Rome detailed the conduct of one unruly prostitute in the ward of Ospedale S. Maria Nuova. In the last four years, this woman, Elvira Landi, had been arrested seven times for violating the prostitution statutes, public health laws, or penal code. With a history of violent behavior during her former visits to the wards, this time she attacked other patients when not being watched. When confined to a private room, she hanged herself. Although revived initially, she died the next day.[237] This highly dramatic incident was not typical, however, of the routine and petty disruption prostitutes, bored and rarely bedridden, fomented in the wards. In some hospitals, prostitutes continued the old practice of slipping out before the end of their treatment, but in others this problem had disappeared.[238]

In the face of insubordination, doctors lacked the wide array of repressive measures available under the statute of 1871 on the sifilicomi. Although second-class patients, prostitutes could no longer be confined to small cells with bread and water or put in straitjackets. In frustration, several directors requested permission from the Division of Public Health to send rebellious prostitutes to prison infirmaries for cure. A series of correspondence among this office, the Division of Prisons, and the Council of State debated the legality of this solution.[239] Although the director of prisons noted that the penitentiary infirmaries were not well equipped to treat venereal disease, both he and the director of public health agreed that they could accommodate prostitutes. According to the Council of State, however, authorities could not send prostitutes who had not been already sentenced for a crime to prison. Undisciplined conduct in the wards did not constitute a grave enough offense for imprisonment. The council charged the Ministry of the Interior with trying to reinstate the Cavour law by giving police powers to doctors. Personnel in the wards, then, had to fall back on persuasion or expulsion of troublemakers to keep order. They retained more power in the case of escaped prostitutes, who could be arrested and returned by police. But some physicians, such as Tommasoli of Palermo, refused to readmit women who had disrupted the ward previously.[240] In conclusion, while the wards did not live up to the rhetoric of liberty and equality of health care for prostitutes, they did lighten the repressive hand of the state. In response, the cooperation of prostitutes with ward doctors increased although not to the extent as in the dispensaries, where they were no longer treated as a separate group.

Evaluation of Public Health Policy

It is difficult to evaluate the overall effectiveness of the medical reforms instituted in 1888. The most concrete indicator—the rate of venereal disease in the population—is not readily accessible.

Table 6.9. *Rates of Venereal Disease in the Military*
(in percents)

	All types of venereal disease	Syphilis only[a]
1867–1869	14.7	
1870	16.0	
1871	13.6	
1872	15.2	
1873	13.5	
1874	11.9	
1875	11.1	
1876	11.4	
1877	10.2	
1878	10.7	
1879	11.5	
1880	11.9	
1881	12.4	
1882	11.0	
1883	10.2	
1884	9.5	
1885	8.6	
1886	8.2	
1887	8.4	.56
1888	7.9	.59
1889	9.9	.86
1890	10.4	1.37
1891	10.3	1.40
1892	10.0	1.45
1893	9.7	1.25
1894	9.2	1.23
1895	8.5	1.20
1896	9.7	1.32
1897	9.3	1.29
1898	9.6	1.33
1899	9.3	1.46
1900	9.0	1.35
1901	8.7	1.40
1902	9.2	1.45
1903	8.5	1.22
1904	8.9	1.34
1905	8.1	1.50

Table 6.9. (continued)

	All types of venereal disease	Syphilis only[a]
1906	7.8	1.40
1907	7.5	1.18

SOURCE: Direzione Generale della Sanità Pubblica, *Il Regolamento 27 luglio 1905, n. 487 e la profilassi delle malattie celtiche dal 1905 al 1908* (Rome: Manuzio, 1910), pp. 152, 153.

[a] Data was not broken down by disease until 1887.

Even Santoliquido admitted that "we do not possess secure, scientific data which could guide us to a firm judgment as to the amount of venereal disease present each year in the population."[241] The state did not require that doctors report incidences of infection except in the case of prostitutes, soldiers, and wet nurses. The statistics of the sifilicomi, dispensaries, and wards do not offer adequate substitutes because the first only admitted prostitutes and the latter two had no record of those patients, presumably from the upper and middle classes, who consulted private doctors. Furthermore, as Santoliquido pointed out, the increasing numbers of admittances to the dispensaries and wards reflected not necessarily rising rates of venereal disease but growing public trust in the new institutions. Once a facility and its physician gained a good reputation, the sick flocked to it willingly. As an alternative measure of public health, he suggested two more reliable indicators: the diffusion of venereal disease in the military and the mortality from syphilis.

Examined regularly like the prostitutes, soldiers with venereal disease were not likely to escape detection, and the Ministry of War kept continuous health records on its troops. Furthermore, "since they are spread throughout the entire kingdom, in the large and small towns, and have the same probability of infection as the rest of the population," military personnel constituted a relatively reliable sample from which the state could project larger trends.[242] According to military statistics, rates of venereal disease dropped from 14.7 percent in the years 1867–1869 to 7.5 percent in 1907 (Table 6.9).[243] The decline was not consis-

Table 6.10. *Rates of Syphilis in Garrisons of Eight Communes, 1899*

City	Size of garrison	Number with syphilis	Percentage with syphilis
Bologna	7,133	72	1.0
Florence	6,915	58	.8
Genoa	8,895	51	.6
Milan	11,077	86	.8
Naples	15,452	451	2.9
Palermo	9,129	214	2.3
Rome	13,990	258	1.9
Turin	15,801	161	1.0

SOURCE: Ispettorato Generale della Sanità Pubblica, *Malattie infettive e diffusive e profilassi della sifilide e delle malattie veneree: Anno 1899* (Rome: Mantellate, 1901), p. 133.

NOTE: No garrison was stationed in Venice.

tent, however, for there was a short reversal around 1889–1890, possibly owing to the confusion associated with the introduction of the Crispi legislation. The picture was not so bright in the case of syphilis alone; there the figures, after 1890, oscillated between 1.2 and 1.5 percent.[244] Provincial breakdowns showed syphilis to be more widespread in southern communes, like Naples and Palermo, than in the North (Table 6.10).

Mortality rates, only available for the kingdom as a whole beginning in 1888, show a pattern similar to that for veneral disease in the military: an initial decline, temporary reversal in the early 1890s, and then a steady drop (Table 6.11). For every 10,000 inhabitants, .64 died of syphilis in 1888 as opposed to .52 in 1907.[245] Figures for the sixty-nine provincial capitals were triple those for the nation as a whole, reflecting the relative scarcity of syphilis in the countryside. Of the nine major cities, Naples and Rome turned in the highest totals, while Turin, Bologna, and Venice came last (Table 6.12). When compared with other fatal diseases, syphilis exhibited a rather low mortality rate.[246] Tuberculosis was at least twenty times as deadly, while typhus, diptheria, measles, malaria, scarlatina, malignant tumors, small pox, and pellegra also killed significantly more of the nineteenth-

Table 6.11. *Mortality Rates from Syphilis*
(per 10,000)

	Kingdom	Provincial capitals only (69)
1888	.64	1.82
1889	.69	2.06
1890	.71	2.05
1891	.73	2.15
1892	.71	2.10
1893	.77	2.25
1894	.76	2.11
1895	.74	2.10
1896	.73	2.01
1897	.70	1.97
1898	.70	2.04
1899	.73	2.15
1900	.65	1.85
1901	.60	1.72
1902	.61	1.78
1903	.58	1.75
1904	.56	1.64
1905	.60	1.77
1906	.54	1.52
1907	.52	1.55

SOURCES: Direzione Generale della Sanità Pubblica, *Il Regolamento 27 luglio 1905, n. 487 e la profilassi delle malattie celtiche dal 1905 al 1908* (Rome: Manuzio, 1910), pp. 164; idem, *Annuario statistico italiano* (Rome: G. Bertero, 1912), p. 35.

century population. Only the last two declined sharply enough by the first decade of the twentieth century to become finally less lethal than syphilis.[247] The relative mildness of syphilis is striking in light of the enormous government program erected to combat it, as well as the other two nonmortal venereal diseases. From the point of view of public health, state funding should have been earmarked for tuberculosis, not syphilis. Syphilis symbolized other dangers to the state besides the purely hygienic one.

Fear of national degeneration from "hereditary" syphilis focused attention on the statistics of infant and child mortality. As early as 1887 the state demanded that all babies admitted to

Table 6.12. *Mortality Rates from Syphilis in Nine Communes (per 10,000)*

City	1896–1900	1901	1902	1903	1904	1905	1906	1907	1908
Bologna	2.4	.8	.6	—	.6	.4	.6	.8	.9
Florence	1.6	.9	.9	1.2	1.0	.9	1.0	.8	.9
Genoa	1.4	2.1	1.4	1.2	1.4	1.2	.9	1.4	.9
Milan	2.8	1.5	1.9	2.8	1.3	1.3	1.1	.6	.6
Naples	3.4	2.6	3.2	3.2	3.1	3.3	2.5	2.6	2.2
Palermo	1.2	.7	.4	.7	.8	.5	.5	.8	.7
Rome	2.5	3.0	3.4	2.7	2.5	2.4	1.9	1.8	1.9
Turin	.8	.8	1.0	.4	.5	.4	.7	.5	.7
Venice	.9	.9	.9	.6	.8	1.2	1.3	.9	.7
Kingdom	.7	.6	.6	.6	.6	.6	.5	.5	.5

SOURCE: Direzione Generale della Sanità Pubblica, *Il Regolamento 27 luglio 1905, n. 487 e la profilassi delle malattie celtiche dal 1905 al 1908* (Rome: Manuzio, 1910), p. clx.

foundling homes be accompanied by a certificate attesting to the absence of syphilis in the mother.[248] Alarmed that infected children might contaminate commercial wet nurses, or vice versa, the Division of Public Health ordered surveillance on wet nurses and began to require that all doctors report cases of syphilis contracted by these women.[249] As historian Gianna Pomata has argued, the alarmism about syphilis served as an excuse to discipline a group of women whom doctors classified as analogous to prostitutes on account of their "promiscuous" nursing of many babies.[250] It also prompted the government to gather mortality rates for syphilis by age group (Table 6.13). According to official figures, an outstanding 70 percent of all deaths from syphilis occurred in children aged five and under, with by far the largest proportion taking place before the age of one.[251] This supposed concentration of deaths in the early years throws suspicion on the published mortality rates inasmuch as the cause of infant deaths has always been notoriously difficult to diagnose. Misdiagnosis may have inflated these government statistics. Taken at face value, syphilis declined steadily among children, a possible indicator of the success of the public health program.[252] On the other hand, improvements in diagnostic techniques may have accounted for the apparent declining incidence of a disease that had

Table 6.13. *Mortality Rates from Syphilis by Age*

Year[a]	Total number of deaths	Percentage by age	
		Five and under	Over five
1888	1,907	77	23
1889	2,084	78	22
1890	2,134	75	25
1891	2,233	75	25
1895	2,313	72	28
1896	2,307	72	28
1897	2,205	69	31
1898	2,247	69	31
1899	2,354	71	29
1900	2,117	67	33
1901	1,965	67	33
1902	2,009	66	34
1903	1,919	67	33
1904	1,849	66	34
1905	1,986	65	35
1906	1,814	63	37
1907	1,757	63	37

SOURCE: Direzione Generale della Sanità Pubblica, *Il Regolamento 27 luglio 1905, n. 487 e la profilassi delle malattie celtiche dal 1905 al 1908* (Rome: Manuzio, 1910), p. 165.
[a]Data was not collected by age for the years 1892–1894.

never really been widespread. Until the Wasserman test, fear of congenital syphilis prompted doctors to attribute other types of death to this cause.

A cautious assessment of the military and mortality figures suggests that venereal disease in general was decreasing while no clear pattern emerged for syphilis. Did the health of prostitutes follow this same pattern? Although the available statistics are limited to the decade from 1898 to 1908, they show a marked decline in the proportion of registered prostitutes who underwent cure each year: from 100 percent to 56 percent (Table 6.14).[253] Even at its high point, this period represented an improvement over the era of the sifilicomi, when the number of patients treated annually always exceeded the total of registered prostitutes, and recidivism

219

Table 6.14. *Rates of Venereal Disease for Registered Prostitutes*

| | Number of registered prostitutes | Percentage with venereal disease | | |
		Gonorrhea and chancroid	Syphilis	Total[a]
1898	5,244	69	32	101
1899	5,518	61	29	90
1900	5,548	56	24	80
1901	5,405	59	22	81
1902	5,842	60	21	81
1903	6,208	53	20	73
1904	5,847	50	18	68
1905	5,989	47	19	66
1906	6,685	38	18	56
1907	6,645	42	15	57
1908	6,196	41	15	56

SOURCE: Direzione Generale della Sanità Pubblica, *Il Regolamento 27 luglio 1905, n. 487 e la profilassi delle malattie celtiche dal 1905 al 1908* (Rome: Manuzio, 1910), p. cxxxix.

[a]The total percentage can exceed 100 because some prostitutes were recidivists, that is, they were diagnosed as having venereal disease more than once during the same year.

was high. Furthermore, the percentage of prostitutes diagnosed as having syphilis, as opposed to gonorrhea or chancroid, fell from 31 to 27, although it should be remembered that only 10–20 percent of the patients in the sifilicomi had been admitted for syphilis.[254] Of course, these figures must be regarded with caution since positive diagnosis was not possible in the early period. But, as in the military, an overall decline of venereal disease did correlate with the period of reform begun in 1888.

Finally, the liberalized system benefited the clandestine as well as the registered prostitute. For clandestine prostitutes, treatment was purely voluntary, which encouraged them to seek care in large numbers at the dispensaries. By revealing their profession to be prostitution, they showed their trust in the doctors and their conviction that the health system was in fact separate from the police, so that requesting care would no longer bring arrest. Although police and even some physicians continued to moan about the threat to public health posed by undisciplined clandestine prostitutes, these women probably had more contact with the medical system than ever before. From the medical point of view, the "problem" of clandestine prostitution was fading.

The available statistics on venereal disease, while not always consistent, in no way demonstrate that the easing of regulation after 1888 worsened the health either of the population as a whole or of regulated and clandestine prostitutes. The reform also benefited the public health bureaucracy, for it strengthened its power in relation to its rival, the PS. Under the Cavour law, regulationist and abolitionist doctors alike lamented the subordination of medical personnel to police in the Health Offices. Castiglione, for example, denounced as early as 1872 "that hybrid creation, the Health Office, where a delegate of the PS rules or pretends to rule the hygiene section and the medical examinations as well, so that the doctor ends up becoming his subordinate and almost an accomplice in his errors and abuses [of authority]."[255] With the Crispi law, physicians finally threw off the heavy hand of the police as they became sole arbiters of the dispensaries and wards. Armed with an innovative and progressive policy, the Division of Public Health managed to strip the PS of many of its former prerogatives over prostitutes. By clinging conservatively to the ideology of regulation and denying or excusing any errors committed in its name, the police let the domain of health surveillance slip out of its control. PS administrators recognized their defeat, for according to a government report of 1899, they "looked askance" at the larger role assumed by the health authorities and "protested with indolence."[256] Police continued to patrol the closed houses and arrest streetwalkers in the name of public order and morality. But by medicalizing the issue of prostitution, public physicians had shifted the focus of government policy from police surveillance over registered prostitutes to a medical discipline over all potential victims of venereal disease, that is, the entire population of the kingdom.

In contrast with police, public health doctors changed and modestly improved their relationship with prostitutes between unification and World War I. Physicians no longer submitted women arrested for clandestine prostitution to vaginal examinations as had been routine before 1888 in cases like those of Ballarini and Garagnomi. Streetwalkers now made their own deci-

221

sions as to when and where to seek medical advice. Most took advantage of the new outpatient dispensaries, which treated them and other patients as equals. This voluntary use of the dispensaries by clandestine prostitutes was perhaps the major triumph of the post-1888 health reforms. It showed that freedom rather than force promised to raise the health consciousness of prostitutes. Legal prostitutes practicing in the closed houses enjoyed much less liberty but had the option of choosing private care. Recovery in the new hospital wards proved less humiliating than in the old sifilicomi and therefore elicited greater cooperation from convalescent prostitutes. By treating "respectable" citizens too, the dispensaries and wards contributed to narrowing the social distance between prostitutes and other women. In these ways, the reforms of the Division of Public Health partially dismantled the policy of enclosure, discipline, and surveillance that had constituted a barrior between prostitutes and the rest of society. Yet the medicalization of the problem of prostitution by doctors brought only a temporary period of mitigated regulation; the system returned to repression under Mussolini and was not abolished until the passage of the Merlin Law in 1958.

Conclusion

What does prostitution signify, as it is organized today? It signifies an institution set apart by laws conceived and worked out by men; prostitutes are an abject class, whose only destiny is to satisfy the most brutal male instincts; and until those women who have, by chance, escaped such ignomity raise their voice to protest this male insolence and to extend a sisterly hand to unlucky fallen women, we cannot hope for repentance on the part of the former or rehabilitation of the latter.

Jesse White Mario, 1877

Registration on police lists, which brings serious consequences to a woman and her family, constitutes a degradation of female dignity because the partners of prostitutes, that is, men, are not burdened with either registration or its consequences. Therefore, abolition of this law signals the end of a form of female slavery. Every woman should be satisfied.

Lina Merlin, 1958

The regulation of prostitution, which feminists like Jesse White Mario began to protest immediately after unification, remained Italian state policy for nearly a century. Only in 1958 did Parliament approve an abolitionist law sponsored by the Socialist senator Lina Merlin. Italy finally joined the vast majority of nations that had, in conformity with international resolutions issued first by the League of Nations and later by the United Nations, closed the tolerated brothels. Great Britain had done so in the 1880s, the United States in the 1910s, and France in 1946. That the Italian government moved so slowly to reform prostitution legislation is

223

curious in light of the overall failure of the regulation system to fulfill its objectives. The successive regulationist laws—which included not only those of 1860, 1888, and 1891 but also Fascist statutes of 1923, 1931, and 1940—benefited neither the prostitute nor the state. From an interactionist perspective, the conduct of each party profoundly effected the other in a dialectical process that oppressed prostitutes and crippled government policy.

The passage of the Legge Merlin in 1958, then, did not result from a sudden breakdown in the system, since regulation had never functioned well. Not surprisingly, its effectiveness had continued to decline so that the number of registered prostitutes fell from a peak of 10,422 in 1881 to 4,000 in 1948 and finally to 2,560 in 1958.[1] Nor had the discourse on prostitution changed significantly enough to warrant a reexamination of the question. The parliamentary debates over the Merlin law rehashed for the most part the same positions assumed by regulationists and abolitionists almost a century before. No major insights emerged that might have radically shifted the framework of the discussion and led to the formulation of a new theoretical perspective of a "third" type distinct from the two more traditional ones.

Regulationists, for example, continued to consider prostitution as a necessary safeguard for family life, arguing that "an extramarital affair [with a prostitute] protects marriage much more than a true and proper extramarital relationship."[2] They insisted that prostitutes be enclosed in the tolerated houses to minimize "the spectacle which is certainly not edifying" of public soliciting by streetwalkers.[3] One regulationist warned that, if abolition were victorious, "all the streets of Italy are destined to become 'the streets of Cabiria'" in reference to a film by Federico Fellini.[4] Regulation, they asserted also protected the health of young men since, as one deputy asked, "Who of you does not know that sexual abstinence at a certain age can lead many times to a true poisoning of the organism?"[5] Periodic examinations of prostitutes now protected the public, but the passage of the Merlin law would assure that "all these women acquire the liberty to spread contagion."[6]

Abolitionists asserted the contrary, denying the special exigencies of the male sex drive and citing scientists who attested to the benefits of monogamy. One female deputy taunted her male colleagues for the contradiction between the self-image of their sex as "supermen . . . masters of themselves" and its proclaimed incapacity to resist the sexual instinct: "No, honorable colleagues, we wish to be optimistic. It is true that instincts are strong, but we are convinced that the entire human race is not a herd of pigs."[7] Abolitionists also denied that forced examination protected public health since the sexual activity in the official brothels represented "only a small part of all extramarital sexual relationships."[8] To fight the spread of venereal disease, they proposed that the state rely not on coercion but on sex education and free health care to encourage prostitutes to seek treatment. As one sponsor of the new law pointed out, "Public health cannot be protected by regulation, which can drive women away from the dispensaries for fear of humiliation and [the imposition of] restrictions on their liberty, but by considering venereal disease equivalent to any other contagious disease."[9] Finally, reformers denounced the sexism of registration, and one female legislator proclaimed that the triumph of the Legge Merlin formed an important part of the "more general struggle for a new dignity which all Italian women must wage in order to attain equal rights with men."[10]

Why did the arguments of the abolitionists, which had changed little since the nineteenth century, carry enough weight in 1958 to insure the passage of the Legge Merlin? Part of the answer lies in the medical progress in the field of venereal disease. In the late 1930s and 1940s, the discovery of penicillin and sulfa drugs finally allowed the safe and effective cure of syphilis, gonorrhea, and chancroid. Although health conditions worsened in Italy during World War II, liberation brought a decline in all three types of disease. While this decline was slowed or reversed slightly in the mid-1950s, rates of infection were still far below those preceding the war.[11] That venereal diseases—and even congenital syphilis—had now lost much of their mystery and terror weakened the impact of alarmist appeals by regulationists about the state of public health. With the availability of easy and rapid cure, the abolitionists' proposal to fight disease by developing, without coercion, a new "health consciousness" among the population gained plausibility and acceptance.[12]

Even more important were the radical changes in governmental structure following the fall of fascism and the establishment of the republic. The postwar period saw a realignment of power between the administrative and legislative branches of the state which weakened the traditional strongholds of regulation, the bureaucracies of public security and public health. During the Fascist period, the subordination of the legislature to the executive, typical of the liberal monarchy, became even more pronounced. In fact, Fascist statutes reversed the post-1888 reforms by reinforcing not only police but also medical surveillance over prostitutes. The Mussolini Regulation of 1923 reinstated the requirement that all prostitutes, including "isolated" practitioners working outside the closed houses, carry a special passport enumerating the results of each vaginal examination. Such a stipulation effectively erased the distinction between registering "persons" and "places" that distinguished the Crispi and Nicotera legislation. It also reversed the separation of police and health functions by reasserting PS enforcement of the law on medical passports. Statutes of 1931 and 1940 reconfirmed the duty of police to register brothels and collect information on their employees.[13] This return to the principles of the Cavour Regulation met with little opposition, since the legislature had been reduced to a facade by Benito Mussolini and the Fascist bureaucracy.

After the end of the dictatorship, however, administrative policymaking came under suspicion, and more matters were publicly debated in Parliament including, for the first time in any extensive way, prostitution. During the 1950s, police and even many health personnel continued to voice their opposition to abolition; on theoretical grounds they still subscribed to the Lombrosian conception of the "born prostitute" who needed to be kept under strict surveillance because of her degenerate and criminal tendencies.[14] On a more practical level, abolition threatened to diminish the power and scope of both bureaucracies. But Parliament had historically been more sympathetic to abolition than had the administration, and the open debate in the Chamber finally gave supporters of the Merlin Law an arena in which to be heard.

In the nineteenth century, however, even an open debate might not have assured the passage of a Legge Merlin; by 1958 a new combination of political forces assured its victory. Women had received the vote in 1946 and could now represent their cause in Parliament. No longer outside the central political institutions, feminists from the Communist, Socialist, and Christian Democratic parties participated forcefully in the discussions in the Senate and Chamber of Deputies. Most noteworthy, of course, was Lina Merlin, the woman who persevered for ten years in introducing and reintroducing her legislation until it was finally passed.[15] During her long struggle, she received myriad letters, mostly supportive, from prostitutes who described the crippling effects of the regulation system on their lives. They complained of police harassment, overcharging by doctors, the difficulty of getting off police lists, the barrier to obtaining another type of job owing to the stigma of registration, and the inability of their fiancés, if police or military, to receive the necessary permission to marry. Published in 1958, these "letters from the closed houses" constituted for Merlin the proof that not just feminists, but also prostitutes, clearly wanted the end of regulation.[16]

Despite the incipient integration of women into the political system, it is doubtful that their influence alone could have defeated regulation. Few in number, female senators and deputies were seldom among the party leadership and still had to depend on male support for passage of the new law. They had to contend with parties, Left as well as Right, that did not put a high priority on women's issues. Male legislators seemed to have learned few lessons from their feminist colleagues about changing roles for women. Even the men who most enthusiastically supported the Legge Merlin revealed, in the parliamentary debates, very traditional ideas about the nature of women. Like the Socialist deputy Antonio Berardi, most of them voted for the law not out of a profound belief in the natural equality of the sexes but to free prostitutes to pursue the "highest, most natural, most praiseworthy, and most instinctive aspiration, that of motherhood and the family."[17]

Yet the political spectrum had shifted enough since World War I that abolition could now attract a broad and strong coalition on grounds other than feminism. The parties of the Left had always opposed regulation as class oppression since regulationists preached that the prostitution of lower-class women was a necessary safety valve for the sexual needs of middle-class men. Firm supporters of abolition, the Socialist and Communist parties together commanded almost one-third of the votes in Parliament during the 1950s. In addition, for the first time a major conservative party, the newly established Christian Democrats, threw its support behind termination of registration. Many Christian Democrats were reluctant to dismantle a system that they believed shielded the state from disorder and their respectable, middle-class supporters from moral and physical contagion. As Catholic leaders, however, they could not openly defend the continued legalization and licensing of a sin by the state. The popes had opposed regulation since unification, and the majority of the members of Christian Democracy dutifully, if not always enthusiastically, acquiesced. Furthermore, support of the Legge Merlin was consistent with the traditional campaign of Catholic women's organizations against the victimization of prostitutes by the white slave trade. Stressing the image of the prostitute as a victim, the Christian Democratic deputy Beniamino De Maria drew lively applause and congratulations from his colleagues when he declared that

> we cannot be a democratic Parliament if we do not abolish the regulation of prostitution and lift up from inferiority and unhappiness those poor, unfortunate women who let themselves be exploited by individuals who enrich themselves on poverty and the humiliation of human dignity. We cannot, I repeat, call ourselves representatives of a democratic Parliament if we do not place on a level of human dignity all human beings, rich or poor, no matter what category or social class they belong to.[18]

The Merlin law promised to end the "slavery" of prostitutes to a rich, well-organized, and shadowy group of "interests" that included white slave traders, brothel owners, and madams. Christian Democrats were the majority party in the postwar period, so their decision to join the Left in repealing regulation was decisive.

The eagerness of the Christian Democrats, as well as the Socialists and Communists, to support abolition in the name of democracy can be understood only in the international context. Both the League of Nations and the United Nations had condemned regulation and put pressure on those nations that still had not closed their public brothels.[19] In the legislature, there was general embarrassment over the fact that in 1923 Mussolini, in a

228

reply to an inquiry from the league, had boldfacedly lied by declaring that "regulated prostitution does not exist in Italy."[20] By 1958 Italy was nearly the only regulationist country left in Europe; even France had adopted abolition in 1946. That regulation was associated with authoritarianism and fascism is clear from the words of Renato Tozzi Condivi, the sponsor of the Legge Merlin in the Chamber: "Those who have spoken against the proposed measure sit on the benches of the Right; they are those who have accepted the Constitution but have not understood or have not adhered to the spirit of the Constitutional charter."[21] Italy wished to regain respect and status as a reliable democracy in the international community; approval of the new law was one step in that direction. The final vote in the chamber, 385 for the bill and 115 opposed, showed that there had been defections from the ranks of the supporting coalition. But only the neofascist MSI and part of the Monarchist party had dared publicly to oppose it.

Unlike the Crispi and Nicotera statutes of the late nineteenth century, the Merlin Law was truly abolitionist. Article 1 forbade the establishment of "houses of prostitution," while Article 2 ordered that all existing brothels be closed within six months.[22] To complete the destruction of the regulation system, the new legislation explicitly banned any sort of direct or indirect registration, issuance of medical certificates or "special papers," or medical examination of prostitutes.[23] Stiff penalties fell on procurers, white slave traders, or "anyone who in any way favors or profits from the prostitution of another" in hopes of protecting women from exploitation and coercion by third parties.[24] The law also punished "persons of either sex" who solicited "for the purpose of debauchery" in public places or on the streets.[25] Unlike prohibitionist legislation, however, it did not criminalize the act of prostitution if carried out privately and without the interference of a third party. In concordance with the traditional aims of the reform movement, Merlin intended her law to abolish the regulation of prostitution, not prostitution itself.

Besides the primarily negative purpose of eradicating existing police and medical surveillance, the Legge Merlin promised the creation of two new positive institutions. First, the state finally committed itself to establishing reformatories for both minor and adult prostitutes.[26] The problem of reeducation would be especially pressing upon the closure of the tolerated brothels, when their employees would be turned out onto the streets without jobs and most likely without savings. Abolitionists hoped that many prostitutes might choose this moment for changing their lives if alternative opportunities were available for temporary housing and maintenance while they learned new skills. Second, the law provided for the formation of a "special female corps" of police that would gradually take over functions related to *buon costume* (public morality) and the prevention of juvenile delinquency and prostitution.[27] The appointment of female PS agents would end the sexual harassment and intimidation of prostitutes during routine enforcement of the articles against soliciting. Women (prostitutes) would now interact with women (police) in a process that promised more sensitivity, civility, and justice in the relationship between prostitutes and the state.

Despite intermittent grumblings by unreconstructed regulationists, the Merlin Law has remained on the books for over twenty-five years. The major challenge to it has come only recently and from a group previously left out of formal political debates: prostitutes themselves. On October 13, 1982, in response to continued violence at the hands of American soldiers at the NATO base at Aviano and the failure of Italian police to protect them from it, a group of prostitutes in the northeastern town of Pordenone organized the Committee for the Civil Rights of Prostitutes. Its major aims are to revise the Merlin Law and to open discussion of the issue of prostitution, which members believe has been ignored by feminists as well as less sympathetic sectors of Italian society. Open to women and men, prostitutes and nonprostitutes, the committee has spread to other parts of Italy, especially in the North. It organized, in February 1983, a national convention entitled Prostitution in the '80s: Marginality or Social Question? and consequently began to publish a newspaper entitled *Lucciola*.[28] Several parties of the Left, most notably the Socialist party and the Radical party, have taken up the cause of the committee and introduced modifications of the Legge Merlin into the Italian legislature.[29]

Unlike the regulationists, the prostitutes of the committee do not want to reintroduce the closed houses but in fact praise the Merlin statute for having abolished them. Similarly, they approve the criminalization of procuring and white slave trading and have proposed increasing the current penalties in the case of minors and introducing new punishment in the case of drug-dependent persons. The committee, however objects to the vagueness of the clause directed against anyone who "favors" prostitution. Police have used this stipulation as a pretext for arresting not only landlords, boyfriends, and husbands of prostitutes but also prostitutes themselves. For example, if two women share an apartment, one can be prosecuted for favoring the prostitution of the other. Members of the committee argue that ironically this type of police action has isolated them and thrown them back into the arms of the male underworld rather than freeing them from exploitation as Merlin had intended. Only a man who is already compromised in other illegal activities will dare to rent them a room, usually at an exhorbitant price, or enter into an emotional relationship with them. Furthermore, they denounce the hypocrisy of decriminalizing the act of prostitution but not solicitation, which leaves police free to stop any prostitute on the street or in her car even if she is not disrupting public order. Without court review, PS agents then have the power to apply "administrative" sanctions such as confiscating prostitutes' drivers' licenses, forbidding them to frequent public places, or returning them to their city of birth with a foglia di via (administrative order). According to the committee, prostitutes have to live, advertise, and work somewhere, and their activities, like those of other citizens, should be regulated only by the penal code. Finally, they point out that the two positive institutions formulated in the Legge Merlin, the reformatories for prostitutes and the female police corps, have never been seriously implemented. A law of 1959, for example, funded only a very small corps of female "assistants" and "inspectors" who lack their own offices as well as any clear definition of their duties and position within the larger PS. Thus the state, as in the nineteenth century, has shown its contempt for prostitutes by refusing to fund measures that would protect rather than repress them.

Revolt against marginalization is the main thread running through the discourse and legislative proposals of the committee. According to its secretary, society has tolerated prostitutes only because they fulfilled a functional need and submitted to its repressive logic. Rejecting this role of submission to state authority, she explains, "Today we rebel against this status of marginalization and the role which has been imposed on us [and] we vindicate the right to control our bodies and to carry on our work without, for that reason, being 'ghetto-ized' by a law, like that of Merlin."[30] Prostitutes are revolting against negative labeling by the state and by society in general. The president of the committee has lamented the extreme contempt to which prostitutes are subjected daily by people on the street: as soon as passersby identify a woman as a prostitute, "they consider [her] an informer, intellectually limited, dirty, immoral, [and] sexually unbridled."[31] Prostitutes want to change this perception in the public mind and enter the political, economic, and social mainstream as citizens exercising the full range of rights possessed by other members of Italian society. As a document from the 1983 convention declares, "We claim that which is due other citizens; however, in regard to the possibility of reentering normality, we realize that a battle of only a few months will not suffice."[32] Yet, despite the length of the struggle ahead, prostitutes are determined to make the transition from deviance to normality.

What is most innovative above the committee is that prostitutes have now perceived "the necessity to be protagonists of our struggle."[33] Unlike the earlier abolitionist crusades, prostitutes rather than middle-class feminists lead the movement for legislative reform. Except for Merlin's collection of the "letters from the closed houses," neither side in the historical battle over regulation ever consulted the opinions and wisdom of prostitutes on policy that shaped their lives. Consequently, condescension, ignorance, and sexual fastidiousness have colored even the most sympathetic portraits of the prostitute. Even today, many Italian feminists, while generally supportive of the committee, express ambivalence about the prostitutes' defense of their work as a legitimate means of self-support rather than the ultimate form of female exploitation. Prostitutes profess to not liking their profession but consider it no more degrading than the other limited options open to women that offer less remuneration and free time. They invite a discussion of the Legge Merlin "without false moralism," a quality they believe has previously pervaded the entire discourse on prostitution.[34]

Instead of as victims, the prostitutes of the committee portray themselves as independent, "normal" women who entered their profession by choice. Their self-image differs greatly from the image of the "born" degenerate of the regulationist school or that of the innocent prey of white slave traders so dear to abolitionists. Instead, the president of the committee, while excusing herself for being presumptuous, explains that "we are rather capable; we have never let ourselves become the object of gross repression; we are 'autoregulated,' and we have always been known to defend ourselves a bit and make ourselves a little respected."[35] Even the committee admits that all Italian prostitutes are not now so free; many in Naples and Palermo, for example, are controlled by the Camorra and the Mafia, respectively. But for the first time we are hearing the voices of prostitutes and they are denying the traditional labels: those of idleness, criminality, immorality, female deviancy, and propagators of disease. Perhaps their future testimonies will shed new light on the history of their less political but never passive sisters of the nineteenth and early twentieth centuries.

Notes

Abbreviations

ACS	Archivio Centrale dello Stato
ADB	Associazione Democratica Bolognese
ASB	Archivio di Stato di Bologna
DGPS	Direzione Generale della Pubblica Sicurezza
D.G.San.Pubb.	Direzione Generale della Sanità Pubblica
M.Int.	Ministero dell 'Interno
Pol.Giud.	Polizia Giudiziaria
Pref.	Prefetto
Quest.	Questore

Introduction

1. ASB, Quest., 1886. All translations from the Italian are my own.

2. On the shift in the rates of crime from those against persons to those against property, see Howard Zehr, *Crime and the Development of Modern Society: Patterns of Criminality in Nineteenth-Century Germany and France.*

3. Giovanni Bolis, *La polizia e le classi pericolose della società: Studii*, p. 780.

4. I have treated this subject in more detail in Mary S. Gibson, "The State and Prostitution: Prohibition, Regulation, or Decriminalization?"

5. The only exception is Nevada, where prostitution is legalized and regulated in several rural counties.

6. John H. Gagnon and William Simon, *Sexual Conduct: The Social Sources of Human Sexuality*, p. 218.

7. Historians have been most active in challenging stereotypes about women's nature; the bibliography of women's history is now im-

mense. Less has been accomplished by criminologists and sexologists, although new research on women is now beginning to appear in their fields. For several reviews of biological stereotyping in criminological literature, see Dorie Klein, "The Etiology of Female Crime: A Review of the Literature"; Carol Smart, *Women, Crime, and Criminology: A Feminist Critique*; and Franca Faccioli, "La devianza e la criminalità femminile in Italia." For a similar critique of sex research, see Mary McIntosh, "Who Needs Prostitutes? The Ideology of Male Sexual Needs."

8. The only bibliography on prostitution that, although incomplete, includes historical and cross-national references is Vern L. Bullough et al., *A Bibliography of Prostitution*. For a discussion of some of these works, see Bullough's article "Problems and Methods for Research in Prostitution and the Behavioral Sciences."

9. See, for example, Iwan Bloch, *Die Prostitution*; Gladys Mary Hall, *Prostitution in the Modern World*; Fernando Henriques, *Prostitution and Society*; Paul La Croix, *History of Prostitution*; Ben L. Reitman, *The Second Oldest Profession*; William J. Robinson *The Oldest Profession in the World*; William W. Sanger, *The History of Prostitution: Its Extent, Causes, Effects throughout the World*; Hermann Schreiber [Lujo Basserman], *The Oldest Profession*; George Ryley Scott, *The History of Prostitution*; and Marcel Sicot, *La prostitution dans le monde*. Vern L. Bullough's *The History of Prostitution* contains more careful social analysis than many of its companions but is still flawed by the sweep of its scope.

10. For the growing body of sociological and psychological literature, see the bibliography. I have concentrated on American and Italian contributions to these fields.

11. For France, see Alain Corbin, *Les filles de noce: Misère sexuelle et prostitution (19ᵉ et 20ᵉ siècles)*. For Great Britain, see Frances Finnegan, *Poverty and Prostitution: A Study of Victorian Prostitutes in York*; Paul McHugh, *Prostitution and Victorian Social Reform*; E. M. Sigsworth and T. J. Wyke, "A Study of Victorian Prostitution and Venereal Disease"; Robert D. Storch, "Police Control of Street Prostitution in Victorian England: A Study of the Contexts of Police Action"; and Judith R. Walkowitz, *Prostitution and Victorian Society: Women, Class, and the State*. For the United States, see John C. Burnham, "Medical Inspection of Prostitutes in Nineteenth-Century America: The St. Louis Experiment and its Sequel"; Mark Thomas Connelly, *The Response to Prostitution in the Progressive Era*; Egal Feldman, "Prostitution: The Alien Woman and the Progressive Imagination"; Kay Ann Holmes, "Reflections by Gaslight: Prostitution in Another Age"; Roy Lubove, "The Progressives and the Prostitute"; Robert E. Riegel,

"Changing American Attitudes towards Prostitution (1800–1920)"; and Ruth Rosen, *The Lost Sisterhood: Prostitution in America, 1900–1918.*

The history of German prostitution is not so well documented, but see Richard Evans, "Prostitution, State, and Society in Imperial Germany." Less work has been done on the period before the nineteenth century; several useful articles are James A. Brundage, "Prostitution in the Medieval Canon Law"; Mary Elizabeth Perry, "'Lost Women' in Early Modern Seville"; and Jacques Rossiaud, "Prostitution, Youth, and Society in the Towns of Southeastern France in the Fifteenth Century."

12. Research on Italy is limited. Giorgio Gattei has published two articles, the second of which appeared after the completion of this book. See "Controllo di classi pericolose: La prima regolamentazione prostituzionale unitaria (1869–1888)" and "La sifilide: Medici e poliziotti intorno alla 'venere politica.'" Renzo Villa also includes material on Italy in his articles; see "Sul processo di criminalizzazione della prostituzione nell'ottocento" and "La prostituzione come problema storiografico." A less rigorous account is Romano Canosa, *Sesso e stato.* An interesting collection of documents on abolition can be found in Rina Macrelli, *L'indegna schiavitù: Anna Maria Mozzoni e la lotta contro la prostituzione di stato.* For the Renaissance, see Richard L. Trexler, "La prostitution florentine au XVe siècle: Patronages et clientèles."

13. Michel Foucault, *Discipline and Punish: The Birth of the Prison.*

14. Although justly criticized for their shortcomings, labeling and interationist theories are suited to the analysis of prostitution, which has lacked a clear and consistent legal definition. A "victimless crime," prostitution draws few complainants. The state, therefore, exercises wide discretion in "labeling" certain women as prostitutes, a process that becomes concrete at the street level through "interaction" between suspected prostitutes and police. I share the reservations of the "new criminologists" of Great Britain and the "critical criminologists" of Italy, who have pointed out a tendency toward "idealism" in the labeling and interactionist approaches. Proponents of labeling and interactionist approaches privilege the individual and cultural, rather than the social and material, dimensions of deviancy. Yet, behind the face-to-face encounter lies a larger economic, social, demographic, and political structure that does not determine, but certainly limits and directs, the possible scenario or script between a police officer and a woman charged with prostitution. Thus for both the ruling classes and the prostitute, I describe the "material" milieu in which their attitudes and behavior were rooted. In this way I have tried, in the words of one critical criminologist, "to go beyond the labeling approach, by way of the labeling

approach"; see Alessandro Baratta, "Criminologia critica e riforma penale," p. 363. The journal *La Questione Criminale* and its successor, *Dei Delitti e delle Pene,* have provided the major forum for the discussions of Italian critical criminologists. For the classic statement of the new criminologists of Great Britain, see Ian Taylor et al., *The New Criminology: For a Social Theory of Deviance.*

15. The working charter of the conference can be found in Margo St. James, "First Congress of European and North American Whores" (typescript, Amsterdam, 1984).

Chapter 1: Regulation

1. Bolis, *Polizia,* p. 838.

2. One of the few studies of prostitution during the period before unification is Antonio Sampaoli, *La prostituzione nel pensiero del settecento.*

3. Pierleone Tommasoli, *Prostitution et maladies vénériennes en Italie,* p. 2. Prohibition was also the official policy of Milan; see Macrelli, *Indegna schiavitù,* p. 13.

4. Dr. Jacquot was a physician attached to the French forces stationed in Rome before 1870. He is quoted in Bolis, *Polizia,* pp. 800–801.

5. Jacquot, quoted in Giuseppe Sormani, *Profilassi delle malattie veneree e specialmente della sifilide,* p. 18.

6. Antonio Cutrera, *Storia della prostituzione in Sicilia: Monografia storico-giuridica,* p. 275.

7. Ibid., pp. 272, 274.

8. Bolis, *Polizia,* p. 838.

9. Sormani, *Profilassi delle malattie veneree,* p. 35.

10. Bolis, *Polizia,* pp. 459–460.

11. Carlo M. Cipolla, "Four Centuries of Italian Demographic Development," p. 573; Istituto Centrale della Statistica, *Sommario di statistiche storiche italiane, 1861–1955,* p. 11. Both sources calculate population based on the current geographical boundaries of Italy; the figures, therefore, are slightly higher than the actual resident population of the epoch. For a discussion of the demographic transition in Italy, see Cipolla, ibid., pp. 579–584, and Massimo Livi-Bacci, *A History of Italian Fertility during the Last Two Centuries.*

12. Ufficio del Censimento, *Censimento della popolazione del Regno d'Italia al 10 giugno 1911,* 1:55, 143, 154, 187, 194, 218, 264, 305, 320.

13. This pattern continued to exist into the period following World War II; see Francesco Alberoni, "Aspects of Internal Migration Related to Other Types of Italian Migration," pp. 311–312.

14. On the economic history of nineteenth-century Italy, see Luciano Cafagna, "Italy, 1830–1914"; Gianni Toniolo, ed., *Lo sviluppo economico italiano, 1861–1914*; and Alexander Gerschenkron, *Economic Backwardness in Historical Perspective*.

15. Pierfrancesco Bandettini, "The Employment of Women in Italy, 1881–1951"; Marisa Cinciari Rodano, "La posizione della donna nella vita economica: L'occupazione dal 1900 ad oggi."

16. Joan W. Scott and Louise Tilly, *Women, Work and Family*.

17. Bolis, *Polizia*, p. 461.

18. Ibid.

19. Ibid., p. 462.

20. For a sampling of the new research on social control and the poor in nineteenth-century Italy, see Ercole Sori, ed., *Città e controllo sociale in Italia tra XVIII e XIX secolo*, and Franco Della Peruta, "Infanzia e famiglia nella prima metà dell'ottocento."

21. Bolis, *Polizia*, pp. 460–461.

22. Giovanni Gozzoli, *La prostituzione in Italia*, p. 21.

23. Romano Canosa, *La polizia in Italia dal 1945 a oggi*, pp. 7–98; Dario Melossi and Massimo Pavarini, *The Prison and the Factory: Origins of the Penitentiary System*.

24. Michel Foucault has documented this trend in *La volonté de savoir*. Mario Manfredi and Ada Mangano quote long sections of Italian prescriptive literature, published between 1865 and 1919, on the subject of female sexuality in their *Alle origini del diritto femminile: Cultura giuridica e ideologie*, chaps. 1 and 2. On the social control of female sexuality, see also Gianna Pomata, "Madri illegittime tra ottocento e novecento: Storie cliniche e storie di vita."

25. Giuseppe Tammeo, *La prostituzione: Saggio di statistica morale*, p. 269.

26. Gattei, "Controllo di classi pericolose," p. 755.

27. For a discussion of the "symbol" of the prostitute in England, the United States, and France, see, respectively, Walkowitz, *Prostitution and Victorian Society*, p. 32; Connelly, *Response to Prostitution*, pp. 6–9; and Corbin, *Filles de noce*, pp. 19–24. I disagree with Connelly's conclusion that the prostitute, at the turn of the century, symbolized modernity and therefore that antiprostitution sentiment was linked to a fear of change. A more complex analysis is in order because many characteristics of the image of the prostitute, such as her laziness, lack

of schedule and discipline, and uncleanliness, identified her as part of the premodern, preproletarian, lower-class crowd. Thus the symbol was ambiguous, including both premodern and modern elements.

28. Denis Mack Smith, *Italy: A Modern History*, p. 21.

29. Tommasoli, *Prostitution et maladies vénériennes*, p. 2. McHugh also stresses the military considerations behind the introduction of the Contagious Diseases Acts in England during the 1860s based on a "medico-military" consensus; see his *Prostitution and Victorian Social Reform*, pp. 17–18.

30. Tammeo, *Prostituzione*, p. 38; Sormani, *Profilassi delle malattie veneree*, p. 6.

31. Giuseppe Zino, *Manuale di polizia medica ad uso degli ufficiali sanitari del regno e degli amministratori*, p. 375.

32. Vincenzo De Giaxa, *Igiene pubblica*, p. 372.

33. Sormani, *Profilassi delle malattie veneree*, p. 34.

34. Ibid., p. 31.

35. Foucault, *Volonté de savoir*, p. 164.

36. Smith, *Italy*, p. 24. A. William Salomone also refers to Cavour's machiavellianism in "Statecraft and Ideology in the Risorgimento," p. 21.

37. Salomone, "Statecraft and Ideology," p. 16.

38. Canosa, *Polizia in Italia*, p. 24.

39. Foucault, *Discipline and Punish*, p. 39.

40. Edward Löning, *Polizia dei Costumi*, p. 855.

41. Sormani, *Profilassi delle malattie veneree*, p. 34.

42. Gattei has treated this legislation in "Controllo di classi pericolose," pp. 773–774. See also Bolis, *Polizia*, p. 839, and Tommasoli, *Prostitution et maladies vénériennes*, pp. 2–4.

43. Gattei discusses the contents of the Brussels regulation in "Controllo di classi pericolose," pp. 771–772, as does Villa, "Processo di criminalizzazione della prostituzione," pp. 271–272. Villa goes on to describe the Prussian legislation on prostitution (pp. 272–273).

44. Tommasoli, *Prostitution et maladies vénériennes*, pp. 3–4.

45. Ibid., p. 4; Adolfo Petiziol, *La prostituta: Profilo psicologico, storico, sociale*, p. 55.

46. For a further analysis of this process of Piedmontization, see Denis Mack Smith, "Regionalism," pp. 127–128, and Raymond Grew, "How Success Spoiled the Risorgimento," pp. 45, 52.

47. Smith, "Regionalism," pp. 131–132; John A. Thayer, *Italy and the Great War: Politics and Culture, 1870–1915*, pp. 22–23.

48. William A. Salomone, "Freedom and Power in Liberal Italy," p. 133.

49. Sormani, *Profilassi delle malattie veneree*, p. 8.

50. This was generally true for all the early legislation of united Italy. As Grew wrote of Cavour and his colleagues of the Right, "They stressed the military virtues of discipline and order. The very concepts of unification and liberty had been vigorously and deliberately separated as distinct issues unnecessarily cumbersome when taken together." From "How Success Spoiled the Risorgimento," p. 49.

51. Zino, *Manuale di polizia medica*, p. 375.

52. Giaxa, *Igiene pubblica*, p. 373. See also Giuseppe Profeta, *Sulla prostituzione: 8ª Conferenza*, pp. 2–3.

53. Giambattista Borelli, *Studi sulla prostituzione*, 145. Borelli was an ambiguous figure; he strongly shared the assumptions of the regulationists about male sexuality but not many of their conclusions. He would have to be classified, therefore, more as a reformer than a defender of the Cavour law.

54. Sormani, *Profilassi delle malattie veneree*, p. 37.

55. Ibid.

56. Bolis, *Polizia*, p. 780.

57. Regolamento Cavour (February 15, 1860), art. 65.

58. Ibid., art. 48.

59. Although proponents of the tolerated brothels, regulationists denounced the maltreatment of prostitutes by madams. See, for example, Pietro Castiglione, *Sorveglianza sulla prostituzione e modi per impedire la diffusione della sifilide: Studi storico-statistici e proposte*, p. 116.

60. Regolamento Cavour, art. 56.

61. Ibid., art. 63.

62. Ibid., art. 17.

63. Ibid., art. 45.

64. Ibid., art. 44.

65. Castiglione, *Sorveglianza sulla prostituzione*, p. 88.

66. Foucault, *Discipline and Punish*, pp. 138, 150.

67. Erving Goffman argues that instituting a process of self-mortification is an important strategy for breaking down the independence and sense of self of inmates in total institutions. See *Asylums: Essays on the Social Situation of Mental patients and Other Inmates*, p. 18.

68. Foucault, *Discipline and Punish*, p. 140.

69. Regolamento Cavour, art. 32.

70. Ibid.

71. Foucault, *Discipline and Punish*, p. 177.

72. Castiglione, *Sorveglianza sulla prostituzione*, p. 54.

73. Foucault, *Discipline and Punish*, pp. 184–185.

74. Regolamento Cavour, art. 72.

75. Foucault, *Discipline and Punish*, p. 184.

76. The new forms were prescribed by the Istruzioni provvisorie per regolare il servizio degli Uffici Sanitari issued in 1880 by the minister of the interior.

77. Foucault, *Discipline and Punish*, p. 189.

78. Castiglione, *Sorveglianza sulla prostituzione*, p. 93.

79. Ibid., p. 94.

80. Josephine E. Butler, *Personal Reminiscences of a Great Crusade*, p. 106.

Chapter 2: Abolition

1. Fanny Zampini Salazaro, "Women's Condition in Italy," p. 209.

2. McHugh, *Prostitution and Victorian Social Reform*, pp. 17, 27. For details of the British campaign against the Contagious Diseases Acts, see also Walkowitz, *Prostitution and Victorian Society*.

3. Butler, *Personal Reminiscenses*, p. 19; McHugh, *Prostitution and Victorian Social Reform*, p. 56.

4. Josephine E. Butler, *An Autobiographical Memoir*, p. 14.

5. Butler, *Personal Reminiscences*, p. 146.

6. See Salvatore Saladino, "Parliamentary Politics in the Liberal Era: 1861–1914" p. 30.

7. On the issue of regionalism see the article by Denis Mack Smith, titled "Regionalism," p. 134.

8. Guiseppe Mazzini, quoted in Butler, *Personal Reminiscences*, pp. 26–27.

9. Ibid., p. 25.

10. Ibid., p. 27.

11. Macrelli, *Indegna schiavitù*, pp. 52–53. Franca Pieroni Bortolotti emphasizes the contribution of Morelli to the movement for women's rights in *Socialismo e questione femminile in Italia, 1892–1922*, p. 23.

12. Macrelli, *Indegna schiavitù*, p. 100.

13. Agostino Bertani, *La prostituzione patentata e il regolamento sanitario: Lettera ad Agostino DePretis*.

14. The proceedings of the meeting were published by the ADB under the title *Le donne cadute, la legge e la polizia*.

15. Tommasoli, *Prostitution et maladies vénériennes*, p. 5.

16. Tito mammoli, *La prostituzione considerata nei suoi rapporti con la storia, la famiglia, la società*, p. 136.

17. Giuseppe Nathan quoted in Butler, *Personal Reminiscences*, p. 144.

18. Mammoli, *Prostituzione*, Dedication and p. 136.

19. Macrelli, *Indegna schiavitù*, p. 103

20 Ibid., p. 101.

21. On early Mazzinian feminism, see Franca Pieroni Bortolotti, *Alle origini del movimento femminile in Italia, 1848–1892*, and Judith Jeffrey Howard, "Patriot Mothers in the Post-Risorgimento: Women after the Italian Revolution."

22. The aid given Butler by Protestant ministers in Italy was noted by one of her opponents, Sormani, in *Profilassi delle malattie veneree*, p. 7. Butler also had a familial link to Italy through her sister, Hatty, who was married to an Italian merchant (McHugh, *Prostitution and Victorian Reform*, p. 103). Corbin, in *Filles de noce*, p. 456, has also documented the strength of abolitionism in the Protestant areas of nineteenth-century France.

23. On the development of women's organizations, see Pieroni Bortolotti, *Origini del movimento femminile*; idem, *Socialismo e questione femminile*: and Luciana Capezzuoli and Grazia Cappabianca, *Storia dell'emancipazione femminile*.

24. Mozzoni's letter to Butler, as well as many of her other writings about prostitution, are reprinted in Macrelli, *Indegna schiavitù*, pp. 61–76.

25. Ibid., p. 101.

26. Ibid.

27. Ibid., p. 141.

28. Walkowitz has stressed the importance and originality of the alliance within the British abolitionist movement between working men and middle-class women in *Prostitution and Victorian Society*, p. 6.

29. Quoted in Butler, *Personal Reminiscences*, pp. 173–174.

30. Ibid., p. 181.

31. Mammoli, *Prostituzione*, Forward.

32. Butler, *Personal Reminiscences*, p. 182.

33. Macrelli, *Indegna schiavitù*, p. 115.

34. Ibid., p. 145.

35. In this judgment I differ with Macrelli, who seems to be more convinced by abolitionists' own estimates of lower-class support for their cause; see *Indegna schiavitù*, pp. 102–103.

36. Bertani, *Prostituzione patentata*, p. 8.

37. McHugh notes a similar situation in England. Even though working men's support for abolition was widespread and well organized, their league was "colonised" by middle-class reformers; see McHugh, *Prostitution and Victorian Social Reform*, p. 118.

38. Antonio Gramola, *Le prostitute e la legge*, p. 19.

39. Matilde Dessalles, in ADB, *Donne cadute*, unpaged.

40. Ernesto Nathan, *Le diabolerie e lo stato: Quadro di costumi regolamenti*, p. 34.

41. Mammoli, *Prostituzione*, p. 134.

42. Ibid., p. 144.

43. Gramola, *Prostitute e la legge*, p. 19.

44. Mozzoni quoted in Macrelli, *Indegna schiavitù*, p. 179.

45. Gramola, *Prostitute e la legge*, p. 22.

46. Bertani in ADB, *Donne cadute*, unpaged.

47. Bertani, *Prostituzione patentata*, p. 61.

48. Ibid., p. 54.

49. Nathan, *Diabolerie e lo stato*, p. x.

50. Gramola, *Prostitute e la legge*, p. 8.

51. Nathan, *Diabolerie e lo stato*, p. 29; Aurelio Saffi in ADB, *Donne cadute*, unpaged.

52. Bertani in ADB, *Donne cadute*, unpaged.

53. Ibid.

54. Mammoli, *Prostituzione*, pp. 159–160.

55. Gramola, *Prostitute e la legge*, p. 32.

56. Bertani, *Prostituzione patentata*, p. 28; Corrado Tommasi-Crudeli, *La prostituzione di stato in Italia*, p. 5.

57. Tommasoli, *Prostitution e maladies vénériennes*, p. 28.

58. Abraham Flexner, *Prostitution in Europe*, p. 287. An American, Flexner studied the various types of prostitution legislation in Europe and became a convinced abolitionist.

59. Lorenzo Mei, *Governo e prostituzione*, pp. 3–4.

60. Gramola, *Prostitute e la legge*, p. 29.

61. Bertani in ADB, *Donne cadute*, unpaged.

62. Mozzoni quoted in Macrelli, *Indegna schiavitù*, p. 130.

63. McHugh describes the Ladies Association of England in similar terms: "Poverty was correctly recognized as the main cause of prostitution, but the LNA's preoccupation with morality prevented it from developing responses to this problem." *Prostitution and Victorian Social Reform*, p. 169.

64. Gramola, *Prostitute e la legge*, p. 13; Nathan, *Diabolerie e lo stato*, p. 42; Mei, *Governo e prostituzione*, p. 16.

65. Mozzoni quoted in Macrelli, *Indegna schiavitù*, pp. 132–133.

66. Gramola, *Prostitute e la legge*, p. 35.

67. Mozzoni quoted in Macrelli, *Indegna schiavitù*, p. 140.

68. Tommasoli, *Prostitution et maladies vénériennes*, p. 4; Castiglione, *Sorveglianza sulla prostituzione*, p. 99. Other members of the

commission of 1862 were Paolo Vigliani, Luigi Torelli, Giovanni Bottero, Salvatore Tommasi, and Giovanni Soresina.

69. Castiglione, *Sorveglianza sulla prostituzione*, p. 99.

70. Tommasoli, *Prostitution et maladies vénériennes*, p. 5.

71. Macrelli, *Indegna schiavitù*, p. 50.

72. Salomone, "Freedom and Power in Liberal Italy," p. 134.

73. Tommasoli, *Prostitution et maladies vénériennes*, p. 5.

74. Parlamento, Camera dei Deputati, *Atti Parlamentari*, Documenti, n. 146, p. 1.

75. Giovanni Catella, *Il regolamento 15 febbraio 1860 sulla prostituzione: Estratto del Giornale della R. Accademia di Medicina di Torino*, pp. 10–11.

76. Parlamento, Camera dei Deputati, *Atti Parlamentari*, Documenti, n. 146, p. 1.

77. Ibid. This volume contains Nicotera's speech when presenting the law to the Chamber, a copy of the proposed law, and a statistical appendix on prostitution.

78. Tommasoli, *Prostitution et maladies vénériennes*, p. 6. Anna Garofalo also traces the divisions in the Left over prostitution legislation in "Prostituzione e miseria."

79. Bertani, *Prostituzione patentata*, Dedication.

80. Ibid., p. 12.

81. Ibid., p. 17.

82. Ibid., p. 12.

83. Tommasoli, *Prostitution et maladies vénériennes*, p. 7. For an account of the commission's establishment, see also Commissione Regia per lo Studio delle Questioni relative alla Prostituzione e ai Provvedimenti per la Morale ed Igiene Pubblica, *Relazione, proposte, allegati*, 1:5 (hereafter cited as Commissione Regia (1885), *Relazione, proposte, allegati*). The original members of the committee were Bertani, Francesco Bianchi, Giuseppe Casanova, Francesco De Renzis, Vittorio Giudici, Edoardo Lucchini, Costanzo Mazzoni, Carmelo Patamia, and Sperino; later additions were Enrico Pessina and Pellizzari.

84. Ibid., 1:6; Tommasi-Crudeli, *Prostituzione di stato in Italia*, p. 9; Tammeo, *Prostituzione*, p. 44.

85. Commissione Regia (1885), *Relazione, proposte, allegati*, 1: 91.

86. Ibid., 1:101.

87. Ibid., 1:100.

88. Ibid., 1:95–97.

89. Ibid., 1:101–102.

90. Tommasi-Crudeli, *Prostituzione di stato in Italia*, p. 9; Tommasoli confirms this in *Prostitution et maladies vénériennes*, p. 8.

91. Saladino, "Parliamentary Politics," p. 37.

92. Tommasoli, *Prostitution et maladies vénériennes*, p. 8.

93. Tommasi-Crudeli, *Prostituzione di stato in Italia*, p. 10. This pattern of "lost" reports was not unique to those on prostitution. Thayer notes, for example, that the government (Rudinì and Giolitti) denied any knowledge of the results of the Alvisi-Biagini investigation of banks in 1889, which concluded that they were "grossly mismanaged" (*Italy and the Great War*, pp. 59–60).

94. Tommasoli, *Prostitution et maladies vénériennes*, p. 9.

95. The so-called Regolamento Crispi was issued in three parts: Regolamento Crispi sulla prostituzione (July 26, 1888); Regolamento Crispi sulla profilassi e sulla cura delle malattie sifilitiche (July 26, 1888); and Regolamento Crispi pei dispensari celtici (July 10–26, 1888).

96. Crispi quoted in Smith, *Italy*, p. 136.

97. On the factions of the Left, see Saladino, "Parliamentary Politics," pp. 34–36; Smith, *Italy*, p. 136; and A. William Salomone, *Italy in the Giolittian Era: Italian Democracy in the Making, 1900–1914*, pp. 30–31. Salomone points out that the Right, after 1876, also "ceased to exist as an organized political party" (pp. 13–14).

98. On Crispi's conversion to centralization see Thayer, *Italy and the Great War*, p. 29.

99. Legge di Pubblica Sicurezza 20 marzo 1865, n. 2248.

100. Giorgina Saffi in ADB, *Donne cadute*, unpaged.

101. Ibid.

102. Macrelli, *Indegna schiavitù*, p. 228.

103. McHugh stresses the novelty and importance of the English Ladies Association, which not only was led by women but employed men as abolitionist missionaries; see *Prostitution and Victorian Social Reform*, p. 183.

104. Ibid., pp. 187–202.

105. Brundage, "Medieval Canon Law," pp. 824–845.

106. Paul Larivaille, *La vie quotidienne des courtisanes en Italie au temps de la renaissance: Rome et Venise, XVᵉ et XVIᵉ siècles*, p. 181.

107. More research into popular religion, as opposed to official theology, is necessary to document better the attitudes of the lower clergy toward prostitution. Even a century later, however, sociologists have found a tolerant attitude among parish priests in Italy toward the male "need" for sexual satisfaction with prostitutes. See Norberto Valentini and Clara DiMeglio, *Sex and the Confessional*, pp. 95–96, 116.

108. Parlamento, Camera dei Deputati, *Atti Parlamentari*, n. 5, p. 6117.

Chapter 3: Return to Regulation

1. Zino, *Manuale di polizia medica.* p. 376.
2. Sormani, *Profilassi delle malattie veneree,* p. 37.
3. Pierleone Tommasoli, "Progetto di regolamento sulla polizia dei costumi," p. 5. This unpublished proposal for reform of the laws on prostitution was presented to the Council of State on June 20, 1891. A copy of the project, and the response of the government, are located in ACS, M.Int., D.G.San.Pubb., b. 563, f. 23000-6.
4. Tommasoli, *Prostitution et maladies vénériennes,* p. 14.
5. ACS, M.Int., D.G.San.Pubb., b. 562, f. 23000-6.
6. Ibid., 23000-1.
7. Ibid., f. 23000-6; ibid., b. 1011, f. 2300.
8. Tommasoli, *Prostitution et maladies vénériennes,* p. 18.
9. Tomassoli, "Progetto," p. 4, ACS, M.Int., D.G.San.Pubb., b. 563, f. 23000-6.
10. Tommasoli, *Prostitution et maladies vénériennes,* p. 13.
11. Ibid., pp. 11–12.
12. ACS, M.Int., D.G.San.Pubb., b. 562, f. 23000-1; ibid., b. 597, f. 23500-2.
13. Ibid., b. 562, f. 23000-6.
14. Ibid.
15. ACS, M.Int., DGPS, Pol.Giud., b. 249, f. 10-900.
16. R. Paulucci di Calboli, *Ancora la tratta delle italiane e Conferenza internazionale di Parigi,* p. 14.
17. For an account of the British campaign against white slavery, see Michael Pearson, *The Age of Consent: Victorian Prostitution and Its Enemies,* and Walkowitz, *Prostitution and Victorian Society,* pp. 245—255.
18. Paulucci di Calboli emphasized the wide support of the white slavery campaign across political lines; he claimed that monarchists, intransigent and liberal Catholics, and all branches of socialists supported the cause. See *Ancora la tratta delle italiane,* pp. 13–14.
19. Brian S. Pullan, *Rich and Poor in Renaissance Venice: The Social Institutions of a Catholic State, to 1620*; Luisa Ciammitti, "Conservatori femminili a Bologna e organizzazione del lavoro."
20. ACS, M.Int., DGPS, Pol. Giud., b. 249, f. 10900-21 (1910–1912). Under this archival rubric can be found the statutes or description of the major anti-white slave trade societies in Italy on the eve of World War I.

21. Ibid. On the Buon Pastore, see also Franco Bernocchi, *Prostituzione e rieducazione*, p. 139.

22. ACS, M.Int., DGPS, Pol.Giud., b. 249, f. 10900-21 (1910–1912).

23. Ibid.

24. Ibid.

25. Ibid.

26. Comitato Italiano contro la Tratta delle Bianche, *Relazione per gli anni 1902–1903*, located in ibid.

27. A bibliography of the women's press can be found in Annarita Buttafuoco and Rosanna DeLongis, "La stampa politica delle donne dal 1861 al 1924: Repertorio-catalogo."

28. For two short descriptions of the leagues, see Pieroni Bortolotti, *Socialismo e questione femminile*, pp. 34–35; and Gloria Chianese, *Storia sociale della donna in Italia (1800–1980)*, pp. 39–41. Several themes of *Vita Femminile* have been analyzed by Rosanna DeLongis, "Scienza come politica: *Vita femminile* (1895–1897).

29. Pieroni Bortolotti, *Socialismo e questione femminile*, 114–115; Chianese, *Storia sociale della donna*, 53. For a history of the bulletin *Unione femminile* and the views of Ersilio Majno Bronzini, see Annarita Buttafuoco, "Dalla redazione dell'*Unione Femminile* (1901–1905)."

30. Pieroni Bortolotti, *Socialismo e questione femminile*, pp. 35, 108–109; Chianese, *Storia sociale della donna*, pp. 42, 53.

31. Pieroni Bortolotti, *Socialismo e questione femminile*, p. 27.

32. Ibid., p. 9.

33. Sandra Puccini, "Condizione della donna e questione femminile (1892–1922)," pp. 52–57; Eugenio Garin, "La questione femminile nelle varie correnti ideologiche negli ultimi cento anni," in Società Umanitaria, p. 36. Eric Hobsbawm has documented a "progressive masculinization in the iconography of the labor movement" during the period that witnessed the shift from utopian to Marxist socialism. The image of the woman no longer symbolized revolution but the traditional female role of passive suffering. See Eric Hobsbawm, "Uomo e donna nell'iconografia socialista," 709. Corbin has also noted the ambivalence of French socialists to abolition, which they supported in theory but ignored in practice. See Corbin, *Filles de noce*, pp. 344–353.

34. Pieroni Bortolotti, *Socialismo e questione femminile*, pp. 72, 121; Maria Pia Bigaran, "Per una donna nuova: Tre giornali di propaganda socialista tra le donne."

35. Quoted in Buttafuoco, "Dalla redazione dell'*Unione Femminile*," p. 116.

36. Paulucci di Calboli, *Ancora la tratta delle italiane*, p. 15.

37. ACS, M.Int., DGPS, Pol.Giud., b. 249, f. 10900-21.

38. Ibid.

39. Ibid.

40. Ibid.

41. Comitato Italiano, *Relazione* (1906–1907), p. 5, ACS, M.Int., DGPS, Pol.Giud., b. 249, f. 10900-21.

42. Ibid., (1910), pp. 4–5.

43. Ibid., p. 1.

44. Ibid., p. 7.

45. Ibid., (1904–1905), p. 46.

46. Ibid.

47. Ibid.

48. Ibid., p. 47.

49. Ibid.

50. Ministère des Affaires étrangères, *Conférence internationale pour la repression de la traité des blanches.*

51. ACS, M.Int., DGPS, Pol.Giud., b. 249, f. 10900-21 (1910–1912).

52. Ibid., b. 48, f. 10900-21 (1916–1918).

53. Ibid., b. 249, f. 10900-21 (1910–1912).

54. Ibid.

55. Ibid., b. 48, f. 10900-21 (1916–1918).

56. Ibid.

57. Ibid.

58. A copy of the circular that initiated the interviews, dated March 7, 1913, is located in ibid. For the completed foglietti di indicazione, see ibid., b. 50, f. 10900-21 (1916–1918).

59. Ibid., b. 249, f. 10900 (1910–1912); ibid., f. 10900-21 (1910–1912); ibid., b. 50, f. 10900-21 (1916–1918).

60. Ibid., b. 249, f. 10900-21 (1910–1912).

61. David J. Pivar, *Purity Crusade, Sexual Morality and Social Control, 1868–1900,* p. 132.

62. ACS, M.Int., DGPS, Pol.Giud., b. 50, f. 10900-21 (1916–1918). Of the foglietti I sampled, none contained an admission of being forced into prostitution; instead, they detailed more informal and gradual paths to prostitution.

63. See, for example, Walkowitz, *Prostitution and Victorian Society,* p. 247; Connelly, *Response to Prostitution,* p. 125. Corbin is more convinced of the existence of an extensive white slave trade but believes that it did not differ qualitatively from the traditional circulation of prostitutes among the closed houses; see *Filles de noce,* p. 414.

64. Sormani, *Profilassi delle malattie veneree,* p. 37.

65. Gozzoli, *Prostituzione in Italia*, p. 34.

66. ACS, M.Int., DGPS, Pol.Giud., b. 249, f. 10900-21 (1910–1912).

67. ACS, M.Int., D.G.San.Pubb., b. 562, f. 23000-6.

68. Ibid.

69. Ibid.

70. Ibid., b. 1027, f. 23200.

71. Ibid., b. 562, f. 23000-8.

72. Rocco Santoliquido, *Discours (II Conférence internationale pour la prophylaxie de la syphilis et des maladies vénériennes)*, 1903, p. 15, located in ACS, M.Int., DGPS, Pol.Guid., b. 181, f. 13500.

73. Ibid., p. 14.

74. Ibid., p. 25.

75. Rocco Santoliquido, *Rapport (X Congrès internationale d'hygiene et de demographie)* 1900, p. 11, located in ibid.

76. Santoliquido, *Discours*, p. 20, ACS, M.Int., DGPS, Pol.Giud., b. 181, f. 13500.

77. Ibid., p. 24.

78. Ibid., p. 17.

79. According to Article 17 of the Public Health Law of 1904, the administration had the power to modify the Nicotera law. The resulting regulation, R.D. 27 July 1905, n. 487, was later incorporated into the Testo Unico delle Leggi Sanitari (R.D. 1 August 1907, n. 636). Documentation of the drawing up and approval of the regulation is located in ACS, M.Int., D.G.San.Pubb., b. 1011, f. 23000-1, and ibid., b. 1012, f. 23100.

80. ACS, M.Int., D.G.San.Pubb., b. 1012, f. 23100.

81. Giolitti's government collapsed in March 1905, several months before the final promulgation of the 1905 regulation. By this time, however, the bill had been already formulated and most of the necessary steps in the process of administrative approval had been completed.

82. Salomone, "Freedom and Power," p. 138.

83. Ibid., p. 147.

84. D.G.San.Pubb., *Raccolta sistematica delle leggi, regolamenti ed altre disposizioni sulla sanità pubblica*, 1:634.

85. Corbin, *Filles de noce*, pp. 453–484. I do not think that "neo-regulation" is the appropriate term for describing the theory of Santoliquido as enshrined in the regulation of 1905, for that regulation in fact incorporated quite a few abolitionist precepts. Like the French physicians, however, the Italian public health bureaucracy did succeed in partially "medicalizing" the social control of prostitution, that is, supplanting the police.

86. Connelly, *Response to Prostitution*, p. 12.

87. For an account of this transition from support for abolition to social purity, see Walkowitz, *Prostitution and Victorian Society*, pp. 245–255. Edward J. Bristow has traced the ideological changes within the purity movement in his *Vice and Vigilance: Purity Movements in Britain since 1700*.

Chapter 4: Social Profile of Prostitutes

1. Bolis, *Polizia*, p. 882.

2. Ibid.

3. Salvatore Ottolenghi, *Polizia scientifica: Quadri sinettici delle lezioni tenute nella Scuola di Polizia*, p. 122.

4. For sociological analyses of prostitution in terms of career, see Nanette Davis, "Prostitution: Identity, Career, and Legal-Economic Enterprise"; James H. Bryan, "Apprenticeships in Prostitution"; and Mary Riege Laner, "Prostitution as an Illegal Vocation: A Sociological Overview."

5. Cartenio Pini, *Dati statistici dall'anno 1869 al 1887 sulle visite mediche nelle malattie venereo-sifilitiche in relazione alla questione igienica*.

6. For an overview of research on Italian urbanization, see the articles in Alberto Caracciolo, ed., *Dalla città preindustriale alla città del capitalismo*. Several authors in this collection critique the Anglo-Saxon literature on cities that argues that industrialization leads to urbanization; they point out that in Italy industrialization may have modified cities but did not cause them; see Carlo Carozzi et al., "Processo di crescità urbana in un gruppo di città padane (1880–1970)." Caracciolo, in his own article entitled "Dalla città tradizionale alla città nell'età del capitalismo," uses the terms *traditional* and *modern* to indicate the transition of Italian cities in the nineteenth century.

7. Giorgio Gattei, "Per una storia del comportamento amoroso dei Bolognesi: Le nascite dall'unità al fascismo," pp. 617–618.

8. Ibid., pp. 637–638.

9. Direzione Generale della Statistica, *Censimento della popolazione del Regno d'Italia al 31 dicembre 1881*; idem, *Censimento della popolazione del Regno d'Italia al 10 febbraio 1901*; and Ufficio del Censimento, *Censimento della popolazione del Regno d'Italia al 10 giugno 1911*.

10. Luigi Dal Pane, *Economia e società a Bologna nell'età del Risorgimento: Introduzione alla ricerca*, p. 308.

11. Ibid., pp. 12, 217, 244.

12. Parlamento, Camera dei Deputati, *Atti Parlamentari*, Documenti, n. 146, pp. 14–21; Commissione Regia (1885), *Relazione, Proposte, allegati*, 1:15, 17; ACS, M.Int., D.G.San.Pubb., b. 1011, f. 23000-1; Bolis, *Polizia*, p. 974; L. Jolly, *Polizia Sanitaria*, p. 411.

13. Pietro Gamberini, *Rapporto politico-amministrativo-clinico della prostituzione di Bologna* 1864–1888.

14. This tends to undercut the regulationist argument that the Crispi legislation had been responsible for weaknesses in the government system; more fundamental social and economic forces had already caused many prostitutes to evade registration.

15. Parlamento, Camera dei Deputati, *Atti Parlamentari*, Documenti, n. 146, pp. 14–21.

16. Direzione Generale della Statistica, *Annuario statistico italiano* (1884), p. 707 (hereafter cited as *Annuario statistico*).

17. ASB, Quest., 1886, b. 34.

18. ACS, M.Int., D.G.San.Pubb., b. 600, f. 23569.

19. *Annuario statistico* (1884), p. 707.

20. Parlamento, Camera dei Deputati, *Atti Parlamenti*, Documenti, n. 146, pp. 21–31; Commissione Regia (1885), *Relazione, proposte, allegati*, 1:20; ACS, M.Int., D.G.San.Pubb., b. 1011, f. 23000-1 and b. 1012, f. 23100; Jolly, *Polizia Sanitaria*, p. 411.

21. ACS, M.Int., D.G.San.Pubb., b. 1012, f. 23100.

22. Bolis, *Polizia*, p. 848.

23. Tommasoli, *Prostitution et maladies vénériennes*, p. 28.

24. Gamberini, *Rapporti*, 1864–1886.

25. Achille Breda, *La profilassi delle malattie veneree in Italia*, p. 12; ACS, M.Int., D.G.San.Pubb., b. 600, f. 23562.

26. ACS, M.Int., D.G.San.Pubb., b. 600, f. 23569.

27. Ibid., b. 503, f. 21001-69.

28. Quoted in Gaetano Pini, *Della prostituzione e dei provvedimenti recentemente proposti o adottati a tutela della morale e dell'igiene in Italia e all'estero*, p. 6.

29. The same phenomenon has been noted by historians of prostitution in France and Germany; see Corbin, *Filles de noces*, pp. 42–43, and Evans, "Prostitution, State and Society," pp. 113–114.

30. Gamberini, *Rapporti*, 1864–1888.

31. ACS, M.Int., D.G.San.Pubb., b. 597, f. 23500; ibid., b. 598, f. 23511.

32. Ibid., b. 597, f. 23500. For other cities, see ibid., b. 561, 562, 598, 599, 600, 1012.

33. Ibid., b. 1012, f. 23100.

34. Santoliquido, *Rapport*, p. 10, ACS, M.Int., DGSP, Pol.Giud., b. 181, f. 13500.

35. Ibid.

36. Ibid., p. 11.

37. Parlamento, Camera dei Deputati, *Atti Parlamenti*, Documenti, n. 146, pp. 14–21; Commissione Regia (1885), *Relazione, proposte, allegati*, 1:22; Nathan, *Diabolerie e lo stato*, p. 11; Jolly, *Polizia Sanitaria*, p. 411.

38. Gamberini, *Rapporti*, 1864–1888.

39. ACS, M.Int., D.G.San.Pubb., b. 599, f. 23543; ibid., b. 1027, f. 23200; Tommasoli, *Prostitution et maladies vénériennes*, p. 33; Francesco Poggiali, *Manuale del funzionario di pubblica sicurezza pel servizio degli uffici sanitarii del Regno d'Italia*, app., pp. 8–9.

40. Figures for the population as a whole are taken from Istituto Centrale di Statistica, *Sommario di statistiche storiche dell'Italia, 1861–1975*, p. 12.

41. The young age of female workers is discussed in more detail below.

42. U. Mantegazza and G. Ciuffo, *La prostituzione studiata specialmente in Toscana e Sardegna*, p. 22; Raffaello Gurrieri and Ettore Fornasari, *I sensi e le anomalie somatiche nella donna normale e nella prostituta*, p. 23.

43. ASB, Quest., 1868, b. 50.

44. Ibid.

45. ACS, M.Int., D.G.San.Pubb., b. 599, f. 23543; see also ibid., b. 600, f. 23562.

46. Ibid., b. 1027, f. 23200.

47. Poggiali, *Manuale del funzionario di pubblica sicurezza*, app., pp. 8–9.

48. Santoliquido, *Rapport*, p. 12, ACS, M.Int., DGPS, Pol.Giud., b. 181, f. 13500.

49. Parlamento, Camera dei Deputati, *Atti Parlamenti*, Documenti, n. 146, p. 20; Commissione Regia (1885), *Relazione, proposte, allegati*, 1:17; Nathan, *Diabolerie e lo stato*, p. 11; Poggiali, *Manuale del funzionario di pubblica sicurezza*, app., pp. 1–2; Gurrieri and Fornasari, *Sensi*, p. 21.

50. Gamberini, *Rapporti*, 1864–1888.

51. Figures for women in general are based on the census of 1881 (Direzione Generale della Statistica, *Censimento . . . 1881*).

52. Ibid.

53. Cipolla, "Italian Demographic Development," p. 579.

54. An exception was the commission report of 1885, which found

the civil status of clandestine prostitutes to be the same as that of registered prostitutes. Statistics for clandestine prostitution were based on the women arrested for prostitution. See Commissione Regia (1885), *Relazione, proposte, allegati*, 1:24.

55. Bolis, *Polizia*, p. 868. Bolis believed that an exceptionally high rate of married women in Rome were prostitutes because of its underdeveloped economy and overabundance of celibate men (p. 802).

56. Ibid., p. 868.

57. Statistics for the population in general are based on those in the *Annuario statistico* (1884), p. 60. They refer only to women over the age of five.

58. Parlamento, Camera dei Deputati, *Atti Parlamenti*, Documenti, n. 146, p. 21; Commissione Regia (1885), *Relazione, proposte, allegati*, 1:6; and Poggiali, *Manuale del funzionario di pubblica sicurezza*, app., pp. 1–2.

59. Parlamento, Camera dei Deputati, *Atti Parlamenti*, Documenti, n. 146, pp. 16–21 (for prostitution) and Direzione Generale della Statistica, *Censimento . . . 1881* (for the population in general). Figures refer only to women over the age of five.

60. Howard, "Patriot Mothers in the Post-Risorgimento," p. 254.

61. Gamberini, *Rapporto*, 1868, p. 34.

62. Ibid., p. 35.

63. Ibid.

64. Gozzoli, *Prostituzione in Italia*, p. 22.

65. Parlamento, Camera dei Deputati, *Atti Parlamenti*, Documenti, n. 146, pp. 14–21.

66. Gamberini, *Rapporti*, 1863–1888.

67. Poggiali, *Manuale del funzionario di pubblica sicurezza*, app., pp. 4–7.

68. Commissione Regia (1885), *Relazione, proposte, allegati*, 1:19.

69. Alberoni, "Aspects of Internal Migration," p. 311.

70. For example, see Fabio Giusberti, "Poveri bolognesi, poveri forestieri e poveri inventati: Un progetto di 'rinchiudimento' nel XVIII secolo," p. 348. Giusberti found that, in 1726, 41 percent of those on Bolognese poor lists were not native to the city.

71. Bandettini, "Employment of Women in Italy," p. 371; Nora Federici, "L'inserimento della donna nel mondo del lavoro (Aspetti economici e sociali)," pp. 95–96. These two authors give figures beginning with the year 1881. I have based the statistic of 47 percent for 1861 on the census of that year, but it should be considered a rough estimate since the polling techniques, for this first census of united Italy, were not yet standardized and refined. For Milan, Louise Tilly reports that

the proportion of working women (over the age of 10) dropped from 54 percent in 1881 to 42 percent in 1911; see Louise A. Tilly, "The Working Class of Milan, 1881–1911," p. 126.

72. Bandettini, "Employment of Women in Italy," p. 374.

73. Tilly, "Working Class of Milan," p. 126.

74. Bandettini, "Employment of Women in Italy," p. 374. The trickiest problem of using the census figures for profession involves the category of female rural workers. As the introduction to the census of 1901 admits, inconsistency characterized the polling of farmwives, who are sometimes listed as farmers and sometimes as housewives. See Direzione Generale della Statistica, *Censimento . . . 1901*, 5:lxxviii.

75. See Direzione Generale della Statistica, *Censimento . . . 1901*, 5:124–125, which gives a breakdown of profession for both sexes in 1882 and 1901.

76. Tilly, "Working Class of Milan," pp. 127–128. In Milan garment making employed the largest proportion of women, followed by domestic service and, finally, textiles.

77. Puccini, "Condizione della donna," p. 12; Federici, "Inserimento della donna," p. 98.

78. Bandettini, "Employment of Women in Italy," p. 369; Federici, "Inserimento della donna," p. 98; Cinciari Rodano, "Posizione della donna," p. 172.

79. Nineteenth-century families tended to be larger than in the past because of the drop in child mortality and consequent survival of more children per family. Family size decreased in the twentieth century after the widespread adoption of birth control.

80. Quoted in Stefano Merli, *Proletariato di fabbrica e capitalismo industriale: Il caso italiano, 1880–1900*, 1:239.

81. Shepard Clough, *Economic History of Modern Italy*, p. 143. One hundred centesimi equal one lira.

82. Macrelli, *Indegna schiavitù*, p. 131. Her source is the report of Anna Maria Mozzoni to the conference of the International Abolitionist Federation in 1877 (for statistics on shirtmakers); for lacemakers, see Merli, *Proletariato di fabbrica*, 1:263.

83. Merli, *Proletariato di fabbrica*, 1:262–263. Long statistical series of women's wages in Italy are not available; scattered figures in other sources tend to support the range suggested by the examples given in the text. See Puccini, "Condizione della donna," p. 14; Tilly, "Working Class of Milan," pp. 246, 447–449; Camilla Ravera, *La donna italiana dal primo al secondo Risorgimento*, pp. 62–63, 91; Mario Romani, *Storia economica d'Italia nel secolo XIX, 1815–1914*, app. 3, 2:336; *Annuario statistico* (1912), pp. 228–229.

84. Pieroni Bortolotti, *Socialismo e questione femminile*, p. 57.

85. Ravera, *Donna italiana*, p. 78.

86. For prices of consumer goods such as food and clothes, from 1861 to 1970, see Istituto Centrale della Statistica, *Sommario di statistiche storiche*, pp. 134–145. For Milanese prices, see Tilly, "Working Class of Milan," p. 167.

87. Tilly, "Working Class of Milan," pp. 258–259; Merli, *Proletariato di fabbrica*, 1:434.

88. The phrase "salari di fame" is used by Puccini, "Condizione della donna," p. 14.

89. Ibid., p. 16.

90. Tilly, "Working Class of Milan," pp. 112–113.

91. Ibid., p. 246.

92. *Annuario statistico* (1912), pp. 228–229.

93. Macrelli, *Indegna schiavitù*, p. 131.

94. Merli, *Proletariato di fabbrica*, 1:259.

95. Ibid., p. 260.

96. Quoted in Pieroni Bortolotti, *Socialismo e questione femminile*, p. 57.

97. Ravera, *Donna italiana*, p. 78.

98. Merli, *Proletariato di fabbrica*, 1:272.

99. Puccini, "Condizione della donna," p. 13.

100. Ibid., p. 15.

101. Tilly, "Working Class of Milan," p. 205.

102. Ibid., p. 306. Even in eighteenth-century Bologna, 59.3 percent of the poor were women, although they formed only 52.2 percent of the population. See Giusberti, "Poveri bolognesi," p. 353.

103. Parlamento, Camera dei Deputati, *Atti Parlamenti*, Documenti, n. 146, p. 21.

104. Gamberini, *Rapporti*, 1863–1885.

105. Parlamento, Camera dei Deputati, *Atti Parlamenti*, Documenti, n. 146, p. 21; Gamberini, *Rapporti*, 1868–1881.

106. Poggiali, *Manuale del funzionario di pubblica sicurezza*, app., pp. 12–13; G. Pini, *Della prostituzione*, unpaged; Mantegazza and Ciuffo, *Prostituzione studiata specialmente*, p. 28. Ovidi reports a slightly higher figure, 18 percent, for the prostitutes in the sifilicomio of Rome. See Ulisse Ovidi, *Relazione statistico-terapeutica sulle prostitute ricoverate nella 1ª sezione del Sifilicomio di Roma dell'aprile al dicembre 1885*, p. 9.

107. Merli, *Proletariato di fabbrica*, 1:253.

108. Parlamento, Camera dei Deputati, *Atti Parlamenti*, Documenti, n. 146, p. 21.

109. Gamberini, *Rapporti*, 1863–1888.

110. Tilly, "Working Class of Milan," pp. 129–130, 149. Both male and female migrants usually found their first urban job in the service sector. While men later moved on to better paying factory employment, there were few alternatives for women, especially as the textile industry declined.

111. Chianese, *Storia sociale della donna*, p. 29.

112. Gamberini, *Rapporti*, 1864–1888.

113. Santoliquido, *Rapport*, p. 12. An early draft of this speech is located in ACS, M.Int., DGPS, Pol.Giud., b. 181, f. 13500.

114. Quoted in Laura Guidi, "Prostitute e carcerate a Napoli: Alcune indagini tra fine '800 e inizio '900," p. 123.

115. Poggiali, *Manuale del funzionario di pubblica sicurezza*, app., p. 1.

116. G. Pini, *Della prostituzione*, unpaged.

117. The likelihood of being orphaned would have decreased throughout the period as life expectancy increased from 35.42 in 1881/1882 to 46.94 in 1910/1912. For more detailed figures on life expectancy, see Cipolla, "Italian Demographic Development," p. 587.

118. The following line of argument has been suggested by Scott and Tilly to explain the rising rates of illegitimacy in late eighteenth- and early nineteenth-century Europe. In polemics with Edward Shorter, they do not believe that increased illegitimacy and prostitution signaled a wave of sexual liberation based on a changed mentality in the lower classes. Rather, they maintain that women continued their traditional behavior after migrating to the cities but were faced with unforeseen consequences, like pregnancy and desertion, stemming from differences in the social and economic environment. See Louise A. Tilly et al., "Women's Work and European Fertility Patterns"; Edward Shorter, "Illegitimacy, Sexual Revolution and Social Change in Modern Europe." On the acceptance of premarital sex in early modern Italy, see Sandra Cavallo and Simona Cerutti, "Onore femminile e controllo sociale della riproduzione in Piemonte tra sei e settecento."

119. According to available statistics, only 15–25 percent of prostitutes had their first sexual experience with a man of the middle or upper classes; see Gurrieri and Fornasari, *Sensi*, p. 22, and Mantegazza and Ciuffo, *Prostituzione studiata specialmente*, p. 38.

120. G. Pini reported that 82 percent of Milanese prostitutes in the sifilicomio had become sexually active before the age of twenty-one; see *Della prostituzione*, unpaged.

121. Walkowitz, *Prostitution and Victorian Society*, p. 20.

Chapter 5: Prostitutes and Police

1. Ottolenghi, *Polizia scientifica*, p. vi.

2. Ibid.

3. For example, in 1866 Prime Minister Ricasoli declared that popular mistrust of the police, justified in the past, no longer had any foundation since the kingdom had become a liberal state; quoted in Bolis, *Polizia*, p. 11. The remarks of Ottolenghi, however, indicate that suspicion of the police continued to exist into the twentieth century.

4. Regolamento Cavour, art. 17.

5. Regolamento Crispi sulla prostituzione, art. 4; Regolamento Nicotera, art. 5.

6. Canosa devotes one chapter to the history of police before World War II in his book, *Polizia in Italia*.

7. Ibid., p. 26.

8. Ibid., pp. 21, 25.

9. Raymond B. Fosdick, *European Police Systems*, p. 191; see also Sheldon Glueck, *Continental Police Practice*, p. 5.

10. On the role of the Italian prefect, see Angelo Porro, *Il prefetto e l'amministrazione perifica in Italia*, and Robert C. Fried, *The Italian Prefects: A Study in Administrative Politics*.

11. Regolamento Cavour, arts. 2 and 3.

12. ASB, Quest., 1866–1867, b. 41–42; ASB, Pref., 1868, b. 12–15; ASB, Quest., 1868, b. 50; ASB, Pref., 1869, b. 14–16; ibid., 1871, b. 4–15; ibid., 1874, b. 4–15; ibid., 1873, b. 13–19; ibid., 1888, b. 6–10.

13. ASC, M.Int., D.G.San.Pubb., b. 562, f. 23000-6.

14. Ibid.; see also ASB, Pref., 1895, b. 13–17.

15. Regolamento Cavour, art. 3. Poggiali also stressed the importance of staffing the Health Offices with police of "the highest level of rectitude, patience, integrity, and firmness" in his *Manuale del funzionario di pubblica sicurezza*, p. 33.

16. ASB, Quest., 1866–1867, b. 41–42; ASB, Pref., 1868, b. 12–15; ASB, Quest., 1868, b. 50; ibid., 1869, b. 59; ASB, Pref., 1869, b. 14–16; ibid., 1871, b. 4–15; ibid., 1874, b. 4–15; ibid., 1873, b. 13–19.

17. ASB, Pref., 1873, b. 13–19; ibid., 1874, b. 4–15.

18. ASB, Quest., 1866–1867, b. 41–42.

19. Ibid., 1868, b. 50.

20. Ibid.

21. Ibid., 1869, b. 66.

22. Ibid.

23. Ottolenghi gave a history of the establishment of the school in

Polizia scientifica. A detailed description of its activities can be found in its *Bollettino*, which began publication in 1910.

24. Fosdick, *European Police Systems*, p. 225; see also Glueck, *Continental Police Practice*, p. 8.

25. Fosdick, *European Police Systems*, pp. 192–193.

26. Cesare Lombroso, *Crime: Its Causes and Remedies*, p. 365.

27. Cesare Lombroso, *Criminal Man*, p. 28.

28. Ibid., pp. 6–7.

29. Salvatore Ottolenghi, *Trattato di polizia scientifica*, pp. vii, viii.

30. Ibid., p. x.

31. Ibid., pp. ix–x.

32. Cesare Lombroso and Guglielmo Ferrero, *The Female Offender*, p. 111.

33. Lombroso, *Crime*, p. 186.

34. Luigi Roncoroni, Review of Pauline Tarnowski, *Prostitution und Abolitionismus*, *Archivio di Antropologia Criminale* 14 (1893): 171. This journal was the main mouthpiece for the positivist school of criminology.

35. Giulio Masini, "La ringoscopia di 50 prostitute"; A. Ascarelli, "Le impronte digitali nelle prostitute," p. 821.

36. Salvatore Ottolenghi, *La sensibilità della donna*.

37. Gurrieri and Fornasari, *Sensi*, p. 347.

38. Ottolenghi, *Polizia scientifica*, p. 122.

39. Lombroso and Ferrero, *Female Offender*, p. 122.

40. Ibid., p. 153.

41. Ibid.

42. Ferrero, Review of Raymond de Rykère, *La criminalité féminine* and Paul Aubrey, *De l'omicide commis par la femme*, p. 572.

43. Lombroso, *Crime*, p. 259.

44. Ibid., pp. 406–407. I obviously disagree with Bulferetti's statement that Lombroso opposed the regulation of prostitution; see Luigi Bulferetti, *Cesare Lombroso*, p. 350.

45. Lombroso, *Crime*, pp. 147–148.

46. Ibid., p. 165.

47. Lombroso and Ferrero, *Female Offender*, p. 154.

48. Lombroso, *Crime*, p. 406.

49. Ettore Botti, *La delinquenza femminile a Napoli*, p. 69. Guidi discusses Botti's view of prostitution in her article "Prostitute e carcerate a Napoli."

50. Salvatore Ottolenghi, *L'insegnamento della polizia scientifica e le funzioni del segnalamento e delle investigazioni giudiziarie nell'amministrazione della pubblica sicurezza in Italia*, p. 9.

51. The figure of 264 Health Offices is for the year 1883; see Commissione Regia (1885), *Relazione, proposte, allegati*, 1:25. Most had been established immediately after unification, for by 1870 there were already 197 Health Offices in the kingdom (Castiglione, *Sorveglianza sulla prostituzione*, p. 68).

52. Mario Licciardelli Galatioto, *La prostituzione e la legge Crispi*, p. 18.

53. Ibid.

54. Gamberini, *Rapporti*, 1864–1886.

55. ASB, Pref., 1864, b. 6–8.

56. Mammoli, *Prostituzione*, p. 106.

57. Regolamento Nicotera, art. 3.

58. Guglielmo Filipponi, *La legislazione italiana in materia di polizia giudiziaria ed amministrativa: Guida teorico-practica*, p. 708.

59. ACS, M.Int., D.G.San.Pubb., b. 597, f. 23500; ibid., b. 600, f. 23562.

60. Regolamento Nicotera, arts. 12–14.

61. In 1899, for example, there were only 5 appeals to the special commission in all of Italy; of the 5, 4 were settled in favor of police and the fifth was withdrawn by the complainant before the final decision. See Ispettorato Generale della Sanità Pubblica, *Malattie infettive e diffusive e profilassi della sifilide e delle malattie veneree: Anno 1899*, p. 98.

62. ACS, M.Int., DGPS, Pol.Giud., b. 181, f. 13600 (1913–1915).

63. ASB, Pref., 1871, b. 4–15.

64. Parlamento, Camera dei Deputati, *Atti Parlamenti*, Documenti, n. 146, pp. 16–21.

65. ACS, M.Int., D.G.San.Pubb., b. 562, f. 23000. These statistics are for January–August 1897.

66. Ibid.

67. ASB, Quest., 1885.

68. Ibid., 1886.

69. Ibid.

70. Ibid.

71. Ibid.

72. Ibid.

73. Ibid.

74. Ibid.

75. Ibid.

76. Ibid.

77. Ibid.

78. Gamberini, *Rapporti*, 1864–1886.

79. ASB, Pref., 1873, b. 13–19; see also ASB, Quest., 1868 and 1869.

80. ASB, Quest., 1885.

81. Ibid.

82. Ibid., 1886.

83. Ibid.

84. Ibid.

85. ASB, Pref., 1873, b. 13–19.

86. ASB, Quest., 1886.

87. Ibid.

88. Ibid.

89. Istituto Centrale della Statistica, *Statistica della criminalità* (1906), p. xxxv.

90. Ibid., pp. 98–107.

91. ASB, Quest., 1886.

92. Ibid., 1885.

93. Ibid. In Rome, according to a list of 1897, the closed houses were concentrated in Campo Marzo near the mausoleum of Augustus, Via dei Coronari, Campo dei Fiori, and Tiburtina near the station (ACS, M.Int., D.G.San.Pubb., 600, f. 235069). Reports from other cities indicate a similar tendency for several brothels to be located on the same street (ibid., b. 597, f. 235001).

94. ASB, Quest., 1885.

95. Santoliquido noted with alarm this acceleration of openings and closings of brothels after 1891 in his report to the Consiglio Superiore della Sanità (High Council of Health); see Ispettorato Generale della Sanità Pubblica, *Malattie infettive: Anno 1899*, p. 98.

96. Bolis, *Polizia*, p. 933.

97. ASB, Pref., 1860–1880, Misc. b. 14.

98. Castiglione, *Sorveglianza sulla prostituzione*, p. 116.

99. A. De Blasio, *Nel paese della Camorra: L'imbrecciata*, pp. 129–130.

100. ASB, Quest., 1886.

101. Ibid., 1865.

102. Ibid.

103. Ibid.

104. Ibid., 1886.

105. ASB, Pref., 1888, ser. 2, b. 6–10.

106. ACS, M.Int., DGPS, Pol.Giud., b. 182, f. 13625 (1913–1915).

107. ASB, Pref., 1890, ser. 2, b. 5–9; ibid., 1888, ser. 2, b. 6–10.

108. ASB, Quest., 1886.

109. Alfredo Niceforo, "La mala vita a Roma e la sua repressione," p. 64. De Blasio published a similar list for Naples in *Nel paese del Camorra*, pp. 189–190.

110. ASB, Quest., 1885 and 1886.

111. Ibid., 1886.

112. Gamberini, *Rapporti*, 1864–1884.

113. ASB, Quest., 1885 and 1886.

114. Commissione Regia (1885), *Relazione, proposte, allegati*, 1:15. Evans noted the same high mobility of prostitutes in Germany in "Prostitution, State and Society," p. 112.

115. Commissione Regia (1885), *Relazione, proposte, allegati*, 1:15.

116. Bolis, *Polizia*, p. 847.

117. Ibid., p. 854.

118. The term is Gamberini's; see *Rapporto*, 1868, p. 33.

119. ASB, Quest., 1886.

120. Ibid., 1885.

121. Ibid., 1886.

122. Eric H. Monkkonen stresses the social service aspect of nineteenth-century policing in *Police in Urban America: 1860–1920*, p. 10.

123. Gamberini, *Rapporti*, 1864–1885.

124. Regolamento Cavour, art. 35.

125. Gamberini, *Rapporti*, 1864–1885.

126. Poggiali, *Manuale del funzionario di pubblica sicurezza*, app., p. 1.

127. ASB, Quest., 1886.

128. Ibid.

129. Ibid.; ASB, Pref., 1863, b. 6–8.

130. ASB, Quest., 1886.

131. Gamberini, *Rapporto*, 1867, p. 26.

132. Ibid.

133. ASB, Quest., 1888.

134. Giovanni Catella, *A proposito di una lettera del Prof. Celso Pellizzari sulla prostituzione e profilassi pubblica della sifilide: Soliloquio di un vecchio medico*, p. 7.

135. ASB, Quest., 1886.

136. Ibid.

137. Ibid.

138. Ibid.

139. Ibid., 1885.

140. Ibid., 1886.

141. Ibid., 1885.

142. ACS, M.Int., D.G.San.Pubb., b. 598, f. 23525.

143. Commissione Regia (1885), *Relazione, proposte, allegati,* 1:20; ASB, Quest., 1866 and 1867; ASB, Pref., 1870, b. 13–16.

Chapter 6: Prostitutes and Doctors

1. ASB, Quest., 1886.
2. Ibid.
3. For an excellent overview of health legislation in the early decades after unification, see Franco Della Peruta, "Sanità pubblica e legislazione sanitaria dall'Unità a Crispi"; see also Jolly, *Polizia Sanitaria,* pp. 398–399; Tommasoli, *Prostitution et maladies vénériennes,* pp. 29–30; Zino, *Manuale di polizia medica,* pp. 13–21. Zino was disappointed in 1888 with the elevation of the administration of public health to only the level of a department within the Ministry of the Interior. Instead, he called for a "Ministry of Health Affairs" [Ministero delle Cose Sanitarie] to coordinate "public hygiene, medical law, and forensic medicine in such a manner as to constitute a major technical-scientific center which would be full of real vitality and not fictitious or incomplete" (ibid., p. 17). This desire, shared by many of his medical colleagues, was not fulfilled until 1958.
4. For the government's philosophy and policy regarding public health assistance, see D.G.San.Pubb., *Ordinamento della pubblica assistenza degli infermi secondo la legislazione sanitaria italiana.*
5. Zino, *Manuale di polizia medica,* p. 155; Della Peruta, "Sanità pubblica," p. 745.
6. Giaxa, *Igiene pubblica,* p. 372.
7. Regolamento generale pei sifilicomi (September 2, 1871), arts. 42–47.
8. Celso Pellizzari, *Prostituzione e profilassi pubblica della sifilide: Lettera aperta a S. E. Francesco Crispi, ministro dell'interno,* p. 10; Castiglione, *Sorveglianza sulla prostituzione,* pp. 126–127; Tommasoli, *Prostitution et maladies vénériennes,* p. 53.
9. Tommasoli, *Prostitution et maladies vénériennes,* p. 53.
10. Celso Pellizzari, *La nuova clinica dermosifilopatica di Siena,* p. 9.
11. Ibid., p. 10.
12. Ibid., p. 6.
13. ASB, Pref., 1860–1880, Misc., b. 14; Castiglione, *Sorveglianza sulla prostituzione,* p. 126.
14. Gamberini, *Rapporto,* 1871, p. 15; see also Bolis, *Polizia,* pp. 970–971.

15. ASB, Pref., 1860–1880, Misc. b. 14.
16. D.G.San.Pubb., *Raccolta sistematica delle leggi*, 1:645.
17. Tommasoli, *Prostitution et maladies vénériennes*, pp. 30–31.
18. De Blasio, *Nel paese della Camorra*, p. 113.
19. ACS, M.Int., D.G.San.Pubb., b. 1011, f. 23001.
20. ASB, Pref., ser. 2, b. 3–10 (1891).
21. ASB, Pref., 1860, b. 3–8.
22. Ibid., 1879, b. 7–15.
23. ASB, Quest., 1885.
24. ASB, Pref., 1873, b. 13–19.
25. Ibid., 1860–1880, Misc., b. 14.
26. Gamberini, *Rapporto*, 1867, p. 17.
27. ASB, Pref., 1879, b. 7–15.
28. ASB, Quest., 1880.
29. ASB, Pref., 1879, b. 7–15.
30. Castiglione, *Sorveglianza sulla prostituzione*, p. 90.
31. Bolis, *Polizia*, p. 964; Gamberini, *Rapporto*, 1867, p. 28; ibid., 1871, p. 13.
32. Breda, *Profilassi . . . in Italia*, p. 43; Tommasoli, *Prostitution et maladies vénériennes*, p. 37.
33. Gamberini, *Rapporto*, 1867, p. 18.
34. Ibid.
35. Zino, *Manuale di polizia medica*, pp. 21–22.
36. Bolis, *Polizia*, p. 963.
37. Sormani, *Profilassi delle malattie veneree*, p. 19. For a similar statement see Zino, *Manuale di polizia sanitaria*, p. 21.
38. Castiglione, *Sorveglianza sulla prostituzione*, p. 91.
39. The curtain was suggested by Epaminonda Abate. Cited in Macrelli, *Indegna schiavitù*, p. 27. See also J. Galligo, *Progetto di regolamento sulla prostituzione per le principali città d'Italia ed in particolare per quelle della toscana*, p. 23, and Giaxa, *Igiene pubblica*, p. 373.
40. Castiglione, *Sorveglianza sulla prostituzione*, p. 91; Sormani, *Profilassi delle malattie veneree*, p. 31; Gamberini, *Rapporto*, 1871, p. 13.
41. ADB, *Donne cadute*, unpaged.
42. Breda, *Profilassi . . . in Italia*, p. 43.
43. Corbin similarly notes that, in the eyes of late nineteenth-century French doctors, "syphilis replaced cholera, and venereal disease symbolized for them the risk of contagion from the lower classes"; *Filles de noces*, pp. 44–45.
44. Pietro Gamberini, *Manuale delle malattie veneree redatto se-*

condo i principii teorico-pratici che si professano allo Spedale di S. Orsola, p. 12.

45. Gamberini, *Rapporto*, 1867, pp. 27–28.

46. Bertani, *Prostituzione patentata*, p. 36.

47. Gamberini, *Manuale*, p. 27.

48. Ibid., p. 26.

49. Enrico Rasori, *I progressi della sifilopatia nel nostro secolo*, p. 5.

50. Ibid.; Nels A. Nelson and Gladys L. Crain, *Syphilis, Gonorrhea and the Public Health*, p. 11; Walter Libby, *The History of Medicine*, p. 367.

51. Rasori, *Progressi*, p. 12.

52. Gamberini, *Manuale*, p. 49.

53. Gamberini, *Rapporto*, 1867, p. 15.

54. Quoted in Rasori, *Progressi*, p. 28.

55. Ibid., p. 21.

56. Ibid.

57. Giuseppe Fermini, *Cognizioni elementari sulla sifilide a chi deve ed a chi vuole conoscerla*, p. 22.

58. Erwin H. Ackerknecht, *A Short History of Medicine*, p. 168.

59. Nelson and Crain, *Syphilis*, p. 88; Ackerknecht, *Short History of Medicine*, p. 168.

60. ACS, M.Int., D.G.San.Pubb., b. 1012, f. 23100; ibid., b. 597, f. 23500-1.

61. Nelson and Crain, *Syphilis*, p. 11.

62. ACS, M.Int., D.G.San.Pubb., b. 1076, f. 24000.

63. Fermini, *Cognizioni elementari*, p. 26.

64. George M. Katsainos, *Syphilis and Its Accomplices in Mischief: Society, the State and the Physician*, p. 251.

65. Fermini, *Cognizioni elementari*, p. 40; Rasori, *Progressi*, p. 35.

66. Gamberini, *Manuale*, p. 54.

67. Fermini, *Cognizioni elementari*, p. 43.

68. Ibid., pp. 22–23.

69. Ibid., pp. 40–41.

70. ACS, M.Int., D.G.San.Pubb., b. 1011, f. 23000-1.

71. Fermini, *Cognizioni elementari*, p. 45.

72. Nelson and Crain, *Syphilis*, p. 88.

73. ACS, M.Int., D.G.San.Pubb., b. 1026, f. 23169.

74. Ibid., b. 1027, f. 23200.

75. Rasori, *Progressi*, p. 47.

76. Pelizzari, *Nuova clinica dermosifilopatica di Siena*, p. 10.

77. Jolly, *Polizia sanitaria*, p. 468.

78. Castiglione, *Sorveglianza sulla prostituzione*, p. 68; Commissione Regia (1885), *Relazione, proposte, allegati*, 2: table D.

79. Castiglione, *Soveglianza sulla prostituzione*, p. 69.

80. ASB, Quest., 1868.

81. ASB, Pref., 1860, b. 3–8.

82. Regolamento Cavour, art. 14.

83. ASB, Pref., 1860–1880, Misc., b. 14.

84. Ibid., 1864, b. 6–8.

85. Ibid., 1867, b. 12–15.

86. ASB, Quest., 1876–1888.

87. Ibid.

88. Castiglione, *Sorveglianza sulla prostituzione*, p. 70.

89. This figure is calculated from the reports of Gamberini for the years 1863–1887.

90. Bertani, *Prostituzione patentata*, p. 58. Regulationists agreed with Bertani that examining doctors were overburdened with work; see Castiglione, *Sorveglianza sulla prostituzione*, p. 123, and Breda, *Profilassi delle malattie veneree*, pp. 19–20.

91. Commissione Regia (1885), *Relazione, proposte, allegati*, 1:73.

92. ASB, Quest., 1876–1888.

93. Ibid.

94. Ibid.

95. Ibid.

96. Ibid.

97. Gamberini, *Rapporto*, 1871, p. 13.

98. Bolis, *Polizia*, pp. 883–884.

99. ASB, Quest., 1886.

100. Phillis H. Williams, *South Italian Folkways in Europe and America*, p. 161. Most of Williams's material on Italy is drawn from the writings of Giuseppe Pitrè, himself a doctor and therefore well acquainted with popular attitudes toward health. He is also considered Italy's first anthropologist, for he collected an enormous treasury of folk beliefs and folk art, the latter of which is on display at the Pitrè Museum in Palermo.

101. Ibid., p. 63.

102. Ibid., pp. 52–53.

103. Joyce Lussu, "La donna nella storia della salute delle masse popolari," p. 109.

104. Marisa Siccardi, "La donna nella medicina popolare e nelle istituzioni assistenziali," p. 115.

105. Bolis, *Polizia*, p. 980. Williams also mentions this belief in the

positive effects of sexual intercourse with a virgin; see *South Italian Folkways*, pp. 167–168.

106. De Blasio, *Nel paese della Camorra*, p. 69.

107. Giovanni Greco, "Aspetti della criminalità comune a Salerno e provincia nel quadrennio 1849–1852," p. 108; Williams, *South Italian Folkways*, pp. 167–168; Gamberini, *Manuale*, p. 52.

108. Gamberini, *Rapporto*, 1867, p. 15.

109. Ibid., p. 24.

110. Gamberini, *Manuale*, p. 52; Greco, "Aspetti della criminalità," p. 108.

111. De Blasio reports that even some doctors in Naples had faith in the remedies of a certain female healer since, as an ex-prostitute, she had survived so many cases of venereal disease during her own life. See *Nel paese della Camorra*, pp. 68–69.

112. ASB, Pref., 1860–1880, Misc., b. 14.

113. Quoted in Macrelli, *Indegna schiavitù*, p. 79.

114. Ibid.

115. Sormani, *Profilassi delle malattie veneree*, p. 16.

116. Ibid., p. 15. For expressions of similar sentiments, see Giaxa, *Igiene pubblica*, p. 374, and Jolly, *Polizia Sanitaria*, p. 411.

117. Pellizzari, *Nuova clinica dermosifilopatica di Siena*, p. 15; Breda, *Profilassi delle malattie veneree*, p. 8.

118. Jolly, *Polizia Sanitaria*, pp. 411–412.

119. ASB, Pref., 1863, b. 6–8.

120. Gattei, "Controllo di classi pericolose," p. 781. Gattei based his calculations on Gamberini's reports for 1863–1886.

121. The sociologist Nanette Davis points out that still today, in the United States, prisons require pap smears of all incoming adolescent females regardless of the charge against them. As in nineteenth-century Italy, the state assumes female deviance to be basically sexual in nature and arbitrarily submits arrested women to a sexual examination as part of the initiation ritual into the status of deviancy. See N. Davis, "Prostitution," p. 266.

122. Castiglione, *Sorveglianza sulla prostituzione*, p. 75; Direzione Generale della Statistica, *Movimento degli infermi negli ospedali civili del regno: Anno 1885–1887*, p. x.

123. Breda, *Profilassi delle malattie veneree*, p. 48. The sifilicomi in the eight cities were the Regio Sifilicomio Femminile and the Sifilicomio S. Lazzaro in Turin, the Regio Sifilicomio in Genoa, the Sifilicomio in Milano, a section of the Ospedale S. Orsola in Bologna, the Regio Sifilicomio in Florence, the Ospedale della Consolazione in Rome, the

Sifilicomio S. Maria della Fede in Naples, and the Regio Sifilicomio in Palermo; see Direzione Generale della Statistica, *Movimento degli infermi: 1884*, p. 116. Venice's lack of a sifilicomio was a legacy of Austrian legislation that had denied aid to the victims of venereal disease.

124. Article 1 of the Regio decreto (royal decree) that provided a prologue to the Regolamento generale pei sifilicomi of September 2, 1871.

125. Direzione Generale della Statistica, *Movimento degli infermi: 1885–1887*, p. xi.

126. Sormani, *Profilassi delle malattie veneree*, p. 34.

127. Pellizzari, *Nuova clinica dermosifilopatica di Siena*, p. 6.

128. Commissione Regia (1885), *Relazione, proposte, allegati*, 1:70. The quotation comes from the director of the Sifilicomio Femminile at Turin.

129. According to Bolis, prison infirmaries made up 47 out of the 116 facilities that provided treatment for prostitutes in 1863; see *Polizia*, p. 974.

130. Gamberini, *Rapporto*, 1861–1862, p. 8.

131. ASB, Pref., 1860–1880, Misc., b. 14.

132. Ibid.

133. Bolis, *Polizia*, p. 976.

134. Breda, *Profilassi delle malattie veneree*, p. 6; see also Galigo, *Progetto*, p. 37.

135. Regolamento generale pei sifilicomi (1871), art. 1.

136. Regio decreto (September 2, 1871), arts. 5, 8.

137. Regolamento (1871), arts. 82–89.

138. Ibid., art. 95.

139. Bolis, *Polizia*, p. 975.

140. Regolamento (1871), art. 85.

141. Sormani, *Profilassi delle malattie veneree*, p. 34.

142. Regolamento (1871), arts. 90, 91.

143. Ibid., art. 94.

144. Commissione Regia (1885), *Relazione, proposte, allegati*, 1:70.

145. Ibid., p. 71.

146. Ibid., pp. 70–72.

147. Quoted in Macrelli, *Indegna schiavitù*, p. 110.

148. G. Pini, *Della prostituzione*, pp. 17–18.

149. Commissione Regia (1885), *Relazione, proposte, allegati*, 1:71.

150. Gozzoli, *Prostituzione in Italia*, pp. 37–38.

151. Bolis, *Polizia*, p. 980.

152. Gozzoli, *Prostituzione in Italia*, p. 38.

153. Commissione Regia (1885), *Relazione, proposte, allegati*, 1:70.

154. ASB, Quest., 1876–1888.

155. Ibid.

156. Ibid.

157. Pellizzari, *Prostituzione e profilassi*, p. 9.

158. Gamberini, *Rapporti*, 1879–1888.

159. C. Pini, *Dati statistici*, unpaged.

160. Commissione Regia (1885), *Relazione, proposte, allegati*, 1: table A. Other reports confirmed that 10–20 percent of the prostitutes in the sifilicomi were syphilitic; see Pellizzari, *Prostituzione e profilassi*, p. 5 (for Pisa); Breda, *Profilassi delle malattie veneree*, p. 9 (Padua); and G. Pini, *Della prostituzione*, appendix (Milan).

161. Parlamento, Camera dei Deputati, *Atti Parlamenti*, Documenti, n. 146, p. 6; Direzione Generale della Statistica, *Risultati dell'inchiesta sulle condizioni igieniche e sanitarie nei communi del regno*, 1:177; *Annuario statistico* (1892), p. 143; Gamberini, *Rapporti*, 1863–1888; Ovidi, *Relazione statistico-terapeutica*, p. 8.

162. Gamberini, *Rapporti*, 1879–1887.

163. Ibid., 1864–1887.

164. For the total number of prostitutes in the sifilicomi, see Parlamento, Camera dei Deputati, *Atti Parlamenti*, Documenti, n. 146, p. 6; Commissione Regia (1885), *Relazione, proposte, allegati*, 2: table A; *Annuario statistico* (1892), p. 143; Direzione Generale della Statistica, *Movimento degli infermi: 1885–1887*, p. x; and Castiglione, *Sorveglianza sulla prostituzione*, p. 73.

165. Bolis, *Polizia*, p. 974; Gozzoli, *Prostituzione in Italia*, p. 18.

166. Williams, *South Italian Folkways*, p. 173.

167. Pomata, "Madri illegittime," pp. 499–500. Pomata looks specifically at the aversion of nineteenth-century women to giving birth in hospitals.

168. Pellizzari, *Prostituzione e profilassi*, p. 9.

169. See n. 165.

170. Regolamento (1871), art. 98.

171. ASB, Pref., 1860–1880, Misc., b. 14.

172. Bolis, *Polizia*, 976; see also Gozzoli, *Prostituzione in Italia*, p. 38.

173. Pellizzari, *Prostituzione e profilassi*, p. 9.

174. Ispettorato Generale della Sanità Pubblica, *Malattie infettive: Anno 1899*, p. 109.

175. Ibid., p. 101.

176. ACS, M.Int., D.G.San.Pubb., b. 1012, f. 23100.

177. ASB, Pref., 1889, ser. 2, 4–6.

178. ASC, M.Int., D.G.San.Pubb., b. 1011, f. 23000-1. A copy of the poster can be found under the same rubric.

179. Ibid.

180. Pietro Ramazzotti, *Parte dei servizi governativi in Milano per la profilassi generale delle malattie veneree: Dispensario celtico-vigilanza sanitaria alle meretrici*, p. 13.

181. Ibid., p. 21.

182. Ispettorato Generale della Sanità Pubblica, *Malattie infettive: Anno 1899*, p. 108 (hereafter cited as *Malattie infettive: Anno 1899*); D.G.San.Pubb., *Malattie infettive e diffusive dall'anno 1901 al 1904 e profilassi delle malattie celtiche dal 1902 al 1904*, p. xliv.

183. Ramazzotti, *Parte dei servizi*, p. 20.

184. D.G.San.Pubb., *Il Regolamento 27 luglio 1905, n. 487 e la profilassi delle malattie celtiche dal 1905 al 1908*, p. cxl (hereafter cited as *Regolamento 1905*).

185. ACS, M.Int., D.G.San.Pubb., b. 1012, f. 23100. These figures are taken from a list of dispensaries existing in 1896. The number in each city varied over time, however, due to closings and openings.

186. Ibid., b. 598, f. 23500-3.

187. *Regolamento 1905*, p. cxli.

188. Ibid.

189. Ibid., p. cxliii.

190. Ibid., p. 84.

191. Ibid. Ramazzotti reported that prostitutes made up 47 percent of the female patients in his dispensary, a figure considerably higher than the national average; see *Parte dei servizi*, p. 39.

192. *Regolamento 1905*, p. 85.

193. Ramazzoti, *Parte dei servizi*, pp. 9–10.

194. ASB, Pref., 1889, ser. 2, 4–6.

195. Ibid.

196. *Malattie infettive: Anne 1899*, p. 109.

197. Ramazzoti, *Parte dei servizi*, p. 13.

198. D.G.San.Pubb., *Malattie infettive . . . 1902 al 1904*, p. xlviii.

199. D.G.San.Pubb., *Raccolta sistematica delle leggi*, 1:97.

200. Statistics are for 1903–1908. See D.G.San.Pubb., *Malattie infettive . . . 1902 al 1904*, pp. 162, 166, and *Regolamento 1905*, pp. 70, 74, 78, 82.

201. D.G.San.Pubb., *Malattie infettive . . . 1902 al 1904*, p. xlix; *Regolamento 1905*, p. cxlvi.

202. Ramazzotti, *Parte dei servizi*, pp. 29–30.

203. *Regolamento 1905*, p. cxlvii.

204. Ramazzoti, *Parte dei servizi*, pp. 29–30.

205. Ibid., p. 14.

206. Ibid.

207. ACS, M.Int., D.G.San.Pubb., b. 562, f. 23000-8.

208. *Regolamento 1905*, p. cxlii.

209. ACS, M.Int., D.G.San.Pubb., b. 562, f. 23000-8. For a breakdown of patients by sex, see *Regolamento 1905*, p. cxliii.

210. ACS, M.Int., D.G.San.Pubb., b. 597, 598, 599, 600.

211. ASB, Pref., 1889, ser. 2, 4–6.

212. ACS, M.Int., D.G.San.Pubb., b. 600, f. 23569.

213. Ibid., b. 599, f. 23543; ibid., b. 598, f. 25500-3.

214. *Malattie infettive: Anno 1899*, p. 109.

215. Until 1902, the public health budgets showed entries for the rent of buildings housing the sifilicomi; see ACS, M.Int., D.G.San.Pubb., b. 1076, f. 24000.

216. *Malattie infettive: Anno 1899*, p. 124; *Regolamento 1905*, p. 150.

217. *Malattie infettive: Anno 1899*, p. 124.

218. Ministero dell'Interno, *Bolletino ufficiale* 21, n. 11 (1912): 479–480.

219. *Regolamento 1905*, p. 150.

220. Ibid.

221. Ibid., for the total patient population in 1899. For the number of prostitutes admitted to the wards in 1899, see *Malattie infettive: Anno 1899*, p. 107.

222. Statistics are for the years 1905–1908; see *Regolamento 1905*, p. clii.

223. Ibid., p. cliii.

224. *Malattie infettive: Anno 1899*, p. 127; D.G.San.Pubb., *Malattie infettive . . . 1902 al 1904*, p. lii; *Regolamento 1905*, pp. clii–cliii. The other two categories, which bring the totals to 100 percent, were "not improved" and those remaining under treatment at the end of each year.

225. *Malattie infettive: Anno 1899*, p. 125.

226. D.G.San.Pubb., *Raccolta sistematica delle leggi*, p. 98.

227. Ibid.

228. ACS, M.Int., D.G.San.Pubb., b. 598, f. 23511.

229. Ibid., b. 598, 599, 600.

230. Ibid., b. 1027, f. 23200; ibid., b. 597, f. 23500.

231. Ramazzotti, *Parte dei servizi*, p. 22.

232. *Malattie infettive: Anno 1899*, p. 107.

233. ACS, M.Int., D.G.San.Pubb., b. 562, f. 23000-8.

234. Ramazzotti, *Parte dei servizi*, p. 40.

235. ACS, M.Int., D.G.San.Pubb., b. 562, f. 23000-8.

236. Ibid., b. 597, f. 23500; ibid., b. 562, f. 23000-6 and f. 23000-7; ibid., b. 1027, b. 23200.

237. Ibid., b. 562, f. 23000-7.

238. Ibid., b. 598, f. 23524; ibid., b. 599, f. 23538.

239. Ibid., b. 562, f. 23000-7.

240. Ibid., b. 597, f. 23500; ibid., b. 599, f. 25343.

241. *Malattie infettive . . . 1902 al 1904*, p. lv.

242. Ibid.

243. *Regolamento 1905*, p. 152.

244. Ibid., p. 153.

245. Ibid., p. 164; *Annuario statistico* (1912), p. 35.

246. D.G.San.Pubb., *Malattie infettive . . . 1902 al 1904*, p. lix; Unione Statistica delle Città Italiane, *Annuario statistico delle città italiane*, 2:8.

247. *Annuario statistico* (1895), p. 93; *Annuario statistico* (1912), p. 35.

248. Pomata, "Madri illegittime," p. 506.

249. ACS., M.Int., D.G.San.Pubb., b. 1076, f. 24000.

250. Pomata, "Madri illegittime," pp. 509–510.

251. This figure is the average for the years 1888–1907 with the exception of 1892–1894, when the government failed to collect information by age; see *Regolamento 1905*, p. 165.

252. Ibid. According to official figures, syphilis caused 1,473 deaths per year among children in 1888 but only 1,103 by 1907.

253. Ibid., p. cxxxix.

254. Ibid.

255. Castiglione, *Sorveglianza sulla prostituzione*, p. 100.

256. ACS, M.Int., D.G.San.Pubb., b. 1011, f. 23000.

Conclusion

1. Cesare Gerin et al., *Aspetti medico-sociali della prostituzione con particolare riferimento alle attuali norme di legge*, p. 15.

2. Filippo Franchi, "Sulla sessualità maschile nei riguardi del problema delle case di tolleranza," in *La piaga sociale della prostituzione*, p. 90.

3. Parlamento, Camera dei Deputati, *Atti Parlamentari*, Discussioni, 44:39314. The speaker was Angelo Rubino, PNM (Monarchist party).

4. Ibid., p. 39327 (Giuseppe Calabro, MSI—Italian Social Movement, the Neofascist party).

5. Ibid., p. 39366 (Alfredo Cucco, MSI).

6. Ibid., p. 39314 (Rubino).

7. Ibid., p. 39326 (Gigliola Valandro, DC—Christian Democratic party).

8. Parlamento, Senato, *Atti Parlamentari*, Resoconto delle sedute della 1ª Comm. permanente, p. 321.

9. Ibid.

10. Parlamento, Camera dei Deputati, *Atti Parlamentari*, Discussioni, 44:39329 (Gisella Floreanini della Porta, PCI—Italian Communist party).

11. Gerin, *Aspetti*, pp. 22–30.

12. Parlamento, Camera dei Deputati, *Atti Parlamentari*, Discussioni, 44:39320 (Beniamo De Maria, DC).

13. For the Fascist legislation in prostitution, see the Appendix to Lina Merlin and Carla Barberis, eds., *Lettere dalle case chiuse*.

14. For doctors see the articles in *La piaga sociale della prostituzione*; for police see Guglielmo Di Benedetto, "Il capitolo del meretricio nel T.U. delle leggi di P.S."

15. Angelina Merlin was born in 1889 near Padua. A high school teacher, she joined the Socialist party in 1919 and collaborated on the *Difesa delle Lavoratrici*, a socialist feminist periodical. After refusing to take the Fascist oath, she was dismissed from teaching, arrested twice, and spent five years under house arrest in Sardinia. A participant in the resistance, she entered the directorate of the PSI in 1945 and was among the founders of the leftist feminist organization Unione Donne Italiane (Union of Italian Women). She was elected to the Senate in 1948.

16. Merlin and Barberis, *Lettere dalle case chiuse*.

17. Parlamento Camera dei Deputati, *Atti Parlamentari*, Discussioni, 44:393232 (Antonio Berardi, PSI).

18. Ibid., p. 39321 (De Maria).

19. The United Nations condemned the tolerated houses in a resolution of 1947 and a convention passed on March 21, 1950.

20. Parlamento, Senato, *Atti Parlamenti*, Resoconto, p. 309.

21. Parlamento, Camera dei Deputati, *Atti Parlamentari*, Discussioni, 44:39346 (Renato Tozzi Condivi, DC). Tozzi Condivi was referring to the Monarchist and Neofascist parties, which opposed the foundation of the Republic after World War II.

22. Legge 20 febbr. 1958, n. 75: Abolizione della regolamentazione della prostituzione e lotta contro lo sfruttamento della prostituzione altrui (Legge Merlin).

23. Legge Merlin, arts. 5, 7.

24. Ibid., art. 3.

25. Ibid., art. 5.

26. Ibid., art. 8.

27. Ibid., art. 12.

28. *Lucciola* translates as "firefly," the euphemism applied to Italian prostitutes because of the fires they built in the winter to keep warm on the streets. The first issue, published in July 1983, has articles explaining the founding of the committee and summarizing the proceedings of the first convention.

29. The Radical party was founded in the 1970s to promote New Left issues such as peace, the eradication of world hunger, ecology, and feminism.

30. "Dichiarazione della Segretaria, Pia, del Comitato dei Diritti Civili delle Prostitute," December 21, 1982 (typescript, Pordenone, 1982).

31. "Relazione di Carla, Presidente del Comitato dei Diritti Civili delle Prostitute al 1 Convegno Nazionale," February 19–20, 1983, at Pordenone, p. 7 (typescript, Pordenone, 1983).

32. Ibid., p. 2.

33. Ibid., p. 8.

34. "Dichirazione della Segretaria, Pia."

35. "Relazione di Carla, Presidente," p. 6.

Bibliography

Archives

ACS   (Archivio Centrale dello Stato, Rome)
ASB   (Archivio di Stato di Bologna)

Government Publications

Commissione Regia per lo Studio delle Questioni relative alla Prostituzione e ai Provvedimenti per la Morale ed Igiene Pubblica, *Relazione, proposte, allegati.* 2 vols. Florence: Casa di Patronato per Minorenni, 1885.

Direzione Generale della Pubblica Sicurezza. *Bollettino della Scuola di Polizia Scientifica.* Rome: Mantellate, 1910–1920.

Direzione Generale della Sanità Pubblica, *Malattie infettive e diffusive dall'anno 1901 al 1904 e profilassi delle malattie celtiche dal 1902 al 1904.* Rome: Manuzio, 1907.

————. *Ordinamento della pubblica assistenza degli infermi secondo la legislazione sanitaria italiana.* Rome: G. Bertero, 1910.

————. *Raccolta sistematica delle leggi, regolamenti ed altre diposizioni sulla sanità pubblica in vigore a tutto il 31 dicembre 1905.* Rome: Manuzio, 1906.

————. *Il Regolamento 27 luglio 1905, n. 487 e la profilassi delle malattie celtiche dal 1905 al 1908.* Rome: Manuzio, 1910.

Direzione Generale della Statistica. *Annuario statistico italiano.* Rome: Elzeviriana, 1878.

————. *Annuario statistico italiano.* Rome: Botta, 1881–1888.

————. *Annuario statistico italiano.* Rome: G. Bertero, 1889–1926.

————. *Censimento della popolazione del Regno d'Italia al 10 febbraio 1901.* 5 vols. Rome: G. Bertero, 1902–1904.

————. *Censimento della popolazione del Regno d'Italia al 31 dicembre 1881.* 2 vols. Rome: Bodoniana and Botta, 1883.

––––––. *Censimento generale (31 dicembre 1861)*. Turin: Tipografia Letteraria, 1864.

––––––. *Movimento degli infermi negli ospedali civili del regno: Anno 1884, 1885–1887*. Rome: Camera dei Deputati, 1886, 1888.

––––––. *Risultati dell'inchiesta sulle condizioni igieniche e sanitarie nei comuni del regno*. 3 vols. bound in 2. Rome: Ospizio di San Michele, 1886.

––––––. *Statistica dei ricoverati in ospedali pubblici e privati e in altri istituti di assistenza nell'anno 1898*. Rome: G. Bertero, 1900.

Ispettorato Generale della Sanità Pubblica. *Malattie infettive e diffusive e profilassi della sifilide e delle malattie veneree: Anno 1899*. Rome: Mantellate, 1901.

Istituto Centrale della Statistica. *Statistica dei riformatori*. Rome: Mantellate, 1904–1915.

––––––. *Statistica della criminalità*. Rome: Stamperia Reale, 1890–1895, 1906.

––––––. *Statistica della criminalità*. Rome: Ludovico Cecchini, 1907–1915.

––––––. *Statistica delle carceri*. Rome: Mantellate, 1881–1915 with gaps.

––––––. *Sommario di statistiche storiche dell'Italia, 1861–1975*. Rome: F. Failli, 1976.

––––––. *Sommario di statistiche storiche italiane, 1861–1955*. Rome: Istituto Poligrafico dello Stato, 1958.

Parlamento, Camera dei Deputati. *Atti Parlamentari*. Discussioni, legislatura II, Anno 1957–1958. Rome: Camera dei Deputati, 1958.

––––––. *Atti Parlamentari*. Documenti, sessione 1876–1877. Rome: Camera dei Deputati, 1877.

––––––. *Atti Parlamentari*. Sessione 1887–1888. Rome: Camera dei Deputati, 1888.

Parlamento, Senato. *Atti Parlamentari*. Resoconto delle sedute della 1ª Commissione permanente, Legislatura II, 1953–1958. Rome: Senato, 1958.

Ufficio del Censimento. *Censimento della popolazione del Regno d'Italia al 10 giugno 1911*. 3 vols. Rome: G. Bertero, 1914.

Unione Statistica delle Città Italiane. *Annuario statistico delle città italiane*. Florence: Alfani e Venturi, 1906–1916.

Books and Articles

Accati, Luisa. "Lo spirito della fornicazione: Virtù dell'anima e virtù del corpo in Friuli, fra '600 e '700." *Quaderni Storici* 14 (1979): 644–672.

Bibliography

Ackerknecht, Erwin H. *A Short History of Medicine.* New York: Ronald, 1955.

Adler, Freda. "The Oldest and Newest Profession." In Freda Adler and Rita James Simon, eds., *The Criminology of Deviant Women,* pp. 213–222. Boston: Houghton Mifflin, 1979.

Agostin, Tibor. "Some Psychological Aspects of Prostitution: The Pseudo Personality." *International Journal of Psycho-Analysis* 26 (1945): 62–67.

Alberoni, Francesco. "Aspects of Internal Migration Related to Other Types of Italian Migration." In Clifford J. Jansen, ed., *Readings in the Sociology of Migration,* pp. 285–316. Oxford: Pergamon, 1970.

Amicis, Tommaso de. *Rendiconto statistico speciale delle affezioni osservate e curate nel Deambulatorio e nella Clinica D-S della R. Università di Napoli.* Naples: Angelo Trani, 1910.

Antonini, Claudia, and Buscarini, Marilena. "Le coscritte dell'amore: Intervento istituzionale e prostituzionale negli ultimi decenni del XIX secolo." Thesis, University of Bologna, 1981–1982.

Ascarelli, A. "Le impronte digitali nelle prostitute." *Archivio di Antropologia Criminale* 27 (1906): 812–821.

Associazione democratica bolognese. *Le donne cadute, la legge e la polizia.* Bologna: Assoguidi, 1881.

Bandettini, Pierfrancesco. "The Employment of Women in Italy, 1881–1951." *Comparative Studies in Society and History* 2 (1960): 369–374.

Baratta, Alessandro. "Criminologia critica e riforma penale." *Questione Criminale* 7 (1981): 349–389.

———. "Problemi sociali e percezione della criminalità." *Dei Delitti e delle Pene* 1 (1983): 15–39.

Becker, Howard S. *Outsiders.* New York: Macmillan, 1963.

Benjamin, Harry. "Prostitution." In Albert Ellis and Albert Abarbanel, eds., *The Encyclopedia of Sexual Behavior,* 2: 869–882. New York: Hawthorn, 1961.

Benjamin, Harry, and Ellis, Albert. "An Objective Examination of Prostitution." *The International Journal of Sexology* 8 (1954): 100–105.

Benjamin, Harry, and Masters, R. E. L. *Prostitution and Morality.* New York: Julian, 1964.

Bernocchi, Franco. *Prostituzione e rieducazione.* Padua: CEDAM, 1966.

Bertani, Agostino. *La prostituzione patentata e il regolamento sanitario: Lettera ad Agostino DePretis.* Milan: E. Quadrio, 1881.

Bigaran, Maria Pia. "Per una donna nuova: Tre giornali di propaganda socialista tra le donne." *Nuova DonnaWomanFemme* 21 (1982): 53–72.

Bloch, Iwan. *Die Prostitution.* 2 vols. Berlin: Louis Marcus, 1912–1925.

Bolis, Giovanni. *La polizia e le classi pericolose della società: Studii.* Bologna: Zanichelli, 1871.

Borelli, Giambattista. *Studi sulla prostituzione.* Rome: Botta, 1881.

Botti, Ettore. *La delinquenza femminile a Napoli.* Naples: Luigi Pierro, 1904.

Bowker, Lee H. *Women, Crime, and the Criminal Justice System.* Lexington, Mass.: Lexington, 1978.

Brandt, Allan M. *No Magic Bullet.* New York: Oxford University Press, 1985.

Breda, Achille. *La profila si delle malattie veneree in Italia.* N.p., n.d.

Bristow, Edward J. *Prostitution and Prejudice: The Jewish Fight against White Slavery.* New York: Schocken, 1983.

———. *Vice and Vigilance: Purity Movements in Britain since 1700.* Totowa, N.J.: Littlefield, Adams; Rowman and Littlefield, 1977.

Brundage, James A. "Prostitution in the Medieval Canon Law." *Signs* 1 (1976): 825–845.

Bryan, James H. "Apprenticeships in Prostitution." In John H. Gagnon and William Simon, eds., *Sexual Deviance*, pp. 146–164. New York: Harper and Row, 1967.

Bulferetti, Luigi. *Cesare Lombroso.* Turin: UTET, 1975.

Bullough, Vern L. *The History of Prostitution.* New Hyde Park, N.Y.: University Books, 1964.

———. "Problems and Methods for Research in Prostitution and the Behavioral Sciences." In Ailon Shiloh, ed., *Studies in Human Sexual Behavior: The American Scene*, pp. 14–23. Springfield, Ill.: Thomas, 1970.

Bullough, Vern L.; Deacon, Margaret; Elcano, Barrett; and Bullough, Bonnie, eds. *A Bibliography of Prostitution.* New York: Garland, 1977.

Burnham, John C. "Medical Inspection of Prostitutes in Nineteenth Century America: The St. Louis Experiment and Its Sequel." *Bulletin of the History of Medicine* 45 (1971): 203–218.

Butler, Josephine E. *An Autobiographical Memoir.* Ed. W. Johnson and Lucy A. Johnson. 1909. Reprint. Bristol: Arrowsmith, 1928.

———. *Personal Reminiscences of a Great Crusade.* London: Horace Marshall, 1896.

Buttafuoco, Annarita. "Dalla redazione dell'*Unione Femminile* (1901–1905)." *Nuova DonnaWomanFemme* 21 (1982): 101–141.

———. "'Per insofferenza di freno e per miseria': Discole, vaga-bonde e prostitute dell'Asilo Mariuccia di Milano (1902–1914)." *Movimento Operaio e Socialista* 6 (1983): 117–134.

Buttafuoco, Annarita, and DeLongis, Rosanna. "La stampa politica delle donne dal 1861 al 1924: Repertorio-catalogo." *Nuova Donna-WomanFemme* 21 (1982): 73–100.

Cafagna, Luciano. "Italy, 1830–1914." In Carlo M. Cipolla, ed., *The Emergence of Industrial Societies*, 1: 279–328. New York: Har-vester, Barnes and Noble, 1973.

Canosa, Romano. *La polizia in Italia dal 1945 a oggi.* Bologna: Mulino, 1976.

———. *Sesso e stato.* Milan: Mazzotta, 1981.

Capezzuoli, Luciana, and Cappabianca, Grazia. *Storia dell'emancipazi-one femminile.* Rome: Riuniti, 1964.

Caracciolo, Alberto. "Dalla città tradizionale alla città nell'età del capitalismo." In idem, ed., *Dalla città preindustriale alla città del capitalismo*, pp. 155–171. Bologna: Mulino, 1975.

Carozzi, Carlo; Mioni, Alberto; and Rozzi, Renato. "Processo di cres-cità urbana in un gruppo di città padane (1880–1970)." In Alberto Caracciolo, *Dalla città preindustriale alla città del capitalismo*, pp. 199–220. Bologna: Mulino, 1975.

Castiglione, Pietro. *Sorveglianza sulla prostituzione e modi per impedire la diffusione della sifilide: Studi storico-statistici e proposte.* Rome: G. Via, 1872.

Catella, Giovanni. *A proposito di una lettera del Prof. Celso Pellizzari sulla prostituzione e profilassi pubblica della sifilide: Soliloquio di un vecchio medico.* Turin: Roux, 1888.

———. *Il regolamento 15 febbraio 1860 sulla prostituzione: Estratto del Giornale della R. Accademia di Medicina di Torino.* 1887.

Cavallo, Sandra, and Cerutti, Simona. "Onore femminile e controllo sociale della riproduzione in Piemonte tra sei e settecento." *Qua-derni Storici* 44 (1980): 346–383.

Chianese, Gloria. *Storia sociale della donna in Italia (1800–1980).* Naples: Guida, 1980.

Choisy, Maryse. *Psychoanalysis of the Prostitute.* New York: Philo-sophical Library, 1961.

Ciammitti, Luisa. "Conservatori femminili a Bologna e organizzazione del lavoro." *Quaderni Storici* 14 (1979): 760–764.

Cinciari Rodano, Marisa. "La posizione della donna nella vita econ-omica: L'occupazione dal 1900 ad oggi." *Rinascita* 3 (March 1961): 167–180.

Cipolla, Carlo M. "Four Centuries of Italian Demographic Development." In D. V. Glass and D. E. L. Eversley, eds., *Population in History*, pp. 570–587. Chicago: Aldine, 1965.

Clough, Shepard. *Economic History of Modern Italy.* New York: Columbia University Press, 1964.

Cohen, Bernard. *Deviant Street Networks: Prostitution in New York.* Lexington, Mass.: Lexington, 1980.

Cohen, Sherrill. "Convertite e malmaritate: Donne 'irregolari' e ordini religiosi nella Firenze rinascimentale." *Memoria* 5 (1982): 46–63.

Connelly, Mark Thomas. *The Response to Prostitution in the Progressive Era.* Chapel Hill: University of North Carolina Press, 1980.

Corbin, Alain. *Les filles de noce: Misère sexuelle et prostitution (19ᵉ et 20ᵉ siècles).* Paris: Aubier-Montaigne, 1978.

Cott, Nancy. *Bonds of Womanhood: "Women's sphere" in New England, 1780–1835.* New Haven, Conn.: Yale University Press, 1977.

Cutrera, Antonino. *Storia della prostituzione in Sicilia: Monografia storico-giuridica.* 1903. Reprint. Palermo: Editori Stampatori Associati, 1972.

Davis, Kingsley. "The Sociology of Prostitution." *American Sociological Review* 2 (1937): 744–755.

Davis, Nanette. "Prostitution: Identity, Career, and Legal-Economic Enterprise." In James M. Henslin and Edward Sagarin, eds., *The Sociology of Sex: An Introductory Reader*, pp. 195–222. New York: Schocken, 1978.

De Blasio, A. *Nel paese della Camorra: L'imbrecciata.* Naples: Luigi Pierro, 1901.

Della Peruta, Franco. "Infanzia e famiglia nella prima metà dell'ottocento." *Studi Storici* 20 (1979): 473–491.

———. "Sanità pubblica e legislazione sanitaria dall'Unità a Crispi." *Studi Storici* 21 (1980): 713–759.

DeLongis, Rosanna. "Scienza come politica: *Vita femminile* (1895–1897)." *Nuova DonnaWomanFemme* 21 (1982): 35–51.

Di Benedetto, Guglielmo. "Il capitolo del meretricio nel T.U. delle Leggi di P.S." *Rivista di Polizia* 11 (1958): 57–82.

"Donna, devianza e controllo sociale." *Dei Delitti e delle Pene* 1 (1983): 91–166 (special sec.).

Evans, Richard. "Prostitution, State, and Society in Imperial Germany." *Past and Present* 70 (1976): 106–129.

Fabretti, Ariodante, ed. *La prostituzione in Perugia nei secoli XIV e XV: Documenti inediti.* Turin: Private printing, 1885.

Faccioli, Franca. "La devianza e la criminalità femminile in Italia." In Gianni Statera, ed., *Il privato come politica*, pp. 145–189. Cosenza: Lerici, 1977.

Bibliography

Fazio, Eugenio. *L'abrogazione dei regolamenti di sorveglianza sulla prostituzione e l'igiene pubblica.* Naples: N.p., 1876.

Federici, Nora. "L'inserimento della donna nel mondo del lavoro (Aspetti economici e sociali)." In Società Umanitaria, ed., *L'emancipazione femminile in Italia*, pp. 87–127. Florence: Nuova Italia, 1962.

Feldman, Egal. "Prostitution: The Alien Woman and the Progressive Imagination." *American Quarterly* 19 (1967): 192–206.

Fermini, Giuseppe. *Cognizioni elementari sulla sifilide a chi deve ed a chi vuole conoscerla.* Milan: Francesco Marcolli, 1912.

Ferrante, Lucia. "L'onore ritrovato: Donne nella Casa del Soccorso di San Paolo a Bologna (sec. XVI–XVII)." *Quaderni Storici* 53 (1983): 499–527.

Ferrero, Guglielmo. Review of Raymond de Rykère, *La criminalité féminine* and Paul Aubrey, *De l'omicide commis par la femme.* *Archivio di Antropologia Criminale* 12 (1891): 566–573.

Filipponi, Guglielmo. *La legislazione italiana in materia di polizia guidiziaria ed amministrativa: Guida teorico-pratica.* Forlì: Romagnole, 1909.

Finnegan, Frances. *Poverty and Prostitution: A Study of Victorian Prostitutes in York.* Cambridge: Cambridge University Press, 1979.

Fiocca, Giorgio. "Struttura urbana e controllo sociale a Roma nel '700 e nel primo' 800: Mobilità sociale, paesaggio urbano ed enti di sorveglianzo pontifici." In Ercole Sori, ed., *Città e controllo sociale in Italia tra XVIII e XIX secolo*, pp. 380–399. Milan: Angeli, 1982.

Flexner, Abraham. *Prostitution in Europe.* New York: Century, 1914.

Fosdick, Raymond B. *European Police Systems.* New York: Century, 1916.

Foucault, Michel. *The Birth of the Clinic.* Trans. A. M. Sheridan Smith. New York: Random House, Vintage, 1975.

———. *Discipline and Punish: The Birth of the Prison.* Trans. Alan Sheridan. New York: Random House Vintage, 1979.

———. *La volonté de savoir.* Paris: Gallimard, 1976.

Franchi, Filippo. "Sulla sessualità maschile nei riguardi del problema delle case di tolleranza." In *La piaga sociale della prostituzione*, pp. 87–97. Rome: Istituto di Medicina Sociale, 1950.

Fried, Robert C. *The Italian Prefects: A Study in Administrative Politics.* New Haven, Conn.: Yale University Press, 1963.

Gagnon, John H., and Simon, William. *Sexual Conduct: The Social Sources of Human Sexuality.* Chicago: Aldine, 1973.

Galligo, J. *Progetto di regolamento sulla prostituzione per le principali città d'Italia ed in particolare per quelle della toscana.* Florence: Martini, 1860.

Gamberini, Pietro. *Manuale delle malattie veneree redatto secondo i principii teorico-pratici che si professano allo Spedale di S. Orsola.* Bologna: Sassi, 1848.

―――. *Rapporto politico-amministrativo-clinico della prostituzione di Bologna.* Bologna: Gamberini e Parmeggiani, 1864–1888.

Garin, Eugenio. "La questione femminile nelle varie correnti ideologiche negli ultimi cento anni." In Società Umanitaria, ed., *L'emancipazione femminile in Italia,* pp. 19–44. Florence: Nuova Italia, 1962.

Garofalo, Anna. "Prostituzione e miseria." Commissione Parlamentare d'Inchiesta sulla Miseria in Italia *Atti* 9 (1953): 271–294.

Gattei, Giorgio. " Controllo di classi pericolose: La prima regolamentazione prostituzionale unitaria (1860–1888)." In M. L. Betri and A. Gigli Marchetti, eds., *Salute e classi lavatrici in Italia dall'Unità al fascismo,* pp. 763–796. Milan: Angeli, 1982.

―――. "Per una storia del comportamento amoroso dei Bolognesi: Le nascite dall'unità al fascismo." *Società e Storia* 9 (1980): 613–639.

―――. "La sifilide: Medici e poliziotti intorno alla 'venere politica.'" In *Storia d'Italia, Annali,* vol. 7, *Malattia e Medicina,* pp. 741–798. Turin: Einaudi, 1984.

Gebhard, Paul. "Misconceptions about Female Prostitutes." *Medical Aspects of Human Sexuality* 3 (1969): 24–30.

Gerin, Cesare. *Aspetti medico-sociali della prostituzione con particolare riferimento alle attuali norme di legge.* Rome: Istituto Italiano di Medicina Sociale, 1964.

Gerschenkron, Alexander. *Economic Backwardness in Historical Perspective.* Cambridge, Mass.: Harvard University Press, 1962.

Giacomo, Salvatore Di. *La prostituzione in Napoli nei secoli XV, XVI, XVII: Documenti inediti.* Naples: Riccardo Marghieri, 1899.

Giaxa, Vincenzo De. *Igiene pubblica.* Milan: Francesco Vallardi, 1879.

Gibson, Mary S. "The 'Female Offender' and the Italian School of Criminal Anthropology." *Journal of European Studies* 12 (1982): 155–165.

―――. "Prostitution and the Bourgeois Feminist Movement in Italy." In B. B. Cairoli, Robert F. Harney, and Lydia F. Tomasi, eds., *The Italian Immigrant Woman,* pp. 24–30. Toronto: Multicultural Society, 1976.

―――. "The State and Prostitution: Prohibition, Regulation, or Decriminalization?" In James A. Inciardi and Charles E. Faupel, eds., *History and Crime*, pp. 193–208. Beverly Hills, Calif.: Sage, 1980.

Giovanni, Claudio. "L'emancipazione della donna nell'Italia postunitaria: Una questione borghese?" *Studi Storici* 23 (1982): 355–381.

Giusberti, Fabio. "Poveri bolognesi, poveri forestieri e poveri inventati: Un progetto di 'rinchiudimento' nel XVIII secolo." In Ercole Sori, ed., *Città e controllo sociale in Italia tra XVIII e XIX secolo*, pp. 341–362. Milan: Angeli, 1982.

Glover, Edward. "The Abnormality of Prostitution." In A. M. Krich, ed., *Women*, pp. 247–273. New York: Dell, 1953.

Glueck, Sheldon. *Continental Police Practice*. 1926. Reprint. Springfield, Ill.: Thomas, 1974.

Goffman, Erving. *Asylums: Essays on the Social Situation of Mental Patients and Other Inmates*. Garden City, N.Y.: Doubleday, Anchor, 1961.

———. *Stigma*. Englewood Cliffs, N.J.: Prentice-Hall, 1963.

Gozzoli, Giovanni. *La prostituzione in Italia*. Rome: E. Perino, 1886.

Gramola, Antonio. *Le prostitute e la legge*. N.p., 1880.

Greco, Giovanni. "Aspetti della criminalità comune a Salerno e provincia nel quadrennio 1849–1852." In Ercole Sori, *Città e controllo sociale in Italia tra XVII e XIX secolo*, pp. 99–109. Milan: Angeli, 1982.

Greenwald, Harold. *The Call Girl*. New York: Ballantine, 1958.

Grew, Raymond. "How Success Spoiled the Risorgimento." In A. Wm. Salomone, ed., *Italy from the Risorgimento to Fascism*, pp. 38–55. Garden City, N.Y.: Doubleday, 1970.

Guidi, Laura. "Prostitute e carcerate a Napoli: Alcune indagini tra fine '800 e inizio '900." *Memoria* 4 (1982): 116–124.

Gurrieri, Raffaello, and Fornasari, Ettore. *I sensi e le anomalie somatiche nella donna normale e nella prostituta*. Turin: Bocca, 1893.

Guyot, Yves. *La prostitution*. Paris: G. Charpentier, 1882.

Hall, Gladys Mary. *Prostitution in the Modern World*. New York: Emerson, 1936.

Henriques, Fernando. *Prostitution and Society*. 2 vols. Vol. 1, New York: Citadel, 1962; vol. 2, London: MacGibbon and Kee, 1963.

Heyl, Barbara. "Prostitution: An Extreme Case of Sex Stratification." In Freda Adler and Rita James Simon, eds., *The Criminology of Deviant Women*, pp. 196–210. Boston: Houghton Mifflin, 1979.

Hirschi, Travis. "The Professional Prostitute." *Berkeley Journal of Sociology* 7 (1962): 33–49.

Bibliography

Hobsbawm, Eric. "Uomo e donna nell'iconografia socialista." *Studi Storici* 20 (1979): 705–723.

Hollander, Marc H. "Prostitution, the Body, and Human Relatedness." *International Journal of Psycho-Analysis* 42 (1961): 404–413.

Holmes, Kay Ann. "Reflections by Gaslight: Prostitution in Another Age." *Issues in Criminology* 7 (1972): 83–101.

Howard, Judith Jeffrey. "Patriot Mothers in the Post-Risorgimento: Women after the Italian Revolution." in Carol R. Berkin and Clara M. Lovett, eds., *Women, War, and Revolution*, pp. 237–258. New York: Holmes and Meier, 1980.

Jackman, Norman R.; R. O'Toole; and G. Geis, "The Self-image of the Prostitute." *Sociological Quarterly* 4 (1963): 150–161.

James, Jennifer. "Motivations for Entrance into Prostitution." In Laura Crites, ed., *The Female Offender*, pp. 177–205. Lexington, Mass.: Lexington, 1976.

————. *The Politics of Prostitution.* Seattle: University of Washington Press, 1975.

Jolly, L. *Polizia Sanitaria.* Economia Politica, ser. 3, vol. 15, pp. 395–560. Turin: UTET, 1892.

Katsainos, George M. *Syphilis and Its Accomplices in Mischief: Society, the State and the Physician.* Athens: N.p., 1939.

Klein, Dorie. "The Etiology of Female Crime: A Review of the Literature." *Issues in Criminology* 8 (1973): 3–30.

La Croix, Paul. *History of Prostitution.* New York: Covici, Friede, 1931.

Laner, Mary Riege. "Prostitution as an Illegal Vocation: A Sociological Overview." In Clifton D. Bryant, ed., *Deviant Behavior: Occupational and Organizational Bases*, pp. 406–418. Chicago: Rand-McNally, 1974.

Larivaille, Paul. *La vie quotidienne des courtisanes en Italie au temps de la renaissance: Rome et Venise, XVᵉ et XVIᵉ siècles.* Paris: Hachette, 1975.

Libby, Walter. *The History of Medicine.* Boston: Houghton Mifflin, 1922.

Licciardelli Galatioto, Mario. *La prostituzione e la legge Crispi.* Catania: Tipografia dell'Etna di S. D'Urso Condorelli, 1891.

Livi-Bacci, Massimo. *A History of Italian Fertility during the Last Two Centuries.* Princeton, N.J.: Princeton University Press, 1977.

Lombroso, Cesare. *Crime: Its Causes and Remedies.* Boston: Little, Brown, 1912.

————. *Criminal Man.* New York: Putnam's, 1911.

———. "Donna criminale e prostituta." *Archivio di Antropologia Criminale* 10 (1889): 381–382.

———. "Insensibilità in prostitute." *Archivio di Antropologia Criminale* 17 (1896): 165.

———. "Tatto e tipo degenerativo in donne normali, criminali e alienate." *Archivio di Antropologia Criminale* 12 (1891): 1–6.

Lombroso, Cesare, and Guglielmo Ferrero. *The Female Offender*. New York: Appleton, 1909.

Löning, Edgardo. *Polizia dei costumi*. Economia Politica, ser. 3, vol. 15, pp. 851–919. Turin: UTET, 1892.

Lubove, Roy. "The Progressives and the Prostitute." *Historian* 24 (1962): 308–330.

Lussu, Joyce. "La donna nella storia della salute delle masse popolari." In CISO, ed., *Storia della sanità in Italia*, pp. 109–114. Rome: Pensiero Scientifico," 1978.

McHugh, Paul. *Prostitution and Victorian Social Reform*. New York: St. Martin's, 1980.

McIntosh, Mary. "Who Needs Prostitutes? The Ideology of Male Sexual Needs." In Carol Smart and Barry Smart, eds., *Women, Sexuality and Social Control*, pp. 53–64. London: Routledge and Kegan Paul, 1978.

Macrelli, Rina. *L'indegna schiavitù: Anna Maria Mozzoni e la lotta contro la prostituzione di stato*. Rome: Riuniti, 1981.

Mammoli, Tito. *La prostituzione considerata nei suoi rapporti con la storia, la famiglia, la società*. Rocca S. Casciano: Cappelli, 1881.

Manfredi, Mario, and Mangano, Ada. *Alle origini del diritto femminile: Cultura giuridica e ideologie*. Bari: Dedalo, 1983.

Mannheim, Hermann, ed. *Pioneers in Criminology*. Chicago: Quadrangle, 1960.

Mantegazza, U., and Ciuffo, G. *La prostituzione studiata specialmente in Toscana e Sardegna*. Cagliari-Sassari: G. Dessi, 1904.

Masini, Giulio. "La rigoscopia di 50 prostitute." *Archivio di Antropologia Criminale* 14 (1893): 145.

Matza, David. *Becoming Deviant*. Englewood Cliffs, N.J.: Prentice-Hall, 1969.

May, Geoffrey. "Prostitution." In Edwin Seligman, ed., *International Encyclopedia of the Social Sciences*, 12: 593–599. New York: Macmillan, 1933.

Mei, Lorenzo. *Governo e prostituzione*. Rome: Mugnoz, 1878.

Melossi, Dario, and Pavarini, Massimo. *The Prison and the Factory:*

Origins of the Penitentiary System. Totowa, N.J.: Barnes and Noble (Imports and Reprints), 1981.

Merli, Stefano. *Proletariato di fabbrica e capitalismo industriale: Il caso italiano, 1880–1900.* 2 vols. Florence: Nuova Italia, 1972–1973.

Merlin, Lina, and Barberis, Carla, eds. *Lettere dalle case chiuse.* Milan: Edizoni Avanti, 1955.

Millett, Kate. *The Prostitution Papers.* New York: Ballantine, 1971.

Ministère des Affaires étrangères. *Conférence internationale pour la repression de la traité des blanches.* Paris: Imprimerie nationale, 1910.

Monkkonen, Eric H. *Police in Urban America: 1860–1920.* New York: Cambridge University Press, 1981.

Nathan, Ernesto. *Le diabolerie e lo stato: Quadro di costumi regolamenti.* Rome: Forzani, 1887.

Nelson, Nels A., and Crain, Gladys L. *Syphilis, Gonorrhea and the Public Health.* New York: Macmillan, 1938.

Niceforo, Alfredo. "La mala vita a Roma e la sua repressione." *Archivio di Antropologia Criminale* 22 (1899): 62–74.

Nield, Keith, ed. *Prostitution in the Victorian Age: Debates on the Issue from Nineteenth Century Critical Journals.* Westmead, Farnborough: Gregg International, 1973.

Noether, Emiliana P. "The Status of Italian Women's History." *Conference Group in Women's History Newsletter* 3, (1978): 2–4.

Ottolenghi, Salvatore. *L'insegnamento della polizia scientifica e le funzioni del segnalamento e delle investigazioni giudiziarie nell'amministrazione della pubblica sicurezza in Italia.* Rome: Mantellate, 1914.

———. *Polizia scientifica: Quadri sinettici delle lezioni tenute nella Scuola di Polizia.* Rome: Società Poligrafica Editrice, 1907.

———. *La sensibilità della donna.* Turin: Bocca, 1896.

———. *Trattato di polizia scientifica.* Milan: Società Editrice Libreria, 1910.

Ottolenghi, Salvatore, and Rossi, V. *Duecento criminali e prostitute.* Turin: Bocca, 1897.

Ovidi, Ulisse. *Relazione statistico-terapeutica sulle prostitute ricoverate nella 1ª sezione del Sifilicomio di Roma dall'aprile al dicembre 1885.* Rome: Mario Armanni, 1886.

Pane, Luigi Dal. *Economia e società a Bologna nell'età del Risorgimento: Introduzione alla ricerca.* Bologna: Zanichelli, 1969.

Paulucci di Calboli, R. *Ancora la tratta delle italiane e la Conferenza internazionale di Parigi.* Rome: Nuova Antologia, 1902.

Bibliography

Pearson, Michael. *The Age of Consent: Victorian Prostitution and Its Enemies.* Newton Abbott: David and Charles, 1972.

Pellizzari, Celso. *La nuova clinica dermosifilopatica di Siena.* Siena: L. Lazzeri, 1884.

―――. *Prostituzione e profilassi pubblica della sifilide: Lettera aperta a S. E. Francesco Crispi, ministro dell'interno.* Florence: Cenniniana, 1888.

―――. *Una riforma abortita a proposito di un rapporto del Professore Tarnowsky sulla prostituzione in Italia.* Siena: S. Bernardino, 1894.

Perry, Mary Elizabeth. "'Lost Women' in Early Modern Seville." *Feminist Studies* 4 (1978): 195–214.

Pessina, Enrico. "Il diritto penale in Italia da Cesare Beccaria sino alla promulgazione del Codice Penale vigente (1764–1890)." In *Enciclopedia del Diritto Penale Italiano*, 2: 539–768. Milan: Società Editrice Libreria, 1906.

Petiziol, Adolfo. *La prostituta: Profilo psicologico, storico, sociale.* Rome: Edizioni Nazionali, 1962.

La piaga sociale della prostituzione. Rome: Istituto di Medicina Sociale, 1950.

Pieroni Bortolotti, Franca. *Alle origini del movimento femminile in Italia, 1848–1892.* Turin: Einaudi, 1963.

―――. "Per la storia della questione femminile." *Studi Storici* 14 (1973): 450–461.

―――. *Socialismo e questione femminile in Italia, 1892–1922.* Milan: Mazzotta, 1974.

Pini, Cartenio. *Dati statistici dall'anno 1869 al 1887 sulle visite mediche nelle malattie venereo-sifilitiche in relazione alla questione igienica.* Florence: Monnier, 1887.

Pini, Gaetano. *Della prostituzione e dei provvedimenti recentemente proposti o adottati a tutela della morale e dell'igiene in Italia e all'estero.* Milan: Civelli, 1887.

Pitch, Tamar. "Prostituzione e malattia mentale: Due aspetti della devianza nella condizione femminile." *Questione Criminale* 1 (1975): 379–390.

Pitrè, Giuseppe. *Sicilian Folk Medicine.* Lawrence, Kan.: Coronado, 1971.

Pivar, David J. *Purity Crusade, Sexual Morality and Social Control, 1868–1900.* Westport, Conn.: Greenwood, 1973.

Poggiali, Francesco. *Manuale del funzionario di pubblica sicurezza pel servizio degli uffici sanitarii del Regno d'Italia.* Naples: Libreria Nazionale Scolastica, 1868.

Pomata, Gianna. "Madri illegittime tra ottocento e novecento: Storie cliniche e storie di vita." *Quaderni Storici* 44 (1980): 497–542.

Pomeroy, Wardell B. "Some Aspects of Prostitution." *Journal of Sex Research* 1 (1965): 177–187.

Porro, Angelo. *Il prefetto e l'amministrazione perifica in Italia.* Milan: Giuffrè, 1972.

Profeta, Giuseppe. *Sulla prostituzione: 8ª Conferenza.* Palermo: Fratelli Vena, 1897.

Puccini, Sandra. "Condizione della donna e questione femminile (1892–1922)." In Giulietta Ascoli, ed., *La questione femminile in Italia dall '900 ad oggi,* pp. 9–73. Milan: Angeli, 1979.

Pullan, Brian S. *Rich and Poor in Renaissance Venice: The Social Institutions of a Catholic State, to 1620.* Oxford: Blackwell Publisher, 1971.

Ramazzotti, Pietro. *Parte dei servizi governativi in Milano per la profilassi generale delle malattie veneree: Dispensario celtico-vigilanza sanitaria alle meretrici.* Milan: Pietro Agnelli, 1907.

Rasori, Enrico. *I progressi della sifilopatia nel nostro secolo.* Rome: Forzani, 1886.

Ravera, Camilla. *La donna italiana del primo al secondo Risorgimento.* Rome: Edizioni di Cultura Sociale, 1951.

Reitman, Ben L. *The Second Oldest Profession.* New York: Vanguard, 1931.

Riegel, Robert E. "Changing American Attitudes towards Prostitution (1800–1920)." *Journal of the History of Ideas* 29 (1968): 437–452.

Robinson, William J. *The Oldest Profession in the World.* New York: Eugenics, 1929.

Romani, Mario. *Storia economica d'Italia nel secolo XIX, 1815–1914.* 3 vols. Milan: Giuffrè, 1976.

Roncoroni, Luigi. Review of Pauline Tarnowski, *Prostitution und Abolitionismus. Archivio di Antropologia Criminale* 14 (1893): 171–173.

Rosen, Ruth. *The Lost Sisterhood: Prostitution in America, 1900–1918.* Baltimore: Johns Hopkins University Press, 1982.

———. ed. *The Maimie Papers.* Old Westbury, N.Y.: Feminist, 1977.

Rosenblum, Karen E. "Female Deviance and the Female Sex Role: A Preliminary Investigation." In Susan K. Datesman and Frank R. Scarpitti, eds., *Women, Crime and Justice,* pp. 106–128. New York: Oxford University Press, 1980.

Rossiaud, Jacques. "Prostitution, Youth, and Society in the Towns of Southeastern France in the Fifteenth Century." In Robert Forster and Orest Ranum, eds., *Deviants and the Abandoned in French Society*, pp. 1–46. Baltimore: Johns Hopkins University Press, 1978.

Saladino, Salvatore. "Parliamentary Politics in the Liberal Era: 1861–1914." In Edward Tannenbaum and Emiliana P. Noether, eds., *Modern Italy: A Topical History since 1861*, pp. 27–51. New York: New York University Press, 1974.

Salomone, A. William. "Freedom and Power in Liberal Italy." In idem, ed., *Italy from the Risorgimento to Fascism*, pp. 124–148. Garden City, N.Y.: Doubleday, 1970.

————. *Italy in the Giolittian Era: Italian Democracy in the Making, 1900–1914*. Philadelphia: University of Pennsylvania Press, 1960.

————. "Statecraft and Ideology in the Risorgimento." In Edward Tannenbaum and Emiliana P. Noether, eds., *Modern Italy: A Topical History since 1861*, pp. 3–26. New York: New York University Press, 1974.

Sampaoli, Antonio. *La prostituzione nel pensiero del settecento*. Rimini: Cosmi, 1973.

Sanger, William W. *The History of Prostitution: Its Extent, Causes, Effects throughout the World*. New York: Eugenics, 1939.

Scarenzio, Angelo. *Relazione sul dispensario celtico di Pavia e sulle malattie veneree osservatevi durante l'anno 1893*. Pavia: Bizzoni, 1894.

————. *La sifilide ad i vigenti regolamenti contro di essa*. Milan: Bernardoni di C. Rebeschini, 1895.

Scelba, Teresita Sandeschi. "Il femminismo in Italia durante gli ultimi cento anni." In Società Umanitaria, ed., *L'emancipazione femminile in Italia*, pp. 333–345. Florence: Nuova Italia, 1962.

Schreiber, Hermann [Lujo Basserman]. *The Oldest Profession*. London: Barker, 1967.

Schur, Edwin M, and Bedau, Hugo Adam. *Victimless Crimes*. Englewood Cliffs, N.J.: Prentice-Hall, 1974.

Scott, George Ryley. *The History of Prostitution*. New York: Greenberg, 1936.

Scott, Joan W., and Tilly, Louise. *Women, Work and Family*. New York: Holt, Rhinehart and Winston, 1978.

Shoham, Shlomo, and Rahav, Giora. "Social Stigma and Prostitution." *Annales Internationales de Criminologie* 6 (1967): 479–513.

Shorter, Edward. "Illegitimacy, Sexual Revolution and Social Change in Modern Europe." *Journal of Interdisciplinary History* 2 (1971): 237–272.

Siccardi, Marisa. "La donna nella medicina popolare e nelle istituzioni assistenziali." in CISO, ed., *Storia della sanità in Italia*, pp. 115-121. Rome: "Pensiero Scientifico," 1978.

Sicot, Marcel. *La prostitution dans le monde.* Paris: Hachette, 1964.

Sigsworth, E. M., and Wyke, T. J. "A Study of Victorian Prostitution and Venereal Disease." In Martha Vicinus, ed., *Suffer and Be Still*, pp. 77–99. Bloomington: Indiana University Press, 1972.

Smart, Carol. *Women, Crime, and Criminology: A Feminist Critique.* Boston: Routledge and Kegan Paul, 1976.

Smith, Denis Mack. *Italy: A Modern History.* Ann Arbor: University of Michigan Press, 1959.

———. "Regionalism." In Edward Tannenbaum and Emiliana P. Noether, eds., *Modern Italy: A Topical History since 1861*, pp. 125–146. New York: New York University Press, 1974.

Sori, Ercole, ed. *Città e controllo sociale in Italia tra XVIII e XIX secolo.* Milan: Angeli, 1982.

Sormani, Giuseppe. *Profilassi delle malattie veneree e specialmente della sifilide.* Milan: L. Bortolotti, 1882.

Storch, Robert D. "Police Control of Street Prostitution in Victorian England: A Study of the Contexts of Police Action." In David H. Bayley, ed., *Police and Society*, pp. 49–72. Beverly Hills, Calif.: Sage, 1977.

Symanski, Richard. *The Immoral Landscape: Female Prostitution in Western Societies.* Scarborough, Ont.: Butterworth, 1981.

Tammeo, Giuseppe. *La prostituzione: Saggio di statistica morale.* Turin: Roux, 1890.

Taylor, Ian; Walton, Paul; and Young, Jock. *The New Criminology: For a Social Theory of Deviance.* London: Routledge and Kegan Paul, 1973.

Thayer, John A. *Italy and the Great War: Politics and Culture, 1870–1915.* Madison: University of Wisconsin Press, 1964.

Tilly, Louise A. "Urban Growth, Industrialization, and Women's Employment in Milan, Italy, 1881–1911." *Journal of Urban History* 3 (1977): 467–484.

———. "The Working Class of Milan, 1881–1911." Ph.D. dissertation, University of Toronto, 1973.

Tilly, Louise A.; Scott, Joan W.; and Cohen, Miriam. "Women's Work and European Fertility Patterns." *Journal of Interdisciplinary History* 6 (1976): 447–476.

Tommasi-Crudeli, Corrado. *La prostituzione di stato in Italia.* Rome: Mortaro, 1891.

Tommasoli, Pierleone. *Prostitution et maladies vénériennes en Italie.* Brussels: H. Lamertin, 1899.

Bibliography

Toniolo, Gianni, ed. *Lo sviluppo economico italiano, 1861–1940*. Rome: Laterza, 1973.

Trexler, Richard L. "La prostitution florentine au XVe siècle: Patronages et clientèles." *Annales-Èconomies, Sociétés, Civilisations* 36 (1981): 983–1015.

Valentini, Norberto, and DiMeglio, Clara. *Sex and the Confessional*. New York: Stein and Day, 1974.

Villa, Renzo. "La prostituzione come problema storiografico." *Studi Storici* 22 (1981): 305–314.

————. "Sul processo di criminalizzazione della prostituzione nell' ottocento." *Movimento Operaio e Socialista* (1981): 269–285.

Walkowitz, Judith R. *Prostitution and Victorian Society: Women, Class, and the State*. New York: Cambridge University Press, 1980.

White Mario, Jesse. *La miseria in Napoli*. 1877. Reprint. Naples: Quarto Potere, 1978.

Williams, Phyllis H. *South Italian Folkways in Europe and America*. New York: Russell and Russell, 1938.

Winick, Charles, and Kinsie, Paul M. *The Lively Commerce: Prostitution in the United States*. Chicago: Quadrangle, 1971.

Zampa, Raffaello. *I regolamenti sulla prostituzione e la profilassi delle malattie veneree*. Bologna: Zanichelli, 1883.

Zampini Salazaro, Fanny. "Women's Condition in Italy." In National Woman Suffrage Association, *Report of the International Council of Women (March 25–April 1, 1888)*. Washington, D.C.: Rufus H. Darby, 1888.

Zehr, Howard, *Crime and the Development of Modern Society: Patterns of Criminality in Nineteenth-Century Germany and France*. Totowa, N.J.: Littlefield, Adams; Rowman and Littlefield, 1976.

Zino, Giuseppe. *Manuale di polizia medica ad uso degli ufficiali sanitari del regno e degli amministratori*. Milan: Leonardo Vallardi, 1890.

Index

Index

Index

Hata, Sahachiro, 182
Health Law of 1905, 66, 85, 89, 202–203, 250n85
Health Office: closure, 67–68; criticism of, 59; doctors, 171, 172–173, 184–190; in Piedmont, 28–29; police, 32, 34–35, 132–134, 143–144, 146, 156–157
Hobsbawm, Eric, 248n33

International Abolitionist Federation: founding, 41, 47, 54; in Italy, 42–43, 45, 63, 65
Istituto Don Giacomelli, 73
Istruzioni per regolare il servizio degli uffici sanitari, 57
Italian Committee against the White Slave Trade, 77–79

Jacquot, Dr., 14–15

labeling: by abolitionists, 48, 54; by doctors, 168, 184, 190, 211; by police, 129–130; by regulationists, 7, 16, 128; by society, 232; theory of, 8, 237n14
Left (parliamentary): policies, 42, 47, 55, 61, 62; prostitution, 42–44, 227–228, 230
Lega promotrice degli interessi femminili, 45, 74
Leghe di tutela degli interessi femminili, 74
Licciardelli Galatioto, Mario, 143
Lombroso, Cesare, 135–137, 139, 140, 226

Macrelli, Rina, 243n35
madams, 32, 36, 51, 133, 144, 153–154
Majno Bronzini, Ersilia, 76–79, 118
Mammoli, Tito, 44, 46, 48–49, 51, 145
Mazzini, Giuseppe, 42–43
McHugh, Paul, 240n29, 243n37, 244n63, 246n103
Mei, Lorenzo, 52
Merlin Law, 9, 224–233
Merlin, Lina, 223, 273n15
Merli, Stefano, 120, 122
Milan: dispensary, 200, 201; focus of study, 7; growth of, 17–18; police, 132; prostitutes, 126, 147; reformatories, 80; sifilicomio, 68, 194; women, 75, 117, 119–120, 254n71
military, 24, 31, 71, 175–176, 177, 215–216

Ministry of the Interior: dispensaries, 85–87; doctors, 169–170, 172–173; and parliament, 40, 66, 71; police, 132; regulation, 30, 168; statistics, 97. *See also* doctors; police
Monkkonen, Eric, 262n122
Montessori, Maria, 120
morals squad. *See* police
Morelli, Salvatore, 43, 242n11
Mozzoni, Anna Maria: abolition, 45, 47, 49, 53, 54; women's movement, 44–45, 53–54, 74, 75
Mussolini Law, 226, 228–229

Naples: economy, 18; focus of study, 7; migration to, 116; police, 132, 146, 147, 153; prostitutes, 102, 107, 109, 159, 233; venereal disease, 194, 201, 207, 216, 267n111
Napolean I, 15, 24, 132
Nathan, Ernesto, 43, 47, 63
Nathan, Giuseppe, 43–44, 45, 46, 47, 63
Nathan, Sara, 44
Neisser, Albert, 180
Niceforo, Alfredo, 155
Nicotera, Giovanni, 55–57, 69
Nicotera Law: contents, 69–71; health, 171, 184, 199–200; prostitutes, 106, 108–109, 130, 145–146

Ottolenghi, Salvatore, 95, 129, 137–142

Palermo: focus of study, 7; pre-unification, 15; police, 132; prostitutes, 106, 107, 109, 146, 147, 233; reformatories, 80; venereal disease, 68, 182, 194–195, 211, 216
Pane, Luigi Dal, 99–100
parliament: abolition, 42–44, 54–60, 64; commissions, 55–57, 58–60, 97; weakness of, 40, 61–62, 71; after World War II, 226–229. *See also* Left; Right
Pellizzari, Celso, 172, 183, 191, 195, 197–198
Pellizzari, Pietro, 55, 179, 245n83
Peruzzi, Ubaldino, 58
Paulucci di Calboli, R., 247n18
Piedmont (Kingdom of): Piedmontization, 29, 42, 131, 169; prostitution, 13, 23, 174; Risorgimento, 13, 26
Pieroni Bortolotti, Franca, 242n11

Index

sexuality: in Bologna, 98–99; extramarital, 4, 5, 21–22, 148, 155–156, 164–165; female, 48–49, 66, 84, 95-96, 138–139, 140–141; male, 5, 22, 31, 48–49, 63–64, 140, 224–225, 246n107; research on, 6

Shorter, Edward, 257n118

sifilicomio: after arrest, 1–2; closing of, 59, 60, 68, 207; conditions in, 171, 191–199, 268n129, 269n160; criticism of, 43, 59, 60; location, 267n123

Simon, William, 6

Smith, Denis Mack, 25

sociological criminology, 141

Sormani, Giuseppe: regulation 27, 31–32, 65, 83; venereal disease, 30, 176, 193

Sperino, Casimiro, 28, 55, 179, 245n83

syphilis. See venereal disease

Thayer, John, 246n93

Tilly, Louise, 19, 121, 254n71, 257n118

Tommasi Crudeli, Corrado, 59–60, 64

Tommasoli, Pierleone, 67, 68, 109, 172, 213

Tozzi Condivi, Renato, 229, 273n21

Turin: brothels, 147; focus of study, 7; growth of, 17–18; police, 132; venereal disease 191, 193

unification (of Italy). See Risorgimento

Unione Femminile, 75

Unione Internazionale delle Amiche della Giovanetta, 77, 81

United States, 4, 5, 7, 9, 23, 39, 41, 92, 223, 262n122, 267n121

venereal disease: cure of, 181–184, 188–189, 225, 267n111; diagnosis of, 172–174; 177–181; rates of, 159, 195–196, 205–206, 209–210, 213–221,

269n160; and regulation, 1–2, 24–25, 33, 69; syphilis, 170, 178, 179, 180–181, 195–196, 216–219, 264n43, 269n160. See also dispensary; doctors; Health Office; sifilicomio; wards

Venice: brothels, 147; focus of study, 7; police, 132; Risorgimento, 13; venereal disease, 191, 201

Walkowitz, Judith, 47, 127, 242n2

wards (for venereal disease): conditions in, 171, 200, 207–213; establishment, 60, 68, 70, 89

Wassermann, Paul von, 181

White Mario, Jesse, 44–45, 75, 194, 223

white slave trade: campaign against, 71–79, 82–84, 247n18, 249n63; international accords, 66, 80–82; after World War II, 229

Williams, Phillis H., 266n100

women: age of, 107–108; Catholic, 72–73, 82–83; civil status, 110–112; education, 112–113; employment, 19, 117–121, 254n71; independent, 4, 22–23, 33; migration, 17, 20, 116–117, 142, 257n118; and police, 151–152, 164; poverty, 256n102; venereal disease, 203, 205–206, 208–209. See also population; sexuality (female); women's movement

women's movement: abolition, 39, 44–45, 54, 225, 226–227; contemporary, 232; organization, 44–45, 62–63, 73–76; and positivist criminology, 141; white slave trade, 76–79

Zampa, Raffaello, 175, 207

Zampini Salazaro, Fanny, 39

Zino, Giuseppe, 263n3